Mizan Series 1

MUSLIM SUPERHEROES

The Mizan Series

General Editor, Michael Pregill

The Mizan Series is published by the Ilex Foundation in partnership with the Center for Hellenic Studies. The series supports the central mission of the Mizan digital initiative to encourage informed public discourse and interdisciplinary scholarship on the history, culture, and religion of Muslim societies and civilizations.

www.mizanproject.org

MUSLIM SUPERHEROES

COMICS, ISLAM, AND REPRESENTATION

Edited by
A. David Lewis and Martin Lund

Ilex Foundation
Boston, Massachusetts

Center for Hellenic Studies
Trustees for Harvard University
Washington, D. C.

Distributed by Harvard University Press
Cambridge, Massachusetts and London, England

Muslim Superheroes: Comics, Islam, and Representation
Edited by A. David Lewis and Martin Lund

Published by Ilex Foundation, Boston, Massachusetts and The Center for Hellenic Studies, Trustees for Harvard University, Washington, D.C.

Distributed by Harvard University Press, Cambridge, Massachusetts and London, England

Production editor: Christopher Dadian
Cover design: Joni Godlove
Printed in the United States of America

The image on the cover is from a digital painting created by Deena Mohamed, titled *A Superhero in Cairo*.

Library of Congress Cataloging-in-Publication Data

Names: Lewis, A. David, 1977- editor. | Lund, Martin, 1984- editor.
Title: Muslim superheroes : comics, Islam, and representation / edited by A. David Lewis and Martin Lund.
Description: Boston, Massachusetts : Ilex Foundation, [2017] | Series: Mizan series ; 1
Identifiers: LCCN 2017018467 | ISBN 9780674975941 (alk. paper)
Subjects: LCSH: Comic books, strips, etc.--Religious aspects--Islam. | Muslims in literature. | Superheroes in literature. | Superheroes--Islamic countries. | Heroes--Religious aspects--Islam.
Classification: LCC PN6712 .M87 2017 | DDC 741.5/38297--dc23
LC record available at https://lccn.loc.gov/2017018467

To my daughters, my Muslim superheroes. - A. D. L.

To Mei-Ling, forever my little princess. I'll miss you, always. - M. L.

CONTENTS

Whence the Muslim Superhero?

Martin Lund and A. David Lewis

Introduction

MUSLIM SUPERHEROES ARE BECOMING more and more visible, popular, and criticized. Despite what is often claimed in the popular press whenever a new one debuts, their existence is actually neither surprising nor new. The U.S. superhero genre is deeply connected to the vicissitudes of the nation's history and often in a way that highlights how identity, inclusion, and exclusion are negotiated in the U.S. – particularly in relation to major political shifts and cultural anxieties.[1] Indeed, considering the course of geopolitical relations between the U.S. and the so-called Muslim world[2] since the end of World War II as well as American debates about national identity and belonging since the terrorist attacks on September 11, 2001, it is perhaps more surprising that there is not more Muslim representation in the nation's superhero comics, for good and ill.

Still, Muslim superheroes, as a concept and as an experience, seem surprising to the uninformed. Of course, villainous images of Muslims have been normalized over decades to the point where they barely provoke a response.[3] Perhaps the non-threatening Muslims in superhero comics, especially Muslim *as* the superheroes themselves, are so often greeted with surprise due to the inaccurate canard that illustration itself – one half of the image-text nature of comics – is antithetical to Muslim belief. However, even if there were a strict Islamic prohibition against figural imagery, this might not apply to non-Muslim comics creators who are creating representations of Muslims. Further, there is no explicit ban in the canonical Islamic texts and, while avoided in some cultures, figural imagery (even of Muhammad) has, in fact, historically been a staple of Islamic expression in others; the

---

1. See, for example, Wright 2001; Johnson 2011; Lewis 2012.

2. When used to define a space, "Muslim world" most often refers to Muslim-majority parts of the Middle East and North African (MENA) region, as well as to Muslim-majority parts of South Asia, such as Pakistan or Indonesia. However, in a very real sense, the "Muslim world" is not a geographic entity, but rather a global cognitive universe of ideas (see Ackfeldt 2013). It is used here in a broad sense that allows for its reading in both senses while subscribing exclusively to neither.

3. Cf. Michalak 1988; Said 1981; Esposito 1992; Gottschalk and Greenberg 2008.

ban, where it exists, is just one interpretation among many.[4] It cannot be said flatly that "Islam forbids illustration," nor can it be said that comics and Islam are at cross-purposes. Muslims in comics, in reality, prove to be a complicated phenomenon, far from either sentiment.

The purpose of this volume is straightforward but by no means simple: it seeks to investigate the ways in which Muslim superheroes embody, counter, or complicate Western stereotypes of Muslims. Additionally, the essays contained in *Muslim Superheroes* aim to gauge popular audience expectations, across the globe as well as in the looming shadow of Islamophobia. Muslim superheroes are doing more than saving fictional innocents from peril; they are also engaging and influencing real-world comprehension of this world religion, its adherents, and twenty-first-century heroism – and they do so by using narrative, artistic, and generic standards that are rooted in both U.S. and Muslim cultures.

The World Stage of Muslim Superheroes

Despite turning a relatively blind eye (or tin ear) to them through much of the twentieth century, major American comic book publishers like Marvel Comics and DC Comics have featured, in the twenty-first, numerous Muslim superhero characters. Presumably, the publishers' intentions are to diversify their fictional universes and to provide corrective representations of Muslims in a cultural moment that is particularly rife with stereotyping and vilification of Muslims and Islam. More pragmatically, the companies are likely also hoping to capitalize on Islam and Muslims' increased visibility and media profile in recent years. The most notable example to date is Marvel's Kamala Khan, a New Jersey Muslima of Pakistani origin, who in February 2014 joined the publisher's cast of superheroes under the *nom de guerre* Ms. Marvel. Although as a comics character Ms. Marvel might be easy to regard as peripheral or ephemeral – at the time of this writing she has not even saved the universe yet or thwarted an alien invasion – she was excitedly discussed in various mainstream media long before her first appearance. After a commercially and critically successful first year, her image even expanded beyond the comic book page in January 2015, when it was plastered over anti-Muslim ads in San Francisco, illustrating the cultural power such characters can attain.[5] Within the next year, she was invited into the august company of Marvel's flagship superteam, the Avengers.

There are many more Muslim superheroes in the annals of comics, but

4. Cf. Graves 2014; Gruber 2009; 2014; 2015; Gruber and Shalem 2014.
5. Letamendi 2015.

they are less well known, frequently overlooked, and largely misunderstood. Nonetheless, for decades, American publishers and comics creators have felt a need to generate such characters and use them in stories. These U.S. products have been joined, too, in recent years by a growing number of actors in Muslim-majority countries (e.g. indigenous publishers, creators, activists). At the same time, American anti-Islamic pundits increasingly feel a need to claim that Muslim superheroes are another cog in the Islamist machine that, ostensibly, is out to destroy the U.S. Muslim superheroes are a further example, for them, of "creeping Shariah." Objections have arisen, also, from some Islamic commentators and authorities who have reacted negatively to the importation of the U.S. superhero genre and its use in conjunction with Islamic traditions and values. Whatever viewpoint one takes in the current geopolitical climate, it seems clear that Muslim superheroes matter greatly to a large number of Muslims and non-Muslims alike.

The label "Muslim superhero" should here be taken to refer only to the fact that these characters have been inscribed with one or several markers meant to signify a "Muslim" identity, based in one conception of Islam or another. No judgment is given, intended, or implied about the "authenticity" of these characters or conceptions of Islam.[6] Rather, the term as used here acknowledges that both Muslim and non-Muslim creators and critics have had these characters produce, reproduce, represent, and embody one or more of a host of discursively constructed conceptions of Islam and Muslimness.[7]

Starting from that understanding and expanding on our straightforward purpose, the wider aim of this book is threefold. First, it assembles studies of a variety of comics characters and thus begins to outline the history and diversity of Muslim superheroes in comics. Second, it sets out to answer some basic questions about these characters: Why do Muslim superheroes keep being created? What purposes do they serve? Are they, as cartoonist Bosch Fawstin claims, unwanted "enemy propaganda" being "shoved down our throats" from within superhero comics – a genre which otherwise, in his view, is "the one place where good and evil is still being dramatized, week after week?"[8] Or do they respond to a real demand for new representations? Why are more and more Muslim superheroes emerging from contexts where superheroes have not historically been common (yet, perhaps paradoxically,

---

6. That said, we direct the reader to Hussein Rashid's chapter in this volume, in which this matter is discussed in more depth.

7. For introductions to the topic of the discursive construction and reconstruction of Islam(s), see for example Asad 1986; Hjärpe 1997. For insights into the still-understudied idea that non-Muslims similarly discursively construct visions of Islam, see Cato 2012.

8. Fawstin 2014.

have been consistently marginally present)? How do they succeed (and/or fail) in performing their assigned duties as signifiers of one conception of Islam or another? Third, *Muslim Superheroes* sets out to consider the extent of the impact Muslim superheroes have and will continue to have on both the genre and its audiences.

As the chapters in this volume show, there are many answers to these questions, some of them painfully obvious, and others starkly painful. One possible answer, which should be kept in mind as the book progresses, is that these fictional characters are a tangible negotiation of the U.S.'s central – and deeply fraught – national ideals of justice and equality in relationship to Islamophobia ("a *social* anxiety toward Islam and Muslim cultures that is largely unexamined by, yet deeply ingrained in, Americans").[9] This negotiation, of course, operates alongside and in awkward concert with the Muslim world as it, too, comes to terms with the U.S.'s own global influence. The U.S. can use Muslim superheroes to right its relationship with Islam; the Muslim world can use Muslim superheroes to articulate its relationship with the U.S. Indeed, as will be explored in the following pages, Muslim superheroes, globally, occupy a space that is replete with tensions and conflicts, along with the possibility of peaceful resolution, making their study not only relevant, but also important.

Muslim Superheroes and their Discontents

Film critic and political commentator Debbie Schlussel responded to Marvel Comics's late-2013 announcement that it would soon be introducing Ms. Marvel as follows:

> No word on how many IEDs she'll be carrying or how many Jews she'll kill while saving Muslims from accidentally living near a pig farm or a swimming pool that features both sexes swimming at the same time.[10]

Schlussel ends by asking where the Christian and Jewish superheroes are, a telling question both because it shows a lack of knowledge about the topic and because it suggests, erroneously, that Islam is given special treatment by being represented when no other faith is.[11]

---

9. On the conflicting relations, see Michael 2008. Description of Islamophobia from Gottschalk and Greenberg 2008, 5. Emphasis in original.

10. Schlussel 2013.

11. A search in the Comic Book Religion database (http://www.comicbookreligion.com/) on April 6, 2015 garnered 523 Christian heroes, 288 villains, and 510 clergy; 161 Jewish heroes, 56 villains, and 31 clergy; and 65 Muslim heroes, 124 villains, and 10 clergy. As of this publication, however, the database was last updated in September 2014; characters like Ms. Marvel or Nightrunner were not yet catalogued.

Schlussel's tirade, which described the character as Marvel's "Bait-and-Switch Muslima Superjihadista," was just the latest in a series of similar responses to American-made Muslim superheroes. A few years before, when DC Comics created Nightrunner, a French-Algerian Muslim character based in Paris, conservative blogger Warner Todd Huston published a widely read blog post that called the character-creation "PCism run amuck," accusing the publisher of "ignoring the fact that Islam is the single most important factor" in the then-recent French riots.[12] And when, a few years earlier still, a Kuwaiti psychologist and businessman named Naif al-Mutawa created *The 99*, a superhero series with roots in Islamic culture, it was described by some as "a new and particularly insidious form of cultural jihad that is targeting our children."[13]

On the other end of the spectrum, early positive reception of Ms. Marvel was also somewhat inflated. Long before her first appearance, it was claimed that Ms. Marvel would "shatter taboos [and] open the eyes of a new generation of comic book readers to the mostly unseen, unknown complexities of being a Muslim-American woman."[14] One writer prophesied:

> Her very existence will enable readers to see past the "Muslim" tag, into a powerful and flawed multifaceted human being [and that her introduction] gives scope to discuss how America sees power, who can access power and who has the right to be powerful.[15]

Another praised Marvel for introducing the character: "She is strong, she is resilient, she is fierce, she is determined. She is Ms Marvel."[16] As with the negative response, this hopeful tone had precedents. When DC introduced Muslim American Simon Baz as a member of its Green Lantern Corps interstellar police force in 2012, it was repeatedly (and erroneously) claimed that he was America's first Muslim or Arab American superhero and that his introduction was a "major, major breakthrough" in Muslim American representation.[17] In 2010, President Barack Obama famously gave al-Mutawa and *The 99* a "shout-out" for having "captured the imagination of so many young people with superheroes who embody the teachings and tolerance of Islam."[18]

Both types of response are, perhaps, somewhat excessive in the mag-

---

12. Huston 2010. For critiques of earlier "Muslim riot" claims, see Cesari 2005; Heneghan 2007.

13. Geller 2011. For more examples, see Santo 2014, 688–690.

14. Jebreal 2013.

15. Janmohamed 2013.

16. Pervez 2013.

17. Anonymous 2012a; 2012b; Molnar 2012.

18. Keyes 2010.

nitude of their claims, but they illustrate the high stakes associated in the American public sphere with Muslim representation a decade and more after the attacks of September 11, 2001. One side sees Muslims as inhuman terror-machines, a monolithic, atavistic threat that is undermining the U.S. through "creeping Islamization" and using "political correctness" to coax "appeasement" from the culture industry; their polar opposites, however, hold an almost-desperate hope that any new positive image could finally be the one that manages to "normalize" Muslims. In neither case have the wishes or fears come true. Muslim superheroes have brought neither doom nor deliverance, but they have opened a wider window into how those in between the extremes can consider the contemporary cultural and geopolitical landscape.

Superhero comics have always had a potboiler sensitivity to major issues in American life, so the existence of American-made Muslim superheroes should be unsurprising given the course of Muslim American history and the superhero industry's attempted but still-in-progress turn toward multiculturalism. In the case of Muslim superheroes, it is an often fumbling finger that tries to take the nation's pulse. Indeed, in many cases, without leaving much of an imprint, Muslim superheroes introduced with much fanfare have soon faded from public view. Publishers cause them to retreat into the periphery of their fictional universe or to submerge in the superhero "Melting Pot," thus assimilating into the genre and making them less distinguishable from other superheroes.[19] They thereby leave less room for (or even contradict their originally intended) cultural specificity.

Certainly, Muslim superheroes are not a *totally* new phenomenon; they have appeared in one form or another since at least March 1944's *Bomber Comics* #1, in which the Muslim superhero Kismet debuted and briefly adventured.[20] In addition to a variety of Muslim and Arabic villains, the list of pre-9/11 Muslim superheroes includes the Archer of Arabia (*Adventure Comics* #250, July 1958), Black Tiger (*Deadly Hands of Kung Fu* #29, October 1976), the first Arabian Knight (*Incredible Hulk* #257, March 1981), the Iraqi superhero team Desert Sword (*New Mutants Annual* #7, August 1991), and Batal (*New Warriors* #58, April 1995). At times, these characters have reproduced, contested, or otherwise engaged stereotypes and hegemonic schemes of Muslim representation; in other, albeit less frequent cases, they have avoided them. In most cases, though, publishers allowed them to fade quickly into obscurity, with no apparent market demand to sustain them.

19. Cf. for example Smith 2001; Lund 2016.
20. Lewis 2014.

Although the comic book superhero is an American creation and one that has only rarely sprung from drawing boards in other countries, Muslim superheroes are not the purview only of American publishers. To the contrary, a number of such characters have in recent years started coming out of Muslim-majority countries. Al-Mutawa and his *The 99* have received much attention from both fans and critics in America, but his work started in Kuwait, where, too, he encountered resistance from religious authorities and, later, became the object of a condemnatory fatwa. (Notably, similar to Simon Baz, some media and much of the scholarship misrepresented al-Mutawa's series as "the first" to include Muslim superheroes when discussing this development.[21]) When *The 99* premiered in 2006, however, it was following in the footsteps of Egyptian publisher AK Comics (2004), whose series had the stated intention of providing Arab role models in superheroic form. Since then, superheroes like the Silver Scorpion (2011) and Buraaq (2011) and superheroines like the Burka Avenger (2013) and Qahera (2013) have also joined the quietly growing roster of international Muslim genre characters.

All of these superheroes – the U.S. ones and the ones created in Muslim-majority countries – waver on the tensions between American and Islamic cultures.[22] Those tensions can manifest in American mainstream publishers creating Muslim characters to entertain with reference to the Orientalist exotic (e.g. Sinbad, the Veil, Kahina the Seer), to attempt a corrective of Islamic representation (Dust), or to address the place of Muslims in the U.S. (Josiah X). Likewise, it can manifest with creators in the Muslim world creating superheroes on an American template to provide role models for youth in the Muslim world (*The 99*, AK Comics) or to critique inequalities in Muslim-majority countries (Qahera, The Burka Avenger). Worse, these tensions can be exploited and augmented, as with creators using the superhero genre to present Islam as a threat and urge resistance to "Islamization" in the West (Fawstin's *The Infidel* [2011], Frank Miller's *Holy Terror* [2011]). This thumbnail sketch of underlying concerns, however, represents a simplification in the extreme, intended only to introduce the subject, the strategies, and the stakes involved in the Muslim superhero. As the next section will show, *Muslim Superheroes* does not exist in a vacuum; a small but growing literature on Muslim superheroes already exists, but much work still needs to be done. The hope, however, is that this collection begins to address what has, as yet, been left unaddressed or unscrutinized.

21. al-Mutawa 2014; Hills 2014; Cadwalladr 2010.
22. For histories of these tensions and their expressions, see for example Sayyid 1997; Esposito 1992; Gottschalk and Greenberg 2008; Shaheen 2009.

Previous Research

Although religious themes and characters have been commonplace through-out comics history, scholarship on comics and religion is a relatively recent phenomenon. Numerous books on the theme emerged over the first decade of the twenty-first century. These works, which almost exclusively present-ed readings of comics through an American Christian or Jewish theological or ethnic lens, were informed by normative or celebratory perspectives.[23] Regardless of their relative scholarly quality, however, these texts helped inspire an interest in the understudied intersection of comics and religion. In their wake, a field of study has emerged and monographs, edited volumes, articles, and online resources are appearing at an ever-growing rate. The field remains largely dominated by studies with focus on Christian and Jew-ish concerns, but it has grown to include, for example, Indian comics which reimagine Hindu epics or, in one collected volume, such diverse traditions as Mormonism, animism, and Gnostic thinking as well as more complex theoretical thinking on the subject.[24] Throughout all of this, however, direct examination of Islam is largely absent.

When it comes to non-superhero comics, the medium's relationship to Islam (and vice versa) has been more thoroughly engaged in scholarship. This collection is not focused on non-superhero comics and Islam, but the scholarship on such works should be noted, just the same, as weaving a sepa-rate but related portion within a shared academic tapestry. Historian Allen Douglas and Arabist Fedwa Malti-Douglas's 1994 study of Arab comic strips, in which they analyzed the political and social impact of their material, included some of the earliest work on Muslim representation and comics for English-speaking, Western audiences.[25] Douglas and Malti-Douglas also later published a short article about a comic strip that dealt with Islamic philosophical issues.[26] Some work has been done on Muslim representations in Evangelical fundamentalist Jack Chick's comic books and propaganda pamphlets known as Chick tracts, but none of this work has been focused entirely on Muslims or Islam, discussing them, instead, in relation to Chick's fundamentalism.[27] A large body of scholarship has also emerged around cartoonist Marjane Satrapi's *Persepolis*, although the majority of this work

---

23. Examples from Christian contexts include Brewer 2004; Garrett 2005; Skelton 2006. Some Jewish-themed examples include Weinstein 2006; Fingeroth 2007; Kaplan 2008. For some critiques about this type of writing, see Lund 2012; 2015b; 2016.

24. McLain 2009; Lewis and Kraemer 2010.

25. Douglas and Malti-Douglas 1994.

26. Douglas and Malti-Douglas 1999.

27. See Varisco 2007; Lund 2015a.

focuses on aspects other than the graphic novel's Islamic representations (e.g. nationalism, remembrance, feminism).[28]

In terms of the concerns of this collection, the timeline for research on Muslims, Islam, and superhero comics is similar and accelerating. While the superhero genre has been the focus of study in twenty academic English-language articles and book chapters available for review, all but one of these texts was written before 2010.[29] The one exception, a 1994 article by Jack Shaheen, a scholar specializing in representations of Arabs,[30] sets out to study Arab caricatures in comics from the early 1950s until the early 1990s. Yet, Shaheen presents only a small number of examples taken from within only a fraction of that period. A distinct lack of contextualization or recognition of growing American fears and anxieties about Muslims and the Muslim world, which were becoming increasingly pronounced in the period discussed, deeply hampers the work. The article's lack of critical substance might explain why further scholarship focused on Islam and superhero comics was so long delayed.

Out of the nineteen remaining articles, two are similar, but in one case more critically substantial, surveys to that of Shaheen's; seven are single-character analyses; three are comparative readings; and seven are focused on *The 99*. The first survey, written by scholar Jehanzeb Dar and published in 2010, discusses Islamophobia in U.S. superhero comics in a broad way. While it has some issues related to its claims and style, it brings Shaheen's survey up to date and is a foundational text for the subfield.[31] The second survey, published in 2011 and written by comics scholar Fredrik Strömberg, analyzes a selection of popular, American-made Arab and Muslim superheroes since September 11, 2001.[32] Strömberg's article considers the history of tensions and conflicts between the U.S. and the Muslim world, places the comics in their cultural context, and considers previous research on Muslim and Arab representations. Although the selection is small, the article remains one of the most critically insightful works on Muslim superheroes and should be considered as an important stepping-stone for future research, this volume included.

The earliest single-character study is a comparative reading of the

---

28. See, for example, Naghibi and O'Malley 2005; R. G. Davis 2005; Chiu 2008; Chute 2008; Leigh 2011; Brock 2012.

29. This number is based on a series of comprehensive scholarly database searches via Lund University, Linnaeus University, CUNY, and the Bonn Online Bibliography for Comics Research, made between February 2015 and July 2016.

30. Shaheen 1994.

31. Dar 2010.

32. Strömberg 2012.

Egyptian superhero Zain, published by AK Comics, which focuses on changes made in the translation of the comic from Arabic to English, and how each
version has a different purpose.[33] It is good scholarship, but the analysis is
too formal to be of much use in future work. Later single-character studies
discuss the Marvel characters Dust and Janissary, respectively; both articles
are more descriptive than analytical and lack a critical interpretive edge.
The Dust article discusses the markers of her religious identity, her "doubly
liminal" status as superhero and Muslim in the West, and her marginalization as a woman. But it does so in a way that fails to relate the character to
a larger context, focusing instead almost exclusively on Dust's role within
the comics and her relationship to other characters, not to the world of her
readers.[34] The Janissary text is problematic for similar reasons, as well as for
its attempts to place an American-made character within what the authors
call the Turkish "secular-Islamic dichotomy," and because it blurs contexts
of production and reception.[35]

The remaining character-studies are devoted to one of two Muslim superheroines: Ms. Marvel and Qahera. There is one full-length article that
analyzes Muslim masculinities and femininities in the *Ms. Marvel* series and,
while it could have been an interesting contribution to the field, it is hampered by too many underdeveloped assumptions about the context and
storytelling to be truly useful.[36] The other two pieces are shorter research
notes: in the first, feminist scholar Miriam Kent makes a strong argument
for how Ms. Marvel has been shorn of what makes her different by review-
ers who seem to display a fondness for assimilation; in the second, comics
scholar Ernesto Priego presents a highly personal approach to the series'
first issues and offers questions for further research.[37] Both are good but
too brief to truly delve into their subjects. Kamala is also one of the subjects
of a comparative reading in a book on superheroines by political scientist
Carolyn Cocca, but her Muslimness is barely mentioned.[38] Finally, Qahera
appears in three pieces: she is the subject of a research note about Qahera's
struggles with the Ukrainian feminist group FEMEN and the epistemic violence the group perpetuates against Muslim women, as well as of two brief
comparative readings, in which her identity as a superheroine is secondary
to her being a veiled woman or an expression of the revolution in Egypt.[39]
Thus, while both characters have attracted scholarly attention, most likely

33. van Leeuwen and Suleiman 2010.
34. J. Davis and Westerfelhaus 2013.
35. Erhart and Eslen-Ziya 2014.
36. Khoja-Moolji and Niccolini 2015.
37. Kent 2015; Priego 2016.
38. Cocca 2016, 183–214.
39. Ivey 2015; Duncan 2015; Jones 2014, 183–198.

because of their high visibility in recent years, they have yet to be studied with much depth.

As for studies of *The 99*, the micro-field is better cultivated. Studies have appeared that discuss the series' female characters as corrective representations of Muslim women,[40] the various characters as representing different aspects of everyday life in the Arab and Muslim world alongside a sense of universalism,[41] the series' possible negotiations between historical Muslim epistemologies,[42] and the promises and problems that spring from creating a multinational franchise with an Islamic profile.[43] One of these texts comes to some faulty conclusions because it regards the Muslim women in the series as representing "strategic self-positioning" by Muslim women, when the collaborative creation – largely by white, male, American hands – of the stories is undeniable;[44] another assumes a too-pronounced Islamic intention, which leads the authors to be blind to the universalist message that the series' creator has been vocal about trying to convey.[45] Notwithstanding these flaws, these articles all represent critical steps forward for the cultural placement of *The 99* in particular and of Muslim superheroes in general.

Other articles on *The 99* are less productive overall but provide useful touchstones toward what is being attempting with this volume.[46] Collectively, all these 2010–2016 articles paint a picture of an emerging field that is still experiencing growing pains and is in search of a foundation from which to grow. By embodying different perspectives and employing different methodologies (such as feminist scholarship, philosophy, reception studies, and close readings), they suggest some fruitful avenues to pursue in this process. Foremost among these considerations are the interdisciplinary bridgings between Islamic studies and comics studies; constructive dialogue between scholars and comparative perspectives that bridge different characters, publishers, and contexts; and a broader range of materials studied. The chapters in *Muslim Superheroes* have been collected with all of these considerations in mind.

Disposition

In order to bridge the gaps outlined above and to provide broad coverage of themes and issues, an assortment of scholars and approaches are being

40. Edwin 2012.
41. Deeb 2012.
42. Clements and Gauvain 2014.
43. Santo 2014.
44. Edwin 2012, 195.
45. Clements and Gauvain 2014.
46. Enderwitz 2011; Meier 2013; Alawadhi 2013.

brought here to bear on the subject of Muslim superheroes; these are not haphazard in their variety but, instead, are meant to be interlocking and in constructive dialogue. The book has been structured to ensure that not only will each chapter be informative and readable in itself, but that together, they progressively build toward a cumulative understanding of the historical and contemporary Muslim superhero, from an international and interdisciplinary perspective. This progression has been set up so that the argument moves from the U.S. mainstream and spans a number of viewpoints before ending in a study of theologically informed comics coming out of Muslim-majority environments.

First, religion scholar Nicolaus Pumphrey analyzes the Marvel character Dust, examining her from a perspective that accounts for her creation and recreation by different authors as well as reader reception. Staying within Marvel's publication history (and the so-called "Marvel Universe," in which the publisher's stories take place), fellow religion scholar Kevin Wanner writes about the Pakistani-British Faiza Hussain (aka Excalibur), focusing on the character's configuration as a model modern Muslim who juggles a variety of cultural roles and affiliations. Wanner then considers this juggling act in terms of how the creative team styles integration of minorities into liberal societies. Rounding off these chapters of single-character close readings focusing on Muslim characters in Western contexts, cultural studies scholars Chris Reyns-Chikuma and Désirée Lorenz study the translation into French of the first volume of the *Ms. Marvel* series. Across the anglophone and francophone manifestations of the hit character, Reyns-Chikuma and Lorenz examine how translators navigate cultural and linguistic differences, why the conservative publisher Panini chose to undertake the project, and how the volume was both presented and received.

Next, two chapters look to a bigger picture of American-made Muslim superheroes. First, historian Dwain Pruitt traces representations of African-American Muslims in three decades of DC Comics. He argues that, in the 1970s, DC created radical straw men inspired by misreadings of Black Nationalism and the Nation of Islam and, only later, slowly moved toward a more nuanced, albeit still problematic, characterization. Fellow historian Mercedes Yanora closes the first half of the book with a chapter on U.S. foreign policy and comics. She highlights how representations of Muslims have mirrored developments in foreign policy and discusses this in relation to notions of gender, Otherness, and citizenship.

Bridging the ostensible divide between the West and the Muslim world, comics scholar Fredrik Strömberg analyzes the comics published by the Egyptian publisher AK Comics and *The 99*, published by the Kuwaiti Teshkeel Media. Through genre analysis, Strömberg shows that, while the two series differed significantly in how they handled generic conventions, both were ultimately hampered by them. Conversely, religion scholar Ken Chitwood focuses on the mixed reception of *The 99*. He looks at how the series and its creator have been used by numerous different actors for different political, social, and religious ends, arguing that how *The 99* and al-Mutawa are reified and represented depends more on how, and by whom, they are received than on their actual content or merit. Then, reversing the trajectory of West to East, anthropologist Aymon Kreil provides a close reading of Qahera, star of the eponymous Egyptian webcomic. In his account, he echoes Reyns-Chikuma and Lorenz's language concerns, this time looking at how an Egyptian superheroine's message is refracted through both English and Arabic iterations.

The penultimate chapter wrestles with superheroes created in more explicit relation to Islamic tradition and theology. Religion scholar Hussein Rashid explores the comics produced by the Indian publisher Sufi Comics. Rashid illustrates how the Sufi Comics super-heroes (*sic*) embody a different set of criteria for heroism, based in Islamic traditions and providing an alternative definition for what gives their heroes such power.

Finally, we, the editors, return to provide some concluding remarks and compelling linkages. In synthesizing a number of the conclusions presented in the preceding pages, we demonstrate how *Muslim Superheroes* concretely adds to the field; identifies areas in which more research is desired; proposes ways forward for the field; and underscores the variety and layers both of popular and scholarly discourse that underlies analyses of Islam in relation to the superhero genre or the comics medium. We also offer suggestions for how to translate the scholarship in these pages into practice, by showing how Muslim superheroes can be brought into the classroom. Our volume is intended as a step forward, not as the final word; the Muslim superhero is not that easily contained.

Works Cited

Ackfeldt, A. 2013. "'I Am Malcolm X' – Islamic Themes in Hip-Hop Video Clips Online." *CyberOrient* 7 (2). http://www.cyberorient.net/article. do?articleId=8630.

al-Mutawa, N. 2014. "The Latest Challenge of 'The 99' Superheroes Is Tackling a Fatwa." *The National*, April 26. http://www.thenational.ae/ thenationalconversation/comment/the-latest-challenge-of-the-99-superheroes-is-tackling-a-fatwa.

Alawadhi, H. 2013. "Reclaiming the Narrative: The 99 and Muslim Superheroes." *International Journal of Comic Art* 15 (2): 268–277.

Anonymous. 2012a. "Simon Baz, the New Green Lantern, Is the Country's First Arab-American Superhero." *Huffington Post*, September 6. http:// www.huffingtonpost.com/2012/09/06/the-new-green-lantern-sim_n_1859031.html?ncid=edlinkusaolp00000003.

———. 2012b. "America's First Muslim Superhero." *Cbc.ca*. September 18. http://www.cbc.ca/books/2012/09/americas-first-muslim-superhero. html.

Asad, T. 1986. *The Idea of an Anthropology of Islam*. Washington D.C.

Brewer, H. M. 2004. *Who Needs a Superhero?: Finding Virtue, Vice, and What's Holy in the Comics*. Grand Rapids.

Brock, J. 2012. "'One Should Never Forget': The Tangling of History and Memory in *Persepolis*." In *Graphic History. Essays on Graphic Novels and/as History*, edited by R. Iadonisi, 223–241. Newcastle upon Tyne.

Cadwalladr, C. 2010. "The 99: The Islamic Superheroes Fighting Side by Side with Batman." *The Guardian*, October 23. http://www.theguardian.com/ books/2010/oct/24/99-islamic-heroes-batman-superman.

Cato, J. 2012. *När islam blev svenskt: föreställningar om islam och muslimer i svensk offentlig politik 1975-2010*. Lund.

Cesari, J. 2005. "Ethnicity, Islam, and Les Banlieues: Confusing the Issues." *Social Science Research Council*, November 30. http://riotsfrance.ssrc. org/Cesari/.

Chiu, M. 2008. "Sequencing and Contingent Individualism in the Graphic, Postcolonial Spaces of Satrapi's *Persepolis* and Okubo's *Citizen 13660*." *English Language Notes* 46 (2): 99–114.

Chute, H. 2008. "The Texture of Retracing in Marjane Satrapi's *Persepolis*." *Women's Studies Quarterly* 36 (1/2): 92–110.

Clements, J., and R. Gauvain. 2014. "The Marvel of Islam: Reconciling Muslim Epistemologies through a New Islamic Origin Saga in Naif al-Mutawa's *The 99*." *The Journal of Religion and Popular Culture* 26 (1): 36–71.

Cocca, C. 2016. *Superwomen: Gender, Power, and Representation.* New York and London.

Dar, J. 2010. "Holy Islamophobia, Batman! Demonization of Muslims and Arabs in Mainstream American Comic Books." *Counterpoints* 346: 99–110.

Davis, J., and R. Westerfelhaus. 2013. "Finding a Place for a Muslimah Heroine in the Post-9/11 Marvel Universe: New X-Men's Dust." *Feminist Media Studies* 13 (5): 800–809.

Davis, R. G. 2005. "A Graphic Self: Comics as Autobiography in Marjane Satrapi's *Persepolis.*" *Prose Studies* 27: 264–279.

Deeb, M-J. 2012. "*The 99*: Superhero Comic Books from the Arab World." *Comparative Studies of South Asia, Africa and the Middle East* 32 (2): 391–407.

Douglas, A., and F. Malti-Douglas. 1994. *Arab Comic Strips: Politics of an Emerging Mass Culture.* Bloomington.

———. 1999. "Islamic 'Classics Illustrated': Regendering Medieval Philosophy in a Modern Tunisian Strip." *International Journal of Comic Art* 1 (2): 98–106.

Duncan, J. 2015. "Beyond the Veil: Graphic Representation of Islamic Women." *The Compass* 1 (2). http://scholarworks.arcadia.edu/thecompass/vol1/iss2/4.

Edwin, S. 2012. "Islam's Trojan Horse: Battling Perceptions of Muslim Women in *The 99.*" *Journal of Graphic Novels & Comics* 3 (2): 171–199.

Enderwitz, S. 2011. "'The 99': Islamic Superheroes – A New Species?" In *Transcultural Turbulences: Towards a Multi-Sited Reading of Image Flows,* edited by C. Brosius, and R. Wenzlhuemer, 83–95. Berlin and New York.

Erhart, I., and H. Eslen-Ziya. 2014. "Janissary: An Orientalist Heroine or Role Model for Muslim Women?." In *Heroines of Comic Books and Literature: Portrayals in Popular Culture,* edited by M. Bajac-Carter, N. Jones, and B. Batchelor, 95–106. Lanham.

Esposito, J. L. 1992. *The Islamic Threat: Myth or Reality?* New York.

Fawstin, B. 2014. "The Post-9/11 'Muslim Superhero' Invasion." *Bosch Fawstin,* February 19. http://fawstin.blogspot.com/2014/02/the-post-911-muslim-superhero-invasion.html.

Fingeroth, D. 2007. *Disguised as Clark Kent: Jews, Comics, and the Creation of the Superhero.* New York.

Garrett, G. 2005. *Holy Superheroes!: Exploring Faith & Spirituality in Comic Books* Colorado Springs.

Geller, P. 2011. "86 'The 99'." *WND,* October 10. http://www.wnd.com/2011/10/354477/.

Gottschalk, P. and G. Greenberg. 2008. *Islamophobia: Making Muslims the Enemy*. Lanham.

Graves, M. S. 2014. "Islam and Visual Art." In *The Oxford Handbook of Religion and the Arts*, edited by F. Burch Brown. Oxford.

Gruber, C. 2009. "Between Logos (Kalima) and Light (Nur): Representations of the Prophet Muhammad in Islamic Painting." *Muqarnas: An Annual on the Visual Culture of the Islamic World* XXVI: 229–62.

———. 2014. "IMAGES." In *Muhammad in History, Thought, and Culture: An Encyclopedia of the Prophet of God*, edited by A. Walker, and C. Fitzpatrick, 298–94. Santa Barbara.

———. 2015. "The Koran Does Not Forbid Images of the Prophet." *Religionsvetenskaplig Internettidskrift*. Also published in *Newsweek*. January 9. http://www.newsweek.com/koran-does-not-forbid-images-prophet-298298.

Gruber, C., and A. Shalem. 2014. "Introduction: Images of the Prophet in a Global Context." In *The Image of the Prophet between Ideal and Ideology: A Scholarly Investigation*, edited by C. Gruber, and A. Shalem, 1–9. Berlin.

Heneghan, T. 2007. "Why We Don't Call Them 'Muslim Riots' in Paris Suburbs." *Reuters Blogs*, November 29. http://blogs.reuters.com/faithworld/2007/11/29/why-we-dont-call-them-muslim-riots-in-paris-suburbs/.

Hills, C. 2014. "A Saudi Fatwa Shuns the First Comic Book to Feature Muslim Superheroes." *Public Radio International*, March 28. http://www.pri.org/stories/2014-03-28/saudi-fatwa-shuns-first-comic-book-feature-muslim-superheroes.

Hjärpe, J. 1997. "What Will Be Chosen from the Islamic Basket?" *European Review* 5 (3): 267–274.

Huston, W. T. 2010. "Batman's Politically Correct European Vacation." *Publicus Forum*, December 23. http://www.publiusforum.com/2010/12/23/batmans-politically-correct-european-vacation/.

Ivey, C. L. 2015. "Combating Epistemic Violence with Islamic Feminism: Qahera vs. FEMEN." *Women's Studies in Communication* 38 (4): 384–387.

Janmohamed, S. 2013. "Hallelujah! Even Muslim Women Can Now Be Superheroes." *The Telegraph*, November 6. http://www.telegraph.co.uk/women/womens-life/10430505/Even-Muslim-women-can-be-superheroes.-Hallelujah.html.

Jebreal, R. 2013. "Meet the Muslim Ms. Marvel: Kamala Khan's Fight Against Stereotypes." *The Daily Beast*, November 8. http://www.thedailybeast.com/articles/2013/11/08/meet-the-muslim-ms-marvel-kamala-khan-s-fight-against-stereotypes.html.

Johnson, J. K. 2011. "Terrified Protectors: The Early Twenty-First Century Fear Narrative in Comic Book Superhero Stories." *Americana: The Journal of American Popular Culture (1900-Present)* 10 (2). http://www.american-popularculture.com/journal/articles/fall_2011/johnson.htm.

Jones, R. B. 2014. *(Re)thinking Orientalism: Using Graphic Narratives to Teach Critical Visual Literacy*. New York.

Kaplan, A. 2008. *From Krakow to Krypton: Jews and Comic Books*. Philadelphia.

Kent, M. 2015. "Unveiling Marvels: Ms. Marvel and the Reception of the New Muslim Superheroine." *Feminist Media Studies* 15 (3): 522–527.

Keyes, C. 2010. "Comic book publisher praised for reflecting 'tolerance of Islam'." *CNN.com*, May 11. http://www.cnn.com/2010/LIVING/04/27/kuwait.comics/.

Khoja-Moolji, S. S., and A. D. Niccolini. 2015. "Comics as Public Pedagogy: Reading Muslim Masculinities through Muslim Femininities in *Ms. Marvel*." *Girlhood Studies* 8 (3): 23–39.

Leigh, G. 2011. "Witnessing *Persepolis*: Comics, Trauma, and Childhood Testimony." In *Graphic Subjects. Critical Essays on Autobiography and Graphic Novels*, edited by M. A. Chaney. Wisconsin Studies in Autobiography, 157–163. Madison.

Letamendi, A. 2015. "Meet the Muslim Superhero Fighting Bigotry on San Francisco Buses." *The Guardian*, February 1. http://www.theguardian.com/books/2015/feb/01/meet-the-muslim-superhero-fighting-bigotry-on-san-francisco-buses.

Lewis, A. D. 2012. "The Militarism of American Superheroes after 9/11." In *Comic Books and American Cultural History*, edited by M. Pustz, 223–236. New York.

———. 2014. "Kismet Seventy Years Later: Recognizing the First Genuine Muslim Superhero." *ISLAMiCommentary*, March 19. http://islamicommentary.org/2014/03/kismet-seventy-years-later-recognizing-the-first-genuine-muslim-superhero/.

Lewis, A. D., and C. H. Kraemer, eds. 2010. *Graven Images: Religion in Comic Books and Graphic Novels*. New York.

Lund, M. 2012. "Gud i fyrfärgstryck. Om tecknade serier, moral och teologi." *Religionsvetenskaplig Internettidskrift* 2 (13).

———. 2015a. "'[A] Matter of SAVED or LOST': Difference, Salvation, and Subjection in Chick Tracts." In *Comics and Power: Representing and Questioning Culture, Subjects and Communities*, edited by R. P. Cortsen, E. La Cour, and A. Magnussen, 177–196. Newcastle upon Tyne.

———. 2015b. "The Mutant Problem: *X-Men*, Confirmation Bias, and the Methodology of Comics and Identity." *European Journal of American Studies* 10 (2). http://ejas.revues.org/10890.

———. 2016. *Re-Constructing the Man of Steel: Superman 1938–1941, Jewish Ameri-can History, and the Invention of the Jewish-Comics Connection*. New York.

McLain, K. 2009. *India's Immortal Comic Books: Gods, Kings, and Other Heroes.* Bloomington.

Meier, S. 2013. "'Truth, Justice, and the Islamic Way': Conceiving the Cos-mopolitan Muslim Superhero in *The 99*." In *Transnational Perspective on Graphic Narratives: Comics at the Crossroads*, edited by D. Stein, S. Denson, and C. Meyer, 181–193. London.

Michael, J. 2008. *Identity and the Failure of America: From Thomas Jefferson to the War on Terror*. Minneapolis.

Michalak, L. 1988. *Cruel and Unusual: Negative Images of Arabs in American Popular Culture*. 3rd ed. Washington D.C.

Molnar, L. 2012. "First Muslim Superhero in 'Green Lantern'." *Daily Gossip*, September 5. http://www.dailygossip.org/first-muslim-superhero-in-green-lantern-4433.

Naghibi, N., and A. O'Malley. 2005. "Estranging the Familiar: 'East' and 'West' in Satrapi's Persepolis." *ESC: English Studies in Canada* 1 (2): 223–247.

Pervez, S. 2013. "Why We all Should Marvel at this Muslim Superhero." *The Independent*, November 14. http://www.independent.co.uk/voices/comment/why-we-all-should-marvel-at-this-muslim-superhero-8932359.html.

Priego, E. 2016. "Ms Marvel: Metamorphosis and Transfiguration of the 'Minority' Superhero." *The Winnower*. https://thewinnower.com/papers/2746-ms-marvel-metamorphosis-and-transfiguration-of-the-minority-superhero#submit.

Said, E. W. 1981. *Covering Islam: How the Media and the Experts Determine How We See the Rest of the World*. New York.

Santo, A. 2014. "'Is It a Camel? Is It a Turban? No, It's The 99': Branding Islamic Superheroes as Authentic Global Cultural Commodities." *Television & New Media* 15 (7): 679–695.

Sayyid, B. 1997. *A Fundamental Fear: Eurocentrism and the Emergence of Isla-mism*. London and New York.

Schlussel, D. 2013. "Marvel Comics Adds Muslim Chick Superhero (to Ap-pease Marvel's Muslim Chick Editor)." Debbieschlussel.com, November 5. http://www.debbieschlussel.com/67082/marvel-comics-adds-mus-lim-chick-superhero-to-appease-marvels-muslim-chick-editor/.

Shaheen, J. G. 1994. "Arab Images in American Comic Books." *Journal of Popular Culture* 28 (1): 123–133.

———. 2009. *Reel Bad Arabs: How Hollywood Vilifies a People*. Northampton.

Skelton, S. 2006. *The Gospel According to the World's Greatest Superhero*. Eugene.

Smith, M. J. 2001. "The Tyranny of the Melting Pot Metaphor: Wonder Woman as the Americanized Immigrant." In *Comics & Ideology*, edited by M. P. McAllister, E. H. Sewell, Jr., and I. Gordon, 129–50. New York.

Strömberg, F. (2011), "'Yo, rag-head!': Arab and Muslim Superheroes in American Comic Books after 9/11," *Amerikastudien/American Studies* 56 (4): 573–601.

van Leeuwen, T., and U. Suleiman. 2010. "Globalizing the Local: The Case of an Egyptian Superhero Comic." In *The Handbook of Language and Globalization*, edited by N. Coupland, 232–254. Chichester.

Varisco, D. M. 2007. "The Tragedy of a Comic: Fundamentalists Crusading against Fundamentalists." *Contemporary Islam* 1 (3): 207–230.

Weinstein, S. 2006. *Up, Up, and Oy Vey!: How Jewish History, Culture, and Values Shaped the Comic Book Superhero*. Baltimore.

Wright, B. 2001. *Comic Book Nation: The Transformation of Youth Culture in America*. Baltimore.

Niqab not *Burqa*:
Reading the Veil in Marvel's Dust

Nicholaus Pumphrey

COINCIDING WITH POPULAR MEDIA TRENDS in the U.S. post-9/11, comic book creators also propagated stereotypical depictions of Muslims as terrorists along with other "well-intentioned-but nevertheless-stereotypical-characters."[1] As early as December of 2001, Marvel Comics responded to the terrorist attacks in New York with *Amazing Spider-Man #36*, by J. Michael Straczynski and John Romita, Jr. Popularly known as the "Black Issue" due to its imageless, all-black cover meant as a sign of mourning, the issue showed the heroes of the Marvel Universe responding to the destruction of the Twin Towers. It contained a scene where some of Marvel's worst supervillains mourned the destruction of the city and the lives lost. Even Doctor Doom, the archenemy of Marvel's Fantastic Four, who has tried on multiple occasions to destroy New York, shed a tear in reaction to the terrorist attacks. Doctor Doom's crying implied that Muslim terrorists were even worse, more destructive, and, significantly, more Other than previous villains of Marvel Comics.[2] Soon after 9/11, Marvel updated Iron Man's origin story and Captain America's modern adventures to have both characters fighting Islamic terrorists.[3]

In December 2002, against this cultural backdrop, Marvel introduced Sooraya Qadir in *New X-Men #133*.[4] Sooraya, codenamed Dust, is a veiled Muslima from Afghanistan. The issue describes her mutant powers as transforming "into sand, and [she] can project herself with enough velocity to flay the skin off you." This power extends to her transforming her entire body and clothing into sand. She was created by writer Grant Morrison and artist Ethan van Sciver in the aftermath of 9/11, in an attempt to satirize the fear that Americans were propagating and to create a misunderstood hero based on obvious stereotypes that all Muslim women wear *burqas*.[5]

---

1. Strömberg 2011, 574.
2. Straczynski and Romita 2001.
3. Ellis and Granov 2005; Rieber and Cassaday 2002.
4. Morrison and van Sciver 2002.
5. Morrison 2011, 356.

Originally created in 1963, the X-Men are a group of super-powered beings and mutants who have often been used to represent heroes and outcasts. For most of their publication history, the team has been led by Charles Xavier, codenamed Professor X, who has not only trained them but also educated them at his school for gifted youth. The X-Men have fought to keep peace between humans and mutants, often battling both. Grant Morrison's *New X-Men* re-introduced Magneto, one of the series' oldest adversaries, as the primary villain of the series. The veiled Muslima from Afghanistan that Morrison created would add further nuance to what it means to be an outcast after 9/11. She can be read as a hero, while the white male Magneto was the obvious villain.

The way Dust has been characterized and represented under Morrison and after, and the version of her that is most widely known, is a negative reinforcement of the Muslima stereotype, but it could also be read as a positive representation of veiled Muslims. Freelance writer and comic book store owner Eric Garneau and data analyst Maura Foley note that the creation of Dust was part of Morrison's "rebellion against post-9/11 homogenization" and that he left her characterization open-ended.[6] Morrison admits that he had plans for Dust, but the "situation had become so volatile that I just didn't want to touch her after 9/11."[7] As a result, much of her character was developed after Morrison's run ended. She wears a veil that covers her face except for her eyes, a *niqab,* and an *abaya* that covers the remainder of her body, which is mislabeled in many comics as a *burqa* (a *burqa* would cover her eyes).

Six years after Dust's creation, and after numerous references to her *burqa,* in *New X-Men* #42 (November 2007), then-writers Craig Kyle and Chris Yost attempted to rectify the mislabeling of Dust's veil. Their correction was made in a conversation between Dust and her fellow X-Men Pixie and Nehzno:

> Pixie: So why do you wear that burqa? You're so pretty! Everyone's seen you without it now, and it's got to be really, really hot.
>
> Nehzno: It is not a burqa. It is an abaya with a niqab veil. Show respect for Sooraya by learning about her.
>
> Dust: I ... Thank you, Nehzno.[8]

Why did it take six years? Given the post-9/11 climate, this stereotypical depiction of a Muslim woman became prevalent and especially problematic.

6. Garneau and Foley 2014, 182.
7. DeFalco 2006, 235.
8. Kyle et al. 2007c.

However, the veil is a complex symbol that can be read as damning as well as empowering for a character like Dust. As a result, it is not a simple matter to judge Dust's depiction as positive or negative. Rather, to understand her, we need to examine how she opens up for multiple readings. In order to do that, we need first to look at the thing that, in many ways, has come to define her in the popular imagination: the veil.

Reception of the Veil

Feminist theological readings can take many forms. One common strategy, as exemplified by feminist theologian Rosemary Radford Ruether's *Sexism and God-talk*, is to examine a religious doctrine and both show how it is dictated or created by a patriarchal system and how it inhibits women's full humanity or prevents their communion with the divine.[9] Feminist theologians uncover such blatantly male-centric readings and show how they are flawed and thus can be ignored or read in a different light. Another possible feminist way of reading is to take a tradition and show how women already have agency within it, regardless of their position within a patriarchal system, as anthropologist Saba Mahmood does in her book *Politics of Piety*.[10] The politics of the veil continue to be controversial for both Muslims and non-Muslims, especially since its "meanings are not fixed or static across histories and societies," as scholar of Islam Leila Ahmed notes.[11] Outsiders often understand women being forced to cover their head as an obvious sign of an oppressive patriarchal system. This mode of thinking reached its peak in the U.S. directly after 9/11. In a radio address on November 17, 2001, First Lady Laura Bush stated that,

> Afghan women know, through hard experience, what the rest of the world is discovering: The brutal oppression of women is a central goal of the terrorists [...] civilized people throughout the world are speaking out in horror – not only because our hearts break for the women and children of Afghanistan, but also because in Afghanistan we see the world the terrorists would like to impose on the rest of us [...] the fight against terrorism is also a fight for the rights and dignity of women.[12]

Bush's comments were well received by like-minded Americans, who saw

9. Ruether 1983.
10. Mahmood 2010.
11. Ahmed 2011, 212.
12. Bush 2001.

Islam as oppressing women through religious dress such as the veil, but the comments also sparked critical commentary by many scholars of Islam.[13]

As a result, in the past decade, the veil has become a major point of discussion in Islamic Studies, to the point that it has become "so overinvested with meaning that one can no longer speak of it in any simple way."[14] Ahmed writes, "As the burka [*sic*] of Afghanistan became a pervasive image in the media, so also did the subject of women in Islam, and in particular the 'oppression of women in Islam,' emerge as a salient theme in relation to issues of war and the moral rightness of war, and even in explanations of why America had been attacked."[15] The veil became the symbol and signifier of Muslim women, and especially of the "violence Islam has inflicted upon women."[16]

The two most common scholarly debates regarding the history of the veil center on whether or not it is culturally appropriated from pre-Islamic Arabia and whether the practice of veiling empowers women, respectively. Many feminist scholars of Islam and the Qur'an claim that the prescription to veil existed prior to Islam, in Christianity, Judaism, and pre-Islamic Arabia, as a cultural and social construct meant to control women. Islamic studies scholar Asma Barlas believes that a view of the Qur'an that generalizes and universalizes the prescription of veiling does not take into account the "temporal/spatial contexts of the Qur'an's teachings."[17] Most of the prevailing ideas about veiling come from interpretations of two Surahs: Surah 24 and Surah 33. However, the Qur'an does not give a commandment to veil; instead it speaks of modesty. Qur'an scholar Amina Wadud states:

> The Qur'an acknowledges the virtue of modesty and demonstrates
> it through the prevailing practices. The principle of modesty is
> important – not the veiling and seclusion which were manifestations
> particular to that context [fifth-century century Arabia]. These were
> culturally and economically determined demonstrations of modesty.[18]

According to scholars like Wadud, if the veil is a culturally driven symbol and not a Qur'anically driven one, then it should not be a mandatory Islamic prescription.

Although some scholars claim that the veil is an obvious sign of subju-

13. Oliver 2007.
14. Barlas 2002, 57.
15. Ahmed 2001, 222.
16. Mahmood 2005, 195.
17. Barlas 2002, 53.
18. Wadud 1999, 10.

gation in a patriarchal system, some scholars see veiling as a liberating act, of having agency and power by actively choosing it. Scholars such as Saba Mahmood believe that Muslim women can embrace the veil and still operate within an empowered feminist identity. These women do not see the veil as a symbol of oppression, but as a symbol of the submission to Allah.[19] Leila Ahmed notes that "widely viewed as the emblem of Islamic patriarchy and oppression, [the veil] had come to signal a call for gender justice (of all things) and a call for equality for minorities."[20]

Ahmed, who often argues against mandatory veiling, believes that the reclamation of the veil as a symbol of empowerment and cultural/religious heritage can only exist in a post-9/11 America and Europe. In the discourses of geopolitics the reemergent veil is an emblem of many things, prominent among which is its meaning as the rejection of the West, she states, adding that "the reemergent veil attests, by virtue of its very power as a symbol of resistance, to the uncontested hegemonic diffusion of the discourses of the West in our age."[21] As a result, the veil is a dynamic text that is read and authored by both wearer and audience. It can be a symbol of subjugation to a patriarchal system, but it can also be read as a symbol of agency or power, as well as a symbol of identity against oppressive stereotypes. As a result, and as noted above, the depiction of Dust historically is complicated, and she can be read in multiple ways.

History of Dust

Dust has been defined through five major stages and one recent depiction: her creation by Grant Morrison and Ethan van Sciver; her role in *New X-Men: Academy X* (July 2004–Dec. 2005) written by Nunzio DeFilippis and Christina Weir, and drawn by Randy Green, Staz Johnson, Michael Ryan, Paco Medina, and Aaron Lopresti; the four part mini-series *New X-Men: Hellions* written by DeFilippis and Weir and drawn by Clayton Henry (July 2005–Oct. 2005); the end of *New X-Men* by writers Craig Kyle and Chris Yost, and drawn by Mark Brooks, Paco Medina, Duncan Rouleau, Mike Norton, Skottie Young, Niko Henrichon, and Humberto Ramos (Jan. 2006–March 2008); Marc Guggenheim's *Young X-Men* (2008–2009), with artists Yanick Paquette, Ben Oliver, and Rafa Sandoval contributing; and finally, her most recent appearance as of this writing, in *E is for Extinction*, written by Chris Burnham and Dennis Culver and drawn by Ramon Villalobos (June 2015–September 2015).

19. Mahmood 2005.
20. Ahmed 2011, 211.
21. Ahmed 2011, 235.

In this long history, Dust has gone through periods where she has been a major character and periods where had only the occasional appearance. She is very much a product of the post-9/11 world and the attempt by comic book authors and artists to interact with contemporary issues of terrorism, war, and Islamophobia. Historian Jeffery K. Johnson writes:

> As the leaders and marketers of the war on terror encouraged Americans to be afraid, comic book superheroes advised readers to trust no one, not even themselves. Once again, superheroes became a product of the society that created them and presented a mirror for Americans to view themselves.[22]

The subtexts of the "real world" needed to become overt in the post-9/11 world.

Grant Morrison admits that he, too, depicts more realism; however, with Dust he attempted to create a critique of the dominant narrative.[23] The first suggestion of Dust, even before her official first appearance, came in *New X-Men* #115, where a similarly garbed student is depicted in a classroom in the all-mutant utopia Genosha. The civilization and most of its inhabitants are destroyed in this issue by a giant, mutant-killing robot called a Sentinel. The student that is briefly seen is not Dust herself, but her appearance shows that Morrison or van Sciver were contemplating a veiled character before Dust's official creation. Dust was created by Morrison specifically to be an answer to the post-9/11 paranoia and to complicate the clear divisions between hero and terrorist. He has said that,

> Over its forty-issue run, *New X-Men* turned into a diary of my own growing distrust of a post-9/11 conformity culture that appeared to be in the process of greedily consuming the unusual and different.[24]

In Dust's first official appearance, in December 2002, the X-Man Wolverine rescues her from slave traders in Afghanistan, some of whom have had their skin stripped from their bones because they tried to lift her veil.[25] In this same issue, Professor X convinces a hijacker named Mohammed to not hijack an airplane.

Psychology scholar Jehanzeb Dar believes that Dust is an example of the "Western male gaze" which solely focuses on Muslim women as oppressed, by not only their religion but also their men, and in need of saving by a

22. Johnson 2011.
23. Morrison 2011, 347.
24. Morrison 2011, 356.
25. Morrison and van Sciver 2002.

Western male hero, which happens in this case to be Wolverine.[26] This moment echoes post-colonial scholar Gayatri Spivak's critical summary of the Western narrative: "white men are saving brown women from brown men."[27] About Dust's battle against the slave traders, Dar asks, "Since there weren't any 'good Muslim men' around to take a stand against the Taliban's perverted behavior, who better to rescue her than Wolverine, or rather, 'Western democracy?'"[28] After her rescue, Dust is practically voiceless and can only say the eponymous *turaab*, Arabic for "dust."

With Dust's creation, the reader is introduced to a stereotypical caricature of a Muslima hero in contrast to a stereotypical depiction of a Muslim terrorist. Morrison parallels the two in order to complicate the classification of "good Muslims" and "bad Muslims," but still creates a stereotypical portrayal. In "Grant Morrison's Mutants and the Post-9/11 Culture of Fear," Eric Garneau and Maura Foley write that, "The complex world Morrison constructs pulls from and sheds a light on the political climate of post-9/11 America, particularly the cultural cost of the War on Terror."[29] Morrison specifically takes the stereotypical depiction of a veiled woman and uses it to create conflict. The reader recognizes the stereotype, but then questions it as soon as she reads Dust's story.

With *New X-Men: Academy X,* Nunzio DeFilippis and Christina Weir took over the writing of Dust. In this series, she is integrated fully into the X-Men school. She joins a particular training squad, the Hellions, and is given a roommate, Surge. In many of the Dust stories during the DeFilippis and Weir run, she attempts to compete against the other team and tries to fit in with her classmates while being Muslim.

In the December 2005 "Yearbook" special for *New X-Men,* Dust is voted "Most Mysterious." Her biographical entry states that, after being placed in a "special class" at the Xavier Institute, "She continued to wear her traditional burqa, seen by many as a sign of the oppression of women under the Taliban, and few at the school understood her." This emphasizes that her "*burqa*" is a major issue for her perception by her peers.[30] The fact that Dust's veil is not a *burqa* shows the authors' limited knowledge and furthers the stereotypical depiction of Muslim women in comics. The authors contrast American gender stereotypes against what they believe are conservative Muslim standards through Dust's roommate Noriko (Surge), a young, flirtatious mutant

---

26. Dar 2010, 107.
27. Spivak 1988, 298.
28. Dar 2010, 107.
29. Garneau and Foley 2014, 179.
30. DeFilippis et al. 2005b.

who wears as little clothing as possible. In their first meeting in the August 2004 issue, Dust says she does not understand American music, and Surge responds with the following:

Surge: Yeah, whatever. And speaking of things we don't *understand...*is that outfit you're wearing *actually* a *Burqa*?

Dust: Yes. It is *traditional* in Afghanistan to –

Surge: Cover yourself from head to toe in *shame* and be *subservient* to men?

(Dust removes the veil.)

Dust: No. The Burqa is about *modesty*. There are *boys* and *men* on campus. And it is not right for me to show off by *exposing* myself or my flesh to them.

Surge: Are you saying I expose too much flesh?

Dust: I do not *judge* the way you dress. I only ask that you do the *same* for me.

Surge: You know what? You *do* judge me. You just said that exposing flesh is *showing off.* I don't need to be lectured by someone who's setting women back *fifty years* just by walking around like *that.* [31]

After this heated exchange, Surge slams the door. Later, when she encounters Cyclops, a longtime X-Man and headmaster of the school, she tells him she needed to "get some air," because she was frustrated over the fact he gave her a "*religious nut* for a room-mate!"[32] English scholar Rich Shivener asserts that this issue shows American sentiment about Muslims during the war in Afghanistan.[33] Surge represents American ignorance towards Muslim women. She confirms a widespread and misguided fear and distrust of Islam, especially considering a Pew survey, which claims that seventy-four percent of Americans do not have in-depth knowledge of Islam.[34] Surge, then, understands Dust in the same way as any average American.

Surge continues to question the veil, and in the December 2004 issue of *New X-Men* she states, "You wear the burqa because you're told to. You come down here because Julian [her team leader] told you to. You make me *sick!* Do you *always* do what you're told?"[35] This Dust has virtually no agency. She

31. DeFilippis et al. 2004a.
32. DeFilippis et al. 2004a.
33. Shivener 2014.
34. Pew Research 2009.
35. DeFilippis et al. 2004b.

seems to wear her *niqab* because of her indoctrination in the religion and follows orders blindly. Dar states:

> Her reasoning to cover herself is somewhat inaccurate and stereotypical [...] Quite frequently, Dust speaks about "protecting herself from men," which not only make men sound [*sic*] lustful and perverted, but it also sexualizes herself and makes her an object of desire [...] It is her religion that divides her from others, which not only plays into stereotypes about how "religion divides," but also how Islam in particular places "harsh restrictions" on Muslim women in general. Almost every time the reader sees Dust, she is praying and asking God for forgiveness for whatever sin she may have committed. Unfortunately, Dust fulfills the negative stereotype that Islam is restrictive and that God is someone to constantly ask forgiveness from, especially if you're a woman.[36]

Dust's depiction throughout the DeFilippis and Weir run is constantly in flux, and, as Dar suggests, she is often sexualized. In several instances, the reader is allowed to view her under the *niqab* and *abaya*. In *New X-Men* #6, drawn by Michael Ryan, she is completely naked, covered only by her hands and some well-placed plant life.[37] This act seems to satisfy the male gaze, by stripping away the female Oriental Other's *burqa* and giving a view of the "beautiful" woman hiding underneath, an oversexualized view based on the mystery of the *burqa*. In other instances, Dust's clothing is tight-fitting, showing off her hips or even the outline of her breasts, working in the direct opposite of the *niqab*'s purpose. This is true of Paco Medina's art in various issues. This dissonance becomes especially ironic in the July 2005 issue, *New X-Men* #14, wherein Dust, drawn in such a sexualized way, refuses to attend a school dance because of her modesty.[38] Another noteworthy example can be found in *New X-Men* #19, the last issue of the DeFilippis and Weir run. Set in an alternate timeline called "House of M," where Marvel's mutants have been granted their deepest desires, Dust is depicted without her *niqab*, wearing instead a tight top and a miniskirt. In a state of induced confusion and anger, she accuses her closest friend of changing her, since she once had "faith" and "morals."[39]

New X-Men ended with a 26-issue run by Craig Kyle and Chris Yost, in which the writers attempted to shift how Dust was portrayed. Kyle and Yost increased her appearances and made her one of the series' major characters.

36. Dar 2010, 108.
37. DeFilippis et al. 2004b.
38. DeFilippis et al. 2005a.
39. DeFilippis et al. 2005b.

They focused on her in particular in one story arc, making her an opposite to the mutant-hating, fanatical preacher William Stryker. In this storyline, Kyle and Yost intentionally contrast the fanatical religion of Reverend William Stryker with the peaceful religion of Dust. Stryker's first appearance was in the graphic novel *God Loves, Man Kills*, where he attempts to eradicate mutants after his son is born one.[40] Stryker uses religious language to condemn mutants as sinful. He eventually becomes a televangelist and attempts to kill Kitty Pryde, a Jewish X-Man, on television.[41] He frequently quotes the Bible in justification of his actions, and he represents the potentially destructive nature of Christian fundamentalism.

In *New X-Men*, Stryker has used technology from the future to plan the death of all mutants. Killing Dust is pivotal for his plan to succeed, because her mutation has the potential to be very powerful, and so she would pose too serious a threat if she were allowed to live. In Stryker's eyes, Dust is doubly sinful, both because of his view of mutants as abomination and because of her religion. After Stryker's plot to kill Dust fails, the two engage in a forceful exchange:

Stryker: The *Muslim* ... I don't understand ... God showed me your death ... I made it happen, you *abomination* ... *I killed you!*

Dust: Be silent! No God would condone such horror! Such hatred! You are the abomination![42]

In August of 2006, it was still common for Americans to see Islam as violent.[43] Kyle and Yost use Dust to show that fundamentalism exists in all religions, which has long been a common liberal reaction to Muslim stereotypes.[44] They bolster this argument by depicting Stryker as a white, male Christian, killing people in the name of his cause, and contrasting him with the veiled Muslima hero.

Kyle and Yost also emphasize Dust's Islamic beliefs more than previous writers had. Although they make mistakes, the main reason for adding more religion content seems to be to accurately depict Dust's tradition. In the March 2006 issue, she confirms that she is Sunni, after being asked by another character.[45] In the May issue, she says prayers or makes exclamations in Arabic, often with no translation.[46] When William Stryker bombs a

40. Claremont and Brent 1982.
41. Rennaker 2014.
42. Kyle et al. 2006c.
43. Esposito 2011.
44. Armstrong 2000.
45. Kyle et al. 2006a.
46. Kyle et al. 2006b.

bus as it is leaving the school, killing several mutant teenagers, she says the traditional Islamic funeral prayer for them. Dust also uses Arabic in the July issue *New X-Men* #38, when she travels to a hell-dimension called Limbo and encounters the demon Belasco, whom she calls Shaitan. [47]

Kyle and Yost also attempt to correct the previous mistake of calling Dust's clothes a *burqa* in the aforementioned conversation between Dust, Nehzno, and Pixie.[48] This is an attempt to correct the continuity and to make a statement informing readers, and it includes a value judgment on the previous authors, which is further emphasized when the villains in the story continue to call the veil a *burqa*. Although the conversation about Dust's *niqab* is meant to correct such errors, her depiction is almost more problematic than the art during DeFilippis and Weir's *New X-Men*. Artist Paco Medina continues to draw her with the tight, form-fitting *niqab*. One scene in *New X-Men* #24 is particularly noteworthy for its extremely provocative close-up view of Dust from behind.[49] In issue #27, also drawn by Medina, the reader again gets to see Dust without her *niqab*, as a beautiful girl in her underwear.[50]

Following *New X-Men*, Marc Guggenheim's twelve-issue story-arc, *Young X-Men*, traces the lives of a few teenage X-Men from *New X-Men*, primarily Dust, the chameleon-like Anole, the precognitive Blindfold, and a rock-skinned character named Rockslide, alongside a group of mutants created specifically for this story. One of the major new characters is Ink, a human who receives powers once he is tattooed by a mutant tattoo artist. The main plot revolves around the group of mutants being tricked by the X-Men leader Cyclops, in actuality an imposter named Donald Pierce. Pierce, a mutant-hating cyborg, wants the group to kill the original New Mutants, a young X-Men team created in the 1980s. In the end of the story, Dust dies but is soon resurrected by Ink using a newly acquired resurrecting power that leaves him comatose.

In *Young X-Men*, Dust assumes the role of a moral compass, as though her religious identity makes her the most ethical character. In several instances, Dust corrects Rockslide when he makes sexist comments.[51] Much like Kyle and Yost, Guggenheim also makes attempts to discuss both Islamophobia and radical Islam. In issue #6, the X-Men have imprisoned Pierce, and Dust begins discussing religion with him. Pierce states: "You're perversions. You

---

47. Kyle et al. 2007b.
48. Kyle et al. 2007c.
49. Kyle et al. 2007b.
50. Kyle et al. 2007c.
51. Guggenheim and Paquette 2008.

in particular, Sooraya, with your unholy, oppressive religion." Dust responds, "I enjoy talking to you, Mr. Pierce. Your unbridled prejudice and hate, to say nothing of your tragic misunderstanding of Mohammed's teachings ... it reminds me of home."[52] In the next issue, she responds to Pierce, again specifically addressing Islamophobia and its relation to anti-mutant bigotry: "I'm a mutant and a Muslim, Mr. Pierce. I know something of bigotry. And *bigots*. There's no greater satisfaction for one than to have their prejudices justified by a minority's self-hatred."[53] In Guggenheim's construction, Dust's character represents a multilayeredness of identities and oppressions, by being a woman, a mutant, and a Muslim.

Dust's clothing is very different under Guggenheim and his artists, and it even contributes to a mild loss of identity in a few issues. The first major alteration, done by artist Yanick Paquette, is the addition of a yellow sash and yellow gloves, which serves to make Dust's *abaya* into an X-costume.[54] In issues #8–9, Rafa Sandoval draws her *abaya* as less of a cloak and more as a cape: she is here visibly wearing a black and yellow X-costume underneath, and the *abaya* is open and flowing behind her.[55] However, in issue #10, artist Ben Oliver draws her again wearing the traditional *abaya*, but it is in his version slightly form-fitting.[56] The last notable depiction of Dust comes in issue #11, where Pierce convinces her to free him. Following this, the narrative jumps into a dystopian future, where she is the most powerful mutant alive, bent on eradicating the mutant population. Much like in the "House of M" episode by DeFilippis and Weir, she has here exchanged her *niqab* for a tight and revealing halter top.[57] As a result of all the inconsistent visual depictions, the talks with the bigoted Pierce, which are poorly motivated in terms of characterization, and Dust's turn to evil in the series' potential future, it is hard to determine if Guggenheim's attempt to expose bigotry and Islamophobia was successful.

At the time of writing, one of the most recent representations of Dust is the *E is for Extinction* series from 2015, written by Chris Burnham and Dennis Culver and drawn by Ramon Villalobos. The book is meant to be an alternate take on Grant Morrison and artist Frank Quitely's eponymous story arc that ran in *New X-Men* #114–117. In this story, set several years into the future of an alternate timeline, the classic X-team, led by Cyclops, fights Magneto's team, of which Dust is a member. Although the story arc only lasted four

52. Guggenheim and Oliver 2008a.
53. Guggenheim and Oliver 2008b.
54. Guggenheim and Panquette 2008.
55. Guggenheim and Sandoval 2009ab.
56. Guggenheim and Oliver 2009.
57. Guggenheim and Sandoval 2009c.

issues, two major alterations to Dust occur. First, her outfit as depicted by Villalobos looks more like a *burqa,* in that it completely obscures her face and has only a tiny slit for her eyes. Second, she is much more assertive than in her other depictions, and even seems to be the leader of the team. In issue #2, after Cyclops has tried to convince her that she and her teammates are being misled by Magneto, she responds, with more assertiveness than ever before,

> Your argument would be far more compelling if you weren't
> just caught trying to hypnotize us into believing we were being
> manipulated! You come into our school in the middle of the night
> shooting lasers – This is why you never accomplish anything, Scott
> Summers![58]

In five different representations, Dust has been depicted along different lines, which makes it possible to read her and her veil in multiple ways.

Dust as Damaging or Empowering

What makes the reception of serialized superhero comics so interesting is that it is exceedingly rare for any one writer or artist to depict a character alone. Further, readers will accept some characterizations and depictions and reject others, based on their own diverse readings. Still, there is an officially "sanctioned" continuity, which exists on multiple levels. Comics scholar Richard Reynolds identifies what he calls "serial continuity" as a type of continuity that emerges when one comic follows another in a series.[59] Each new comic builds upon earlier ones, and the continuity established thereby should, in theory, stay consistent.

However, as the different iterations of Dust discussed above show, she is not static, nor is any other similar character: her various characterizations are, in certain aspects, widely different from each other. Her writers and artists have, at times, clearly worked at cross-purposes. This complicates the reading of Dust and her depiction of the veil. English and comics scholar Neil Shyminski emphasizes that most comic book readers are white, cis-male heterosexuals and that the X-Men allow "privileged white males to appropriate a discourse of marginalization."[60] If Shyminsky's reading is right, Morrison, DeFilippis and Weir, Kyle and Yost, Guggenheim, and Burnham and Culver are writing primarily for a white male audience. All

---

58. Burnham et al. 201
59. Reynolds 1992, 38.
60. Shyminksy 2006, 389.

are communicating through potentially damaging stereotypes, and all are fraught with mistakes.

Journalist and comics scholar Fredrik Strömberg writes,

> Because images are a part of a narrative flow in comics and are not meant to be viewed separately from the text, cartoonists have often simplified their characters, making them more iconic and easily identifiable.[61]

As a result, comics have "a tendency to employ stereotypical features."[62] Communications scholars Julie Davis and Robert Westerfelhaus note:

> Depicting religious identity is easiest, especially for those outside the tradition, when that identity is tied to an easily recognizable visual index, such as the distinctive garb and grooming practices of the Amish or Hassidic Jews. Such visual elements are used to draw attention to characters' religious identity in films and television.[63]

Kyle and Yost may have attempted to elevate Dust and correct earlier errors in the text, but one mention of the proper terminology is not going to change the readers. Regardless, barring changes in comics industry hiring practices, Muslim men and Muslim women are predominantly going to be portrayed from an outsider perspective and through stereotypes. Strömberg writes that most post-9/11 Arab and Muslim superheroes

> seem to have been created to resist stereotypical or racist configurations of Arabs and/or Muslims as terrorists, submissive veiled women, and so on. Yet despite this attempt, these representations still partake in the Othering of these ethnic and religious groups by reinforcing stereotypes of 'the Oriental.'[64]

Islamic studies scholars Peter Gottschalk and Gabriel Greenberg state that it is the disembodied veil, and not the woman herself, that represents Islam. [65] Dust's *niqab*, as well as her ability to transform into faceless sand, reaffirms this reading of the "invisible" Muslim woman.

The X-Men are often read as an allegory of diversity and a metaphor for civil rights; however, this might be more a case of editorial attempts to control the readers or readers only understanding diversity as non-diverse

---

61. Strömberg 2011, 574.
62. Strömberg 2011, 574–575.
63. Davis and Westerfelhaus 2013, 802.
64. Strömberg 2011, 576–577.
65. Gottschalk and Greenberg 2008, 54.

outsiders. The works of comics scholar Joseph Darowski show that the political and historical issues of American society usually have allegorical equivalents within comics.[66] Similar to Shyminsky, Darowski's book *X-Men and the Mutant Metaphor* shows that statistically the X-Men comics have not contained the ethnic and gender diversity that is usually attributed to them, and that, as a result, it is a stretch for white cis-male heterosexual mutants to be read, for example, as reflective of the African American experience, as empowering to women, or as representative of the LGBTQ community.[67] Darowski explains that, for the most part, when conservative political ideals are common in American society, X-Men are mainly white males and the villains are minority groups. When the team has been less dominated by white, straight mutants, the effect has often been very tokenistic, as for example in *Giant Size X-Men* #1, where the team was composed of an international array of mutants. Similarly, it is only to be expected that the X-Men should include a Muslim character in the post-9/11 context, even if it is likely that it, too, will be tokenistic or stereotypical.

Nonetheless, as noted, reading Dust is not as simple as it might appear at first glance. One reading of Dust, especially emphasized by Kyle and Yost, is that she indeed has agency and the ability to choose. By depicting her as an empowered character, it seems that the writers complicate the stereotypical depiction of Muslims, or at least they were trying to. American studies scholar Nolween Mignant suggests that characters like Dust actually acquire "a new power over language, word, and action."[68] She writes that, "in fact, the 9/11 events seem to have had the paradoxical effect of leading Hollywood to become more sophisticated in the way it depicts Arabs and Muslims. Far from being radicalized, the representation became 'more nuanced' and 'more balanced.'"[69] Davis and Westerfelhaus similarly see Dust's Otherness as a way to enter into American culture:

> By situating Dust within the monomyth metanarrative informing the superhero genre, she is afforded a liminal license that permits her entry into American mainstream culture, even though some of her beliefs and practices are perceived by some to be at variance with the culture's core values [...] In introducing Dust, Marvel managed to make a place within its universe for a Muslimah superheroine, but that place is a small one, far removed from its narrative center.[70]

66. E.g. Darowski 2014a; 2014b.
67. Darowski 2014b.
68. Mignant 2014, 179.
69. Mignant 2014, 168.
70. Davis and Westerfelhaus 2013, 807.

Based on this reading, the character of Dust sometimes creates an example of a hero who does not conform to the "normative" American standard. Granted, no iteration is free of stereotype. DeFillipis and Weir position her as an alien Other. Conversely, Guggenheim's Dust is willing to debate religious politics of bigotry and fundamentalism. Looking at the newest – though "alternative" – version of Dust in *E is for Extinction*, she is an assertive and free-speaking leader.

Furthermore, the options for reading Dust extend beyond her printed characterizations, and are to a significant degree dependent on context. Islamic studies scholar, feminist, and Muslim American Kecia Ali states that she does not want to cover herself, and that she does not "dwell on veiling in my thinking, writing or teaching about Islam."[71] However, after the Boston Marathon bombing, she chose to read Dust as an empowering hero, when she donned a Dust costume and raced through the streets during a "Heroes and Villains 5K." When she encountered a puzzled fellow runner, Ali explained, "I had chosen to run as Dust, a face-veil-and-abaya-wearing X-Men character who happens to be Muslim. I told him this and pointed out, 'I'm a hero, not a villain.'"[72] Even though Ali is conflicted about the veil and debates about whether it reinforces the caricature of Muslim women, she wore the costume to break down stereotypes and to assert that Muslim women can be heroes too. However, judging from the response that she received from her fellow runners, it seems that the complicated stereotype will take more effort to break.

Conclusion

Can a stereotypical Muslim hero be empowering, especially if the majority of U.S. readers are white American males? The simple fact that there is a Muslim character is in itself empowering to Muslims, at least to the extent that it can allow for a discussion of her depiction. Yes, Dust has reinforced the negative stereotype and caricature of Muslim women; however, when she is read amongst the growing roster of Muslim characters within the Marvel Universe, many of whom have appeared after Dust's creation, she can represent the diversity that Muslim women represent. M (Monet St. Croix), for example, is an Algerian French Muslim woman who is powerful and secular, choosing not to veil herself. Still, in recent times of distress, such as in the March 2015 issue of *X-Men*, she still connects to her Muslim background and says the *Basmalah*, meaning "in the name of Allah," which can be found in

71. Ali 2013.
72. Ali 2013.

the opening to the Qur'an and of many *surahs*.[73] Ms. Marvel is a young Muslim American with Pakistani parents, who wears a *hijab* while at the *masjid* but not in public. However, she often is depicted with a scarf tied around her neck draped over her costume like a cape.

Continuity issues are so complex that the reader's response is impossible to predict. The same can be said about the veil. Whether Dust is empowered by choosing to wear the *niqab* or has no agency, the historical scope of her characterization allows readers to give authority to one depiction or another, based on their own lived experience. Regardless of Dust's status as a hero, she reinforces damaging stereotypes that have the potential to bolster negativity towards Muslims. Only an informed reader can see the complexities and significance of a Muslima hero when the cultural milieu is dominated by the Muslim terrorist caricature.

73. Wilson and Boschi 2015.

Works Cited

Ahmed, L. 1992. *Women and Gender in Islam: Historical Roots of a Modern Debate.* New Haven.

———. *A Quiet Revolution: The Veil's Resurgence, from the Middle East to America.* New Haven.

Ali, K. 2013. "Embracing the Veil – If Only for One Day." *Cognoscenti.* May 1. http://cognoscenti.wbur.org/2013/05/01/muslim-women-boston-marathon-bombing-kecia-ali.

Armstrong, K. 2000. *The Battle for God.* New York.

Barlas, A. 2002. *"Believing Women" in Islam: Unreading Patriarchal Interpretations of the Qur'ān.* Austin.

Bush, L. 2001. Radio Address by Mrs. Bush. *The American Presidency Project.* November 17. http://www.presidency.ucsb.edu/ws/?pid=24992.

Burnham, C., D. Culver, and R. Villalobos. 2015. *E is for Extinction,* vol. 1 #2. New York.

Claremont, C., and B. Anderson. 1982. *Marvel Graphic Novel,* vol. 1 #5. New York.

Dar, J. 2010. "Holy Islamophobia, Batman! Demonization of Muslims and Arabs in Mainstream American Comic Books." In *Teaching Against Islamophobia,* edited by J. L. Kincheloe, S. R. Steinberg, and C. D. Stonebanks, 99–110. New York.

Darowski, J., ed. 2014a. *The Ages of the X-Men: Essays on the Children of the Atom in Changing Times.* Jefferson, NC.

———. 2014b. *X-Men and the Mutant Metaphor: Race and Gender in the Comic Books.* Lanham, MD.

Davis, J., and R. Westerfelhaus. 2013. "Finding a Place for a Muslimah Heroine in the Post-9/11 Marvel Universe: New X-Men's Dust." *Feminist Media Studies* 13 (5): 800–809.

DeFalco, T. 2006. *Comics Creators on X-Men.* London.

DeFilippis, N., C. Weir, R. Green, M. Ryan, A. Lopresti, P. Medina, and G. Jeanty. 2004a. *New X-Men,* vol. 2, #2. New York.

———. 2004b. *New X-Men,* vol. 2, #6. New York.

———. 2005a. *New X-Men,* vol. 2, #14. New York.

———. 2005b. *New X-Men,* vol. 2, #19. New York.

———. 2005c. *New X-Men,* vol. 2, Yearbook Special. New York.

DiPaolo, M. 2011. *War, Politics, and Superheroes: Ethics and Propaganda in Comics and Film.* Jefferson, NC.

Esposito, J. L., and I. Kalin. 2011. *Islamophobia: the Challenge of Pluralism in the 21st Century.* New York.

Ellis, W., and A. Granov. 2005. *The Invincible: Iron Man,* vol. 4, #1. New York.

Garneau, E., and M. Foley. 2014. "Grant Morrison's Mutants and the Post-9/11 Culture of Fear." In *The Ages of the X-Men: Essays on the Children of the Atom in Changing Times,* edited by J. J. Darowski, 178–188. Jefferson, NC.

Gottschalk, P., and G. Greenberg. 2008. *Islamophobia: Making Muslims the Enemy.* Lanham, MD.

Guggenheim, M., and B. Oliver. 2008a. *Young X-Men,* vol. 1, #6. New York.

———. 2008b. *Young X-Men,* vol. 1, #7. New York.

———. 2009. *Young X-Men,* vol. 1, #10. New York.

Guggenheim, M., and R. Sandoval. 2009a. *Young X-Men,* vol. 1, #8. New York.

———. 2009b. *Young X-Men,* vol. 1, #9. New York.

———. 2009c. *Young X-Men,* vol. 1, #11. New York.

Guggenheim, M., and Y. Paquette. 2008. *Young X-Men,* vol. 1, #1. New York.

Jenkins, P. and H. Ramos. 2004. *Spectacular Spider-Man*, vol. 2, #17. New York.

Johnson, J. K. 2011. "Terrified Protectors: The Early Twenty-First Century Fear Narrative in Comic Book Superhero Stories." *Americana: The Journal of American Popular Culture (1900-present)* 10 (2). http://www.american-popularculture.com/journal/articles/fall_2011/johnson.htm.

Klock, G. 2002. *How to Read Superhero Comics and Why.* New York.

Kyle, C., K. Yost, P. Medina, M. Brooks, and S. Young. 2006a. *New X-Men,* vol. 2, #22. New York.

———. 2006b. *New X-Men,* vol. 2, #24. New York.

———.2006c. *New X-Men,* vol. 2, #27. New York.

———.2007a. *New X-Men,* vol. 2, #33. New York.

———. 2007b. *New X-Men,* vol. 2, #38. New York.

———.2007c. *New X-Men,* vol. 2, #42. New York.

Mahmood, S. 2005. *The Politics of Piety: The Islamic Revival and the Feminist Subject.* Princeton.

Mingant, N. 2014. "Beyond Muezzins and Mujahideen: Middle-Eastern Voices in Post-9/11 Hollywood Movies." In *Muslims and American Popular Culture,* edited by I. Omidvar, and A. R. Richards, vol. 1, 167–194. Santa Barbara.

Morrison, G. 2011. *Supergods: What Masked Vigilantes, Miraculous Mutants, and a Sun God from Smallville Can Teach Us About Being Human.* New York.

Morrison, G., and E. van Sciver. 2002. *New X-Men,* vol. 1 #133. New York.

Oliver, K. 2009. *Women as Weapons of War: Iraq, Sex, and the Media.* New York.

Pew Research Center. 2009. "Muslims Widely Seen as Facing Discrimination." http://www.pewforum.org/2009/09/09/publication-page-aspxid1398–3/.

Rieber, J. N., and J. 2002. *Captain America,* vol. 4, #1. New York.

Rennaker, J. 2014. "'Mutant hellspawn'" or 'more human than you?' The X-Men Respond to Televangelism." In *The Ages of the X-Men: Essays on the Children of the Atom in Changing Times,* edited by J. J. Darowski, 203–212. Jefferson, NC.

Reynolds, R. 1992. *Super Heroes: A Modern Mythology.* Jackson, MS.

Ruether, R. R. 1983. *Sexism and God-talk.* Boston.

Shivener, R. 2014. "No Mutant Left Behind: Lessons from *New X-Men: Academy X.*" In *The Ages of the X-Men: Essays on the Children of the Atom in Changing Times,* edited by Joseph J. Darowski, 203–212. Jefferson, NC.

Shyminsky, N. 2006. "Mutant Readers, Reading Mutants: Appropriation, Assimilation, and the X-Men." *International Journal of Comic Art* 8 (2): 387–405.

Spivak, G. C. 1988. "Can the Subaltern Speak?" In *Marxism and the Interpretation of Culture,* edited by C. Nelson, and L. Grossberg, 271–313. Urbana and Chicago.

Straczynski, J. M., and J. Romita, Jr. 2001. *Amazing Spider-Man,* vol. 2, #36. New York.

Strömberg, F. 2011. "'Yo, rag-head!': Arab and Muslim Superheroes in American Comic Books after 9/11. *Amerikastudien/American Studies* 56 (4): 573–601.

Wadud, A. 1999. *Qur'an and Woman: Rereading the Sacred Text from a Woman's Perspective.* Oxford.

Wilson, G. W., and R. Boschi. 2015. *X-Men,* vol. 4, #25. New York..

"And, erm, religious stuff":
Islam, Liberalism, and the Limits of Tolerance in Stories of Faiza Hussain

Kevin Wanner

A "Normal" Muslim?

[She is a] Muslim super heroine of Pakistani descent[....] From the moment of her introduction [..., she] is immediately likeable. A superhero fangirl, a normal person encountering an extraordinary world – we are supposed to identify with her. A Muslim woman who isn't criminalized, or intended as an object of the audience's pity, but is normalized and made identifiable![1]

Anyone familiar with the recent publishing history of Marvel Comics might assume that this quotation refers to the premiere of the American teenager Kamala Khan in *Ms. Marvel* #1, published in February of 2014.[2] It dates, however, from 2010 and refers instead to the introduction of the lesser-known – but, in some ways, more pioneering – British superhero Faiza Hussain in *Captain Britain and MI13* #1, published in May of 2008 by Marvel.[3] These characters have so much in common that the former may be regarded as a corporately-sanctioned plagiarism of the latter: aside from being female, young, and Muslim, both are only daughters of Pakistani immigrants; one is a doctor, while the others' parents aspire for her to go into medicine; both speak in a breathless, colloquial style studded by youthful slang and coinages;[4] both possess powers of radical body manipulation that they deploy sparingly and usually defensively; both dislike violence and killing; and both are ardent fans of superheroes, before and after they join their ranks.

These characters were also designed to elicit the kind of reaction found

1. Ayaan 2010.
2. Wilson and Alphona 2014a.
3. Cornell and Kirk 2008a. The comics waver on the punctuation of the name of the titular UK intelligence agency; I have used the rendering that appears on covers, and which seems standard for its real-life counterparts, MI5 and MI6.
4. E.g. Faiza's "evilfying" and "berserkery" (Cornell and Kirk 2008a; 2008c), and Kamala's catchphrase "embiggen!" (Wilson and Alphona 2014b).

in the opening quotation. Faiza's creator, Englishman Paul Cornell, has stated in interviews his desire to "keep it person first, belief system second," to make her "an everyday religious person who you won't hear anything religious from until it would naturally come up. Which is hardly ever."[5] He aimed to make her a "real person" and not a representation the British Muslim world in its entirety. "I want people to adore her, not to be pleased she's there as part of a quota system."[6] Cornell assembled a "Faiza Hussain oversight team" of four British Muslim women to advise him on how to depict someone like them and, it seems fair to suggest, provide some guarantee of authenticity that his own identity as a white, male Anglican could not.[7] Online reactions attest to readers responding to Faiza in the spirit in which she was conceived. At last, they gush, here is a superhero who is Muslim and yet "normal," "identifiable," "believable, relatable,"[8] "interesting [...] in her own right,"[9] "vibrant, individual,"[10] and "really very human."[11]

Bubbling just beneath the surface of Faiza's creation and reception are assumptions about what counts as a "real" or "normal" person, what an "everyday religious person" is like – even what it is to be "human." These assumptions, I submit, are those that dominate in and indeed define liberal societies. I define "liberalism," following philosopher and legal scholar Paul W. Kahn, as an ideology that holds "belief in the equality and liberty of every person" and "the idea of tolerance" as "fundamental."[12] A social order founded in liberalism, Kahn continues,

> seeks to regulate behavior among individuals who do not agree on the sources of meaning in their lives. Liberalism requires [...] that individuals be able to take the same attitude toward their own conception of the good that they take toward others[.... T]hey cannot be so bound to it that its realization is the measure of every judgment and act.[13]

Clearly, this ideology has tremendous ramifications for religion. As a legacy of Enlightenment thinkers' solution to the problem of inter-Christian conflict in post-Reformation Europe, liberalism sets deliberate limits on re-

---

5. Tramountanas 2008, Richards 2008.
6. Richards 2008.
7. They are named and thanked in Cornell and Kirk 2008b; 2008d.
8. Ayaan 2010.
9. The Sword is Drawn 2015.
10. Napier 2015.
11. Ads 2015.
12. Kahn 2005, 6, 68.
13. Kahn 2005, 116.

ligion's power in society. To describe the forms religion takes on the two sides of this division, historian of religions Bruce Lincoln proposes a less partisan pair of labels than the one of "moderate" versus "fundamentalist" (or "extremist," "terrorist," etc.) that tends to predominate in media, political, and everyday discourses. To substitute for the former term, he suggests "minimalism" be used for any social practice or organization that limits "religion to an important set of (chiefly metaphysical) concerns, protects its privileges against state intrusion, but restricts its activity and influence to this specialized sphere." To replace the latter term(s), he proposes that "maximalism" be used to refer to "the conviction that religion ought to permeate all aspects of social, indeed of human existence."[14]

As Lincoln stresses, minimalism has become an ethical and often legal norm in the "secular nation-state, which learned to derive its legitimacy from the people it governed rather than God."[15] In such states, religion loses its coercive power, is irrelevant to one's status as citizen, and is regarded as remaining within its proper bounds when it operates as a set of non-testable beliefs, optional moral guidelines, and ritual practices – which is to say, symbolic or magical in intent – and as a basis for voluntary association. Under liberal regimes, scholar of religion Russell McCutcheon writes, a "position is allowed to count as religious [...] if, *and only if*, it is politically ineffectual and reserved only for some posited interior, personal struggle of faith."[16] Or, as political scientist Wendy Brown puts it, "religion as domination, tyranny, or source of irrationality and violence is presumed to transform, where the individual reigns, into religion as a choice and as a source of comfort, nourishment, moral guidance, and moral credibility."[17] Liberal orders characteristically strive to sustain a condition of cultural pluralism, in which self-determining individuals with "crosscutting identities" of religion, ethnicity, class, gender, and so on, interrelate on a common foundation of mutual respect and toleration.[18]

In what follows, I will argue that Faiza, both in *Captain Britain and MI13* – which lasted fifteen issues and one annual from 2008–2009 – and in appearances in other comics since, has been an exemplar of minimalist religiosity. I will further suggest that much of the positive reaction to her stems from her usefulness for rebutting claims that Islam is incompatible with liberalism. As political scientist William E. Connolly observes, many Americans and Euro-

14. Lincoln 2006, 5.
15. Lincoln 2006, 58.
16. McCutcheon 2005, 63 (original emphasis).
17. Brown 2006, 301.
18. Baumann 1999, 85.

peans define Muslims as a special minority, as a nation within a nation, that does not honor the post-Enlightenment secular division between private belief and public behavior.[19] To provide just one comics-related articulation of this viewpoint, Bosch Fawstin, vocal critic of Islam and independent comic writer/artist, damns rather than lauds "attempt[s] at normalizing Islam in the West via pop culture"; Islam, Fawstin continues,

> is fundamentally illiberal, but that doesn't matter to liberals in the comic book industry[....] While they claim to value free speech, women's rights, homosexual rights, "tolerance," etc., they throw it all out the window when it comes to Islam[....] A "Muslim superhero," if at all devout, would not act [...] the way the current "Muslim superheroes" are behaving in their comic books[....] What a liberal considers to be a "Muslim superhero" and what a Muslim superhero would be, according to Islam, are two completely different things.[20]

Whatever one makes of Fawstin's assertion of radical incompatibility between Islam and liberalism, his point that they are not identical should be uncontroversial. There are claims and values in Islam – as in other religions, especially ones with pre-modern roots – that do not readily align with those of liberalism. Religious adherents who experience such mismatches as real and significant will have either to choose between the parts of their faith that they perceive liberalism as being opposed to, or else accept the compromise solution of minimalism, which avoids confrontation between religious and competing claims and values by segregating them in separate zones of life, into, roughly, the private versus the public.

Among the female Muslim characters introduced by Marvel in the new millennium, Faiza, I will argue, is the most pronounced example of minimalism. What makes her, as a Muslim, so "normal" and "identifiable" to readers whose own norms and identities have been shaped within and by liberal orders is that she conceals, reveals, and enacts her religion in ways that liberalism deems legitimate and salutary. Furthermore, while Faiza models how to be a Muslim woman in a culturally tolerant society, characters with whom she interacts illustrate, with few but significant exceptions, how others in such a society should regard and treat a Muslim woman. Faiza's stories do not neglect, however, to explore what happens to those who prioritize submission, for themselves as well as sometimes for others, to religious or

19. Connolly 2006, 290–291.
20. Fawstin 2013. Similar rhetoric directed at Teshkeel Comics' *The 99* when it seemed that an animated series featuring these Islamic superheroes would air in the United States is quoted and discussed in Santo 2014, 689.

sectarian dictates over those of tolerance. Thus, my conclusion will consider how *Captain Britain and MI13* suggests, using non-human villains to represent fundamentalist and/or racist ideologies, where some of liberal society's limits lie, in terms both of the kinds of religiosity it can tolerate and of the measures it considers legitimate to employ against those it cannot.

Faiza and Her Religion

The first story arc of *Captain Britain and MI13* tied in to the "Secret Invasion" event, in which, across all of Marvel's line, an army of alien, shape-shifting Skrulls infiltrates and attacks Earth. The series thus begins *in media res* with British superheroes countering this threat. In issue #1, several elements of Faiza's identity are economically introduced. She first appears as a tiny but distinct figure in the background of a panel, gazing skyward at Captain Britain (aka Brian Braddock) fighting Skrulls in London. She is immediately identifiable – at least to those who recognize what this clothing signifies – as a Muslim female by a white scarf that covers her hair, ears, and neck. Henceforth, she is never depicted without this or a similar cloth *hijab*; a chainmail version eventually becomes part of her superhero uniform. This visual cue provides the only concrete indication that Faiza is Muslim until she cries "Allahu akbar. Oh Allahu akbar!" at a dramatic moment in issue #3.[21] Of course, this too is an implicit rather than explicit declaration of her faith.

Faiza's first panels also reveal her profession. Her white coat and stethoscope, as well as her treatment of wounded bystanders, mark her as a physician. The most emphasized component of Faiza's identity in her introductory scene, however, is not her religion, sex, or vocation, but her "fangirlish" enthusiasm for superheroes. After wrenching her attention away from the drama in the sky, she ebulliently tells some rattled ambulance technicians while attending to a casualty: "I saw Captain Britain just now. Easily one of his top ten battles. It was awesome!" "Top ten--!" "Mate! It was up there with the Lord Hawk one! I *so* love British super heroes! Cap, the Knights of Pendragon, Digitek--."[22] Faiza here demonstrates deep knowledge of British superhero minutia, and being a fan of superheroes stays a prominent part of her identity.[23] It is also a trait, as mentioned above, she shares with Kamala. Its significance will be discussed below.

Faiza gains her superpowers near the end of issue #1, when she is struck by a ray from a Skrull vehicle. When she regains consciousness in issue #2,

21. Cornell and Kirk 2008c.
22. Cornell and Kirk 2008a.
23. See e.g. Cornell and Alphona 2009; Ewing and Guice 2013.

she reflexively unleashes these powers on the Black Knight (aka Dane Whitman), who is not only immobilized but also has his clothing, skin, muscle, bone, and organs separated and exposed, like a disassembled anatomical model. He is alarmed but not in pain, and Faiza immediately restores him to his intact state. Later in this issue, she uses her powers to paralyze some Skrulls, and it is here that her religion first figures into dialogue. Unlike her unabashed declaration of superhero fandom, however, Faiza mentions her religion hesitantly and allusively, as one of a litany of reasons why she will not let Dane slay their foes: "You're not going to kill them. I took the Hippocratic Oath. 'Do no harm.' And, erm, religious stuff. And that's the super thing too, right?... Sorry."[24] Faiza's unwillingness to kill becomes another of her defining traits. During the invasion, Captain Britain, wielding King Arthur's sword Excalibur, and MI13's other super-agents dispatch Skrulls in often brutal ways: stabbing and hacking with blades, dismembering with claws, tearing out throats with teeth, etc. When it is over, Captain Britain relinquishes Excalibur, insisting that it "Belongs to someone who never used it to take life."[25] Faiza immediately (and at the subliminal suggestion of a spectral Merlin) pulls the sword from the stone Brian had sunk it into. She has wielded Excalibur ever since, and MI13 director Pete Wisdom later designates this as her codename.[26]

Faiza next mentions her religion in issue #5, as she and Dane approach the home of her parents, both also doctors, in Chelmsford, Essex. They have come to discuss her appointment to British Intelligence's supernatural threat division:

> Everyone's really made me welcome. Except--Mum and Dad.... They're not really onboard yet? They were really scared by the Battle of Westminster Bridge. And in the end, you know... proud, I 'spose. But-- they're not being *told* everything? 'Cos the vetting process is hard on... you know... Muslim families.[27]

This is the only time when Faiza names her religion. That she does so sotto voce (i.e. "MUSLIM FAMILIES" is printed in a smaller font than her normal comments) suggests that it is not something she is comfortable or used to talking about. That she brings it up, moreover, in reference to her government's perception of her and her family is significant. While prejudice against Muslims is here acknowledged to exist in the nation's institutions, it

24. Cornell and Kirk 2008b.
25. Cornell and Kirk 2008d.
26. Cornell and Kirk 2009c.
27. Cornell and Kirk 2008e.

is not evident among its citizens, even those who lead and staff these same bureaucracies. And while there are no hints of a social life for Faiza prior to or apart from the superhero community, in her old job in medicine or new one as a superhero/intelligence agent, her being a Muslim is to all appearances a non-issue.

Other English writers of comics in which Faiza appears have explored this theme differently. Al Ewing depicts governmental suspicion, profiling, and abuse of Muslims more directly in 2015's *Captain Britain and the Mighty Defenders* #2, when an interrogator in the fascist Mondo City says to Faiza,

> You're not from *around* here, creep. I can tell *that* just from *looking* at you.

and accuses her of harboring an *"extemist ideology."*[28] Faiza takes this in stride, however, dismissing his accusations, asserting her human rights, and easily escaping. A third writer, Simon Spurrier, includes Faiza in a mission to a Taliban-controlled region in 2014's *X-Force* #8. Spurrier, however, uses a captioned introduction to immediately and aggressively, if also perhaps ironically, forestall any assumption that her demographics will have anything to do with her part in the story:

> Excalibur: Dr. Faiza Hussain.[...] Ethnicity and faith irrelevant, nondefining, unworthy of media attention, etc.[29]

The only character apart from Faiza ever to name her religion, and the only one who finds it something to worry over, is Dracula. Dracula has a decades-long history in Marvel comics, and he is the villain of the final, six-issue arc of *Captain Britain and MI13*, titled "Vampire State." I will discuss Dracula's role in the series' end below, but here I wish only to address his attitude toward Muslims and others' reactions to it. Dracula first appears in issue #10, meeting with Doctor Doom on the Moon where he has established a base from which to invade the United Kingdom. To persuade Doom to ally with him, Dracula warns that Islam

> will close the gap with the West, in terms of science and superpowered individuals [...]. The realm I would create would [...] serve as a *bulwark* against it.[30]

In what at first seems a non sequitur, Doom responds, "Spare me your racism,

---

28. Ewing and Davis 2015a and 2015b. Mondo City is a thinly-veiled homage to Mega-City One from *Judge Dredd* comics from British publisher 2000 A.D.

29. Spurrier and Kim 2014.

30. Cornell and Kirk 2009a.

'Count.'"[31] Use of this title suggests, however, that Doom perceives Dracula's antipathy for Muslims as dating from his wars as a human aristocrat against the Turks. And indeed, throughout the "Vampire State" story, Dracula is depicted as a dangerous yet also somewhat ludicrous bigot, anachronistically calling Faiza's father a "Moslem"[32] and trying vainly to stir up trouble over her faith. Thus, while Dracula "thinks that everyone else is as much a racist as *he* is,"[33] no one will take his bait. They all look past Faiza's religion.

Returning to the claim that Faiza exemplifies minimalism, I find both negative and positive evidence for this. The negative evidence is the near absence of tradition-specific aspects of Faiza's religiosity. Aside from her *hijab*, these are missing from her on-panel life: she never engages in ritualized prayer or attends mosque, dietary rules or avoidance of alcohol do not come up, and she appears unconcerned with religious restrictions on her choice of partner, let alone friends or general relations. Aside from God being great, no doctrinal content of Islam gets articulated, and she never references the Qur'an or other texts. Now, it could be objected that even though such things are not shown, we can assume they take place off-panel – in the gutters, as it were. After all, Faiza is never shown going to the bathroom either: can we deduce from this that eliminating waste and tending to hygiene are not parts of her life?[34] Such an objection can be used to support my point, however. Lincoln states that a minimalist social order is one wherein religion is restricted to the private sphere.[35] Like whatever goes on in the bathroom, specific religious practices are almost entirely relegated to the unseen portion of Faiza's life.

The minimalist quality of Faiza's religion becomes still more apparent if we compare her with the other female Muslim heroes introduced by Marvel since September 11, 2001. The first such character is Sooraya Qadir (aka Dust), introduced in *New X-Men* #133 in December, 2002.[36] While in intent a progressive representation, Sooraya has been criticized for failing to meet a need for Muslim characters "that have little to do with terrorism, or extremism, or oppression."[37] She is introduced in Afghanistan, transforming into a sandstorm to kill some native thugs threatening to rape her. After she is rescued and enrolled in the X-Men's school in New York, she is criticized for

31. Cornell and Kirk 2009a.
32. Cornell and Kirk 2009a.
33. Cornell and Kirk 2009b.
34. I thank A. David Lewis for raising this objection and thus a chance for me to bolster my case.
35. Lincoln 2006, 59.
36. Morrison and van Sciver 2002.
37. Alsultany 2012, 171.

her *"burqa"*[38] by her roommate, who in her view is "setting women back fifty years just by walking around like that."[39] Given how she is depicted and how other characters treat her, it is not hard to see why Sooraya would strike some readers as "reinforc[ing] a dominant image of Muslim women who either needed to be rescued or who were in a constant state of conflict with pluralist society."[40] She has also been criticized as a stereotype who does little besides represent one sort of Islam: "Other than her religious beliefs, Dust's personality is almost non-existent. What are Dust's hobbies, one may ask? What does she do on her free time? Who sits at her table during lunch breaks? These unanswered questions keep Dust's character underdeveloped and incomplete."[41]

If Sooraya's character is dominated by Islamic traits, and Faiza is all but denuded of them, then Kamala sits somewhere in the middle. Within the first few issues of *Ms. Marvel*, she struggles with prohibitions against bacon and alcohol, and readers are introduced both to parents who seek strictly to limit her contact with boys and to a brother who their mother berates for "dress[ing] like a *penniless mullah*"; she quotes the Qur'an, attends (and questions the practice of gender segregation at) a mosque, and fashions her first costume out of a modest "burkini."[42] Kamala, then, is less of a minimalist representation than Faiza: her religion spills into the public sphere, which for her, initially, is high-school social life. Yet, she ultimately balances the public and private in ways that do not seriously test the limits liberal society sets for religion. Islamic practices and traditions, which are not always easy for her or others to disentangle from ethnic ones, pose persistent but navigable barriers to integration or belonging.[43] When it comes to core beliefs or values, no discordance is obvious. Kamala's Qur'an reference is to surah 5:32, which, as abstracted and paraphrased here, appears to extol the general virtue of saving lives.[44] Another Muslim text she recalls is: "Wherever you are... was circled on a map for you."[45] One thing worth nothing about this reference is that it omits the original's mention of "God." Another is that it is misattributed to the thirteenth-century Persian poet known commonly as Rumi (it is actually by the fourteenth-century Persian poet known com-

---

38. In fact a *niqab*, as noted in Dar 2010, 108. See the article, *"Niqab not Burqa,"* in this volume.

39. DeFillipis, Weir, and Green 2004.

40. Contractor 2012, 111. More specifically on Dust, see Kent 2015, 523.

41. Dar 2010, 108.

42. Wilson and Alphona 2014a-d.

43. Much of this amounts to what Brown calls religion as culture, to choices in "food, dress, music, lifestyle, and contingent values" (2006, 301).

44. Wilson and Alphona 2014b.

45. Wilson and Alphona 2014e.

monly as Hafiz); this is telling, given the extent to which "Americans have come to value Rumi as a source of spiritual wisdom and as an alternative to militant Islamism."[46] Kamala, then, selects from Muslim discourses ecumenically friendly and generically inspirational passages that strengthen her resolve to do what is right.

Much the same description applies to Faiza's expressions of religion, though hers lack any clear links to Islamic texts. These expressions comprise my positive evidence for Faiza's minimalism. In the few instances where Faiza acts or identifies as religious, she does so in ways that are notably generic. Exclaiming "ALLAHU AKBAR" is the equivalent of a Christian, or of many an irreligious person, shouting "Oh God!" in a stressful moment. As for naming "religious stuff" as a reason not to kill, while this suggests that she interprets her specific religion as prohibiting this act, her vague phrasing could be taken to affirm the widespread conviction among liberal subjects/ecumenicists that all authentic faiths preserve a common core of ethical and essentially pacifistic injunctions. For example, Baptist minister and religion professor Charles Kimball asserts in his *When Religion Becomes Evil* that "life-sustaining truths [lie at] the heart of all authentic, healthy [religions]. Whatever religious people may say about their love of God or the mandates of their religion, when their behavior toward others is violent and destructive [...] you can be sure the religion has been corrupted."[47] Clearly, such thinking does not allow for extending tolerance to any who regard violence as a legitimate, let alone laudable, method of defending one's religion or doing the will of one's god(s).

A last instance of Faiza's religiosity surfacing in *Captain Britain and MI13* occurs when she and Dane fall from a destroyed plane. As they plummet through the sky in issue #11, Faiza proposes to repair their bodies in the successive instants that they smash into the ground. Captions record her thoughts as she prepares for this: "She says prayers[...], as she's always said them, to include herself in love, to dedicate herself to doing the best possible thing."[48] The kind of religiosity here on display is akin to that which one critic assigns to the "good Muslim" Amir in the novel *The Kite Runner*, a character who only "invokes religion in sincerely pious desperation – for [...] socially harmless purposes."[49] It also aligns with sociologist Heidi Safia Mirza's characterization of British Muslim women she has interviewed, who "expressed their faith as a private transcendental spiritual space from which

---

46. Anadolu-Okur 2014, 248.
47. Kimball 2008, 47.
48. Cornell and Kirk 2009b.
49. Picht 2014, 206.

they derived an inner strength."[50] Faiza's prayer even resembles remarks made at Stanford University in April, 2015 by Oprah Winfrey, a fervent apostle of the gospel that all authentic faiths are one. Winfrey stated that her life goal has been "to be in that space that I call 'God' [... You] let every step you take move you in the direction of the one thing all religions can agree on, and that is love."[51] In each of these cases, religion has transmuted into spirituality, a more-or-less interchangeable set of prayerful practices and conceptions of a higher power that provide emotional support and bolster internal resolve. In such instances, religion can be understood as observing the limits and purposes assigned to it by liberalism. Faiza clearly joins in such minimalist expression.

Freely-Chosen Impositions, Multicultural Chimeras, and Social Synecdoche

Those who respond positively to Faiza and/or Kamala – and whose subjectivities, I have suggested, have been shaped by and are therefore receptive to the basic premises and values of liberalism, as Kahn, Brown, and others define this – appear to concur about a few things. One is that while it is good for characters to model diversity, this should never be their sole selling-point or focus. Sooraya seems to have fallen flat because she was too clearly intended as a *female Muslim* superhero (and one whose style of Islam was deemed by many to be too conservative and thus problematic), while Faiza and Kamala were conceived and positively received as *superheroes* who *just happen to be* female and Muslim. Readers' warmer embrace of this pair reflects what Brown describes as "that odd but familiar move within liberalism: 'culture' is what nonliberal peoples are imagined to be ruled and ordered by, but liberal peoples are considered to *have* culture or cultures."[52] Faiza's stories in particular seem careful to avoid depicting the "thwarting of individual autonomy with religious or cultural commandments."[53] Her being Muslim – or female, or Pakistani – does not impede her participation in other zones of culture, cultivation of other forms of identity, or association with other sorts of people. And though this is less true of Kamala, who as a teenager has less autonomy, one theme of her comic is how she comes to value and eventually chooses to comport with what she initially perceives as impositions by her protective parents, devout brother, and imposing sheikh.

50. Mirza 2013, 10.
51. I quote a transcript by Amrekeeya 2015.
52. Brown 2006, 299 (original emphasis).
53. Brown 2006, 310.

The one element of Faiza's depiction that could be interpreted as impeding her self-determination is her ubiquitous *hijab*. While Kamala's creators "specifically did not want her to have hijab,"[54] her best friend Nakia Bahadir is asked about hers by their clueless white classmate Zoe Zimmer in *Ms. Marvel #1*:

> Zoe: Your headscarf is so *pretty*, Kiki.[...N]obody *pressured* you to start wearing it, right? Your father or somebody? Nobody's going to, like, *honor kill* you? I'm just *concerned*.
>
> Nakia: Actually, my dad wants me to take it off. He thinks it's a *phase*.
>
> Zoe: Really? Wow, cultures are so *interesting*.[55]

The clear message here is that wearing *hijab* is a choice that girls and women can make for themselves. Readers are thereby informed or reminded that this practice can be viewed as the decision of a free (female) individual, rather than as an encumbrance of (male) authority.

This same point is stressed in many academic studies,[56] and it may also be implied in *Captain Britain and MI13*. In #5, we see that Faiza's mother, Farida, also wears a *hijab*. In this same issue, Faiza's father, Yusuf, says, "I'm not a particularly religious man."[57] While this disclosure is motivated by what else is going on in the scene, the fact that he makes it in the presence of his *hijabi* wife and daughter suggests that they were not pressured by him to adopt this mode of dress. Also worth considering is this exchange between Cornell and a reader:

> Tracy Jackman: You have Faiza Hussain's religious mom hinting happily that Black Knight and Faiza could eventually get married. Are you aware that it is against Islam for a Muslim woman to marry a non-Muslim man[?] Many secular Muslim women in Britain don't care about laws like that, but pretty much all headscarf-wearing ones do.[...] Do you have an explanation?
>
> Cornell: [...] You seem to think that people [...] should conform to a stereotype and not be people.[...] I'm determined that she and her family are going to stay [...] real people with a whole range of responses.[58]

Cornell chafes at the suggestion that Faiza's *hijab* or, by implication, any as-

---

54. Editor and co-creator Sana Amanat, quoted in Dev 2014.
55. Wilson and Alphona 2014a.
56. E.g. Mahmood 2005, 157; Contractor 2012, 83–95; Uddin 2013, 140–141.
57. Cornell and Kirk 2008e.
58. Tramountanas 2008.

pect of her religion might limit her options in life, thereby rendering her less than a "real" person. This is a clear articulation of the liberal view that people are supposed to have culture, not vice versa.

Another thing readers who praise Faiza and Kamala appear to crave in common is characters that are specifically cultural, uniquely individual, and relatably universal, all at once. That this does not strike more people as an odd, even incoherent, set of expectations signals just how hegemonic liberal ideology, in which differences are held to unite rather than divide, and to matter most when they can be shown not to matter to one's place in society, has become. Novelist and journalist Sabaa Tahir in the *Washington Post* expresses this complex of paradoxical desires:

> As a Pakistani American woman, I can relate to Kamala.[...] But I also wanted Kamala to be familiar to everyone.[...] Because it's not just the lonely, comic-book-loving Pakistani teen who needs a hero like Kamala. It's the people who [...] only see a Muslim or a Pakistani instead of a whole person.[...] Kamala could be a Latina or an African American, a descendant of Chinese immigrants or a blonde Daughter of the American Revolution. Her struggles will be familiar to anyone who has tried to figure out where they belong.[59]

Or, as comics critic Noah Berlatsky pithily puts it, "What Makes the Muslim *Ms. Marvel* Awesome: She's Just Like Everyone."[60]

One way to ensure that Faiza and Kamala would be relatable to everyone, or at least everyone who reads comics, was to make them superhero fans. To most ways of thinking, being a fan is a secondary characteristic, one that is less basic or core than such inherited or assigned traits as gender, ethnicity, generational cohort, religion, or nationality. It is also usual to think of these qualities as, unlike fandom, sources of identity, as something you *are* rather than simply *like* or *do*. Such assumptions have been challenged, however. Analysts and participants have increasingly insisted that fandoms (especially ones centering around science fiction, fantasy, or superhero properties with global distribution) constitute genuine communities, ones with a special capacity to bring together people from all walks of life. Scholar of religion Sean McCloud, for instance, describes fandoms "as late modern 'projects of the self', affiliational choices that act to establish self-identity and community during a time when these things are not given,"[61] and fandom scholar Cornel Sandvoss writes that "fandom has become an additional realm of

---

59. Tahir 2014.
60. Berlatsky 2014. For citations of many similar sentiments, see Kent 2015, 524.
61. McCloud 2003, 188.

identity construction alongside" more traditional forms.[62] Further, consider this exchange between American comics journalist Jonah Weiland and Scottish comics writer Grant Morrison:

> Weiland: This is the true power of comics.[...] Who gives a crap about political differences, or religious differences? Cuz once you walk in, it's all about the art, and it's all about love.
>
> Morrison: And that's all that comics, that's all that it ever was.[...] That's what this was always about. We were always this community, and if we can make that global and international, then it's even better.[63]

Returning to Faiza, Cornell emphasized in interviews her superhero obsession over her religion, and he has even called this obsession her "central character point."[64] As for Kamala, *Ms. Marvel* #1 shows her posting online "Avengers fanfiction" in a bedroom filled with superhero paraphernalia.[65] As one essayist opines, this facet of her portrayal

> is important [...] because it builds a solid foundation where the reader and the protagonist feel one in [*sic*] the same[...], part of the collective geek culture that we all love – and this is still before her Muslim heritage and customs come to the fore.[... This] is what geek culture is about – celebrating what we all love and admire together, instead of the lifestyle differences we have.[66]

With both characters, then, there has been an effort to juggle attributes that are likely points of reader identification or alienation. This is done through the (il)logic of liberalism, by combining the culturally specific and thus potentially divisive (religion/ethnicity) with the putatively universal and thus relatable (love for superheroes and/or comics, which themselves are claimed to be "all about love") in "unique" individuals, who yet end up all but identical.[67]

Another thing Faiza's and Kamala's fans and creators seem to share is a conviction that every part, no matter and often in spite of its demographic weight, has the right to represent the social whole. Kamala's synecdochal

---

62. Sandvoss 2005, 62.

63. These comments are transcribed, beginning at 8m20, from comicbookresources 2015.

64. E.g. Richards 2008; DeAngelo, 2008; Jusino 2010.

65. Wilson and Alphona 2014a.

66. McGlynn 2014.

67. Miriam Kent also considers this dynamic, arguing that Kamala's readers' "fondness for assimilation" and "need for the character to be relatable" threaten to "erase individual experiences of marginalized peoples" (2015, 524–525).

function is to stand for her generation of "millennials": she has been positioned and celebrated as a kind of twenty-first-century Peter Parker, a character whose traits of whiteness and maleness once made him the obvious, even only, choice for such a role, but which today practically disqualify him for it.[68] As for Faiza, she comes to stand for her nation and, through it, liberalism or cultural pluralism itself. The simple fact of Faiza's inclusion is signaled when her immigrant father holds Excalibur in *Captain Britain and MI13* #5 and exclaims: "It is of this nation ... and thus ... mine. *Ours.* Astonishing! I'm not a particularly religious man ..., but I can *feel* it ... this is ... blessed.... this is *unconditional acceptance.*"[69] A similar message is conveyed when Captain Britain is (temporarily) killed.[70] Issue #2 opens with Faiza thinking: "When Captain America died, Americans heard about it in the American way: through the media. When *Captain Britain* died, the British felt it in their chests."[71] A panel illustrating this shows three Muslim men grieving. That they and Faiza share in this pathos mystically confirms their Britishness, which is claimed to be more organic or, literally, immediate than its American equivalent. As geographer Jason Dittmer observes, a leitmotif of *Captain Britain and MI13* is the "role of magic in producing territorial bonding"; Britain appears "as something magically real, not the contingent product of human practices but rather a (super)natural feature of reality."[72] Here, the magic lying at Britain's heart affirms the nation's transcendence of its legacy of white, male, Christian privilege (in, notably, a story penned by a white, male Christian).

Yet Britain's magic goes further than this, anointing Faiza – in not just one but *three* alternate realities – as "the living embodiment of all that is British."[73] Thus, she does not simply represent the inclusion of an ethnic/religious minority in a tolerant body politic; she symbolizes the realized promises of liberalism itself, as instantiated in Britain/the British people. As Queen Elizabeth II herself tells Faiza in 2012's *Gambit* #6, "Excalibur represents the Empire and its history far more than *I*. And the sword has chosen *you*."[74] Also present at and acceding to Faiza's election, we recall, was Merlin, another of Britain's ancient mythical totems. And in an alternate reality Britain doomed to be destroyed by a malevolent artificial intelligence in 2013's "Age of Ultron" event, Brian Braddock, fearing he will not survive the

68. See e.g. Schedeen 2014.
69. Cornell and Kirk 2008e.
70. On superheroes' deaths and frequent resurrections, see Lewis 2014.
71. Cornell and Kirk 2008b.
72. Dittmer 2013, 119, 111.
73. Hern 2013.
74. Asmus, Neves, and Barrionuevo 2012.

coming battle, dubs Faiza the new Captain Britain. At first she protests, but when she takes hold of his helmet, she exclaims, *"Oh!* It's ... it's like an old friend."[75]

Faiza's mystical connection to her country even carries over into the world that a near-omnipotent Doctor Doom patches together from remnants of the shattered multiverse in the "Secret Wars" event of 2015–2016. Though neither Britain nor Islam seems to exist in Doom's world, the "Age of Ultron" version of Faiza appears in it with Excalibur in hand and her identities intact in *Captain Britain and the Mighty Defenders*, a two-issue tie-in series. At its conclusion, Faiza's new friends, themselves survivors of worlds they but dimly recall, make her a Union Jack flag. When they admit they "don't know what it *means*," she replies: "It means *good* things, sometimes. And *horrors*--things we can't *forget*. But right *now*... we *all* get to decide what it means."[76] She says this flanked by three women and one man, who between them are black, Hispanic, Asian, and green (or white, since this is She-Hulk). This combination of image and text suggests that Faiza is describing not just Britain but any society that aspires to derive a culturally plural and just future from a history marred by prejudice, racism, exploitation, imperialism, and forced assimilation. Faiza here proclaims, as one fan puts it, "the representational status of us all."[77]

Tolerance's Limits

All of the above doubtlessly plays well to liberal sensibilities. Yet, there is a dark side even to culturally pluralist utopias, one revealed as they form or defend themselves. What, after all, is a tolerant order to do with or about those who refuse to be tolerant? This question points to what many, myself included, see as a paradox inherent in social orders whose dominant value is tolerance. To contradict what Yusuf Hussain says when holding Excalibur, the acceptance proffered by a liberal nation can never be *"unconditional,"* since its forbearance cannot extend to those who are vehemently and especially violently opposed to cultural/religious diversity. Liberalism's intolerance for intolerance often manifests as force. As Connolly asserts, a pluralist is "one who prizes cultural diversity along several dimensions and is ready to join others in militant action, when necessary, to support pluralism against counter drives to unitarianism."[78] Or, as Brown puts it, "[n]onliberal societies and practices, especially those designated as fundamentalist, are not only

75. Ewing and Guice 2013.
76. Ewing and Davis 2015b.
77. Napier 2015.
78. Connolly 2006, 280.

[regarded as] inherently intolerant but as potentially intolerable for their putative rule by culture or religion and concomitant devaluation of the autonomous individual."[79]

While Faiza is largely kept apart from issues of fundamentalism and intolerance, these nevertheless emerge as major themes in *Captain Britain and MI13*. Neither Muslims nor any group of humans represent these things, however. Instead, they are depicted by two armies of monsters that serially seek to conquer the United Kingdom and appropriate its magic for despotic ends. The first are the Skrulls of the "Secret Invasion," who are represented as maximalists, bent on achieving a "holy destiny" of intergalactic and interdimensional conquest.[80] A Skrull who has adopted John Lennon's persona and allied with MI13 responds to another who tells him that their god "loves you" with: "Yeah, yeah, yeah ... look at you. The fundamentalists ... That's what makes me laugh, lads--everything about us Skrulls says we're meant to *fit* in"[81] John is later executed for refusing to rejoin the "the *fascists* who made my *people* into *morons!*"[82] Whether or not these Skrulls are seen as metaphors for Muslim extremists,[83] there is certainly an indication here of how members of a universalist religion who side with liberalism regard those they perceive as hijacking their faith in service of maximalist ends. And since John is celebrated by his adoptive compatriots for brazenly resisting Skrull conformity to the end, his death clearly is meant to mark a victory for or affirmation of what Brown describes as liberalism's "valorization of individual autonomy" over fundamentalism's "valorization of culture and religion at the expense of the individual."[84]

The second invasion force is led by none other than Dracula, who can be understood as a maximalist for vampirism. His "Vampire State" is also called a nation, culture, and civilization, but it is an illiberal one in which all wills are subordinate to his own, and one of his subjects says that after Britain has been conquered, "the next step will be mass conversions."[85] One vampire who resists Dracula's will, however, is a recent "convert," namely Faiza's father, Yusuf. "I will not kill in your name!" he tells Dracula, who responds, "You will have no choice.... In fact, you'll kill your own dau[ghter]."[86] In the end, this "not particularly religious man" remains free of Dracula's control

79. Brown 2006, 303, 310.
80. Cornell and Kirk 2008d.
81. Cornell and Kirk 2008a.
82. Cornell and Kirk 2008c.
83. As is suggested in Jones 2014.
84. Brown 2006, 311.
85. Cornell and Kirk 2009c.
86. Cornell and Kirk 2009d.

and is invited home, now not just as a Muslim but also a vampire who has proven himself still thoroughly British. As Yusuf says to Captain Britain in the series' last line of dialogue, "I could murder for a cup of tea."[87]

In *Captain Britain and MI13*, then, fundamentalists and racists appear as aliens and demons, as backward relics with no place in today's world. With the rare exceptions of dissenters who identify with pluralist Britain, everyone in the Skrull or vampire army exemplifies what Brown calls the "imagined opposite" of the liberal subject: "the radically de-individuated, culturally or religiously bound creature of a fundamentalist order" who is "presumed neither to value tolerance, to be capable of tolerance, nor to be entitled to tolerance."[88] Or, as Kahn states, liberalism makes a "claim of ultimate value [... dividing ...] those who participate in the politics of multi-culturalism [from] those who are perceived as its enemies."[89] Kahn further and provocatively proposes that the violence a liberal nation-state unleashes on its perceived opposites can be unmatched in ferocity, owing to its lack of an extrinsic foundation: for while a "state that understands itself as an expression of a divine or a natural order can look to meanings outside of itself to limit its actions,[...] no principles of restraint on the use of force [...] are implicit in a state that understands itself as the expression of popular sovereignty under the rule of law."[90]

We can perceive this consequence of the self-justifying constitution of liberal nation-states at play in *Captain Britain and MI13*. Not only are fundamentalist and racist outlooks assigned to monsters who suffer deserved annihilation, but the heroes resort to whatever means they deem necessary to attain this end. Several characters' disavowals – such as when Brian says, "Killing ... has to be done, but I loathe it. It's not what I'm *for*," or when the heroic vampire Spitfire tells enemies as she kills them with her fangs, "This is your fault. It's not who I am. It's just who I have to be sometimes."[91] – echo, intentionally or not, the rhetoric of liberal democratic officials and agencies employing unsavory tactics (e.g. "enhanced techniques," aka torture) against those designated terrorists. Even Faiza, "the hero who never *hates*, never *kills*,"[92] makes an exception in the case of the arch-racist Dracula, whom she destroys with Excalibur.[93] We thus find further alignment of Cornell's narrative with Brown's insight that liberal tolerance will tend to "be

87. Cornell and Kirk 2009e.
88. Brown 2006, 315.
89. Kahn 2005, 308.
90. Kahn 2005, 277.
91. Cornell and Kirk 2008a.
92. Ewing and Guice 2013.
93. Cornell and Kirk 2009e. Though, to be fair, he is already undead.

withheld for whole regimes considered to be ruled by culture or religion. This logic effectively insulates all legal practices in liberal orders from the tag of 'barbarism' while legitimating liberal aggression toward [...] regimes deemed intolerable."[94]

Ultimately, piecemeal eradication proves inadequate, and ways are found to ensure that the illiberal contagions are not only eliminated from Britain but prevented from ever entering it again. The Skrull threat ends in #4 when Pete Wisdom sets free Britain's "powers of evil" who grant him "one boon!!!" Wisdom says, "No more Skrulls," and the aliens all burst into flame. Reports confirm that there is "not one skrull left in Britain. Any who try to enter get the same."[95] As for the vampires, MI13 tricks Dracula – as Wisdom says, when "lives and nations are at stake--one *cheats*" [96] – into thinking that an enchanted skull that maintained an anti-vampire barrier around Britain had been destroyed. Thus, when Dracula's space fleet enters British airspace, all of its vampires but Faiza's father, whom Wisdom invites in, also end in fire. Wisdom explains, "This was the only way--the only way to get them *all*."[97]

Two of *Captain Britain* and *MI13*'s story-arcs thus conclude with fantasy realizations of the total and permanent removal from a territory of illiberal, dehumanized others. While this series lasted just two years before being cancelled, it seems to have struck a chord with many readers, and Faiza appears to be a major reason for this. Although Faiza has retreated into the shadow of Kamala, a character who repackages many of her traits in a more saleable, i.e., teenaged and American, form, Marvel seems keen to keep her in play. Like many C-list characters, Faiza is likely to persist through guest and limited appearances and owing to the devotion of a small but adoring fan-base. However, one thing that should temper enthusiasm for a series that successfully used a Muslim character to model minimalist religiosity is that this modeling is presented alongside depictions of extremely violent and radical reactions against groups who, in privileging submission to sectarian identities and values over the liberal dictates of pluralism and tolerance, appear to others to have earned the labels of racist or fundamentalist.

94. Brown 2006, 314.
95. Cornell and Kirk 2008d.
96. Cornell and Kirk 2009e.
97. Cornell and Kirk 2009e.

Works Cited

Ads. 2015. Comment posted to "Hot news: New Captain Britain and the Mighty Defenders Secret Wars series announced without Captain Britain?" *The Captain Britain Fans' Page and Blog.* https://thecaptainbritainblog.wordpress.com/2015/03/24/ hot-news-new-captain-britain-secret-wars-series-announced-without-captain-britain/#comments.

Alsultany, E. 2012. *Arabs and Muslims in the Media: Race and Representation After 9/11.* New York.

Amrekeeya, A. 2015. "Living a Meaningful Life: Oprah Winfrey at Stanford – Full Transcript." *Lahjaty.* http://www.lahjaty. com/%D8%A8%D9%84%D9%88%D9%82/living-a-meaningful-life-oprah-winfrey-at-stanford-full-transcript/.

Anadolu-Okur, N. 2014. "The Enduring Allure of Rumi and Sufism in American Literature." In *Muslims and American Popular Culture Volume One: Entertainment and Digital Culture*, edited by I. Omidvar, and A. R. Richards, 247–266. Santa Barbara.

Ayaan. 2010. "State of the (Superhero) Nation: Faiza Hussein in British Comics." *Muslimah Media Watch.* http://www.patheos.com/blogs/ mmw/2010/08/state-of-the-superhero-nation-faiza-hussein-in-british-comics/.

Baumann, G. 1999. *The Multicultural Riddle: Rethinking National, Ethnic, and Religious Identities.* New York.

Berlatsky, N. 2014. "What Makes the New *Ms. Marvel* Awesome: She's Just Like Everyone." *The Atlantic*, March 20. http://www.theatlantic.com/ entertainment/archive/2014/03/ what-makes-the-muslim-em-ms-marvel-em-awesome-shes-just-like-everyone/284517/.

Brown, W. 2006. "Subjects of Tolerance: Why We Are Civilized and They Are the Barbarians." In *Political Theologies: Public Religions in a Post-Secular World*, edited by Hent de Vries, and Lawrence E. Sullivan, 298–317. New York.

Comicbookresources. 2015. "CBR TV: Grant Morrison Talks Classic Myths, Modern Stories & Humble Bundle." *YouTube.* https://www.youtube. com/watch?v=LczXUhZbL4Y.

Connolly, W. E. 2006. "Pluralism and Faith." In *Political Theologies: Public Religions in a Post-Secular World*, edited by H. de Vries, and L. E. Sullivan, 278–297. New York.

Contractor, S. 2012. *Muslim Women in Britain: De-mystifying the Muslimah.* New York.

Cornell, P. (w), and A. Alphona (a). 2009. "British Magic." *Captain Britain and MI13 Annual #1*.

Cornell, P. (w), and L. Kirk (p). 2008a–e. *Captain Britain and MI13 #1–5*.

———. 2009a–e. *Captain Britain and MI13 #10–15*.

Dar, J. 2010. "Holy Islamaphobia, Batman! Demonization of Muslims and Arabs in Mainstream American Comic Books" In *Teaching Against Islamaphobia*, edited by Joel L. Kincheloe, Shirley R. Steinberg, and Christopher D. Stonebanks, 99–110. New York.

DeAngelo, F. IV. 2007. "British Invasion: Paul Cornell talks about launching Captain Britian [*sic*] and MI: 13 in the heart of Secret Invasion." *Marvel*. http://marvel.com/news/comics/3312/british_invasion.

DeFillipis, N. (w), C. Weir (w), and R. Green (p). 2004. *New X-Men: Academy X #2*.

Dev, A. 2014. "American Muslims Were Proud of Kamala Khan." *The Times of India*, September 15. http://timesofindia.indiatimes.com/city/bengaluru/American-Muslims-were-proud-of-Kamala-Khan/articleshow/42473218.cms.

Dittmer, J. 2013. *Captain America and the Nationalist Superhero: Metaphors, Narratives, and Geopolitics*, Philadelphia.

Ewing, A. (w), and A. Davis (p). 2015a–b. *Captain Britain and the Mighty Defenders #1–2*.

Ewing, A. (w), and B. Guice (p). 2013. *Avengers Assemble #15AU*.

Fawstin, B. 2013. "10 Truths Mainstream Comic Books Evade to Promote 'Muslim Superheroes'." *PJ Media*, December 10. https://pjmedia.com/lifestyle/2013/12/19/10-truths-mainstream-comic-books-evade-to-promote-muslim-superheroes/?singlepage=true.

Hern, A. 2013. "A Marvel comic shows the true face of Britain." *New Statesman*, May 23. http://www.newstatesman.com/culture/2013/05/marvel-comic-shows-true-face-britain.

Jones, D. 2014. "Islamic Invaders: *Secret Invasion* and the Post-9/11 World of Marvel." In *The Ages of the Avengers: Essays on the Earth's Mightiest Heroes in Changing Times*, edited by J. J. Darowski, 165–177. Jefferson, NC.

Jusino, T. 2010. "Countdown to Doctor Who: The Paul Cornell Interview." *Tor*, April 15. http://www.tor.com/2010/04/15/countdown-to-doctor-who-the-paul-cornell-interview/.

Kahn, P. W. 2005. *Putting Liberalism in Its Place*, Princeton.

Kent, M. 2015. "Unveiling Marvels: *Ms. Marvel* and the Reception of the New Muslim Superhero." *Feminist Media Studies* 15: 522–527.

Kimball, C. 2008. *When Religion Becomes Evil*. Rev. ed. New York.

Lewis, A. D. 2014. *American Comics, Literary Theory, and Religion: The Superhero Afterlife*. New York.

Lincoln, B. 2006. *Holy Terrors: Thinking About Religion After September 11*, 2nd ed. Chicago.

Mahmood, S. 2005. *Politics of Piety: The Islamic Revival and the Feminist Subject*. Princeton.

McCloud, S. 2003. "Popular Cultural Fandoms, the Boundaries of Religious Studies, and the Project of the Self." *Culture and Religion* 4: 187–206.

McCutcheon, R. T. 2005. *Religion and the Domestication of Dissent: Or, How to Live in a Less Than Perfect Nation*. London.

McGlynn, A. 2014. "Why Kamala Khan Is the Most Important Superhero in the World." *The Mary Sue*, December 10. http://www.themarysue.com/kamala-khan-important/.

Mirza, H. S. 2013. "'A Second Skin': Embodied Intersectionality, Transnationalism and Narratives of Identity and Belonging among Muslim Women in Britain." *Women's Studies International Forum* 36: 5–15.

Morrison, G. (w), and E. van Sciver (p). 2002. *New X-Men* #133.

Napier, C. 2015. "Marvel's Faiza Hussain: 'Better' as Normal." *Comics Alliance*, April 28. http://comicsalliance.com/marvel-faiza-hussain/.

Picht, S. 2014. "Normalizing Islam: Representations of Good and Bad Muslims in Khaled Hosseini's *The Kite Runner*." In *Muslims and American Popular Culture Volume One: Entertainment and Digital Culture*, edited by Iraj Omidvar, and Anne R. Richards, 197–217. Santa Barbara.

Qureshi, N. 2010. "Quran 5:22, Nazam, and Neglecting Context." *Answering Muslims*. http://www.answeringmuslims.com/2010/05/quran-532-nazam-and-neglecting-context.html.

Richards, D. 2008. "Super Spy Weekend: Faisa Hussain." *Comic Book Resources*, March 9. http://www.cbr.com/super-spy-weekend-faisa-hussain/.

Sandvoss, C. 2005. *Fans: The Mirror of Consumption*. Cambridge.

Santo, A. 2014. "'Is It a Camel? Is It a Turban? No, It's *The 99*': Branding Islamic Superheroes as Authentic Global Cultural Commodities." *Television & New Media* 15 (7): 679–695.

Schedeen, J. 2014. "Between the Panels: Why Ms. Marvel is the New Spider-Man." *IGN*, November 21. http://www.ign.com/articles/2014/11/21/between-the-panels-why-ms-marvel-is-the-new-spider-man.

Spurrier, S. (w), and R.-H. Kim (a). 2014. *X-Force* #8.

Tahir, S. 2014. "MS. MARVEL: Why does Marvel's new reboot succeed? Because its Muslim teen superhero is 'sweet, conflicted and utterly relatable'." *The Washington Post*, February 4. https://www.washingtonpost.com/blogs/comic-riffs/post/ms-marvel-why-does-marvels-new-reboot-succeed-because-its-muslim-teen-superhero-is-sweet-conflicted-and-utterly-relatable/2014/02/04/42908ac8-8-dc6–11e3–95dd-36ff657a4dae_blog.html?utm_term=.b40a7931d3c9.

The Sword is Drawn. 2015. Comment #17 to discussion thread "A NEW
    CAPTAIN BRITAIN COMIC FOR 2016?" *Comic Book Resources*. http://
    community.comicbookresources. com/showthread.php?46713-A-new-
    Captain-Britain-comic-for-2016/page2.
Tramountanas, G. A. 2009. "X-Position: Paul Cornell." *Comic Book Resources*,
    September 23. http://www.cbr.com/x-position-paul-cornell-5/.
Uddin, S. F. 2013. "Navigating Between the Religious and the Secular: Re-
    sponding to the Muslim 'Woman Question' in Diasporic Britain." Ph.D.
    dissertation, University of California. Los Angeles.
Wilson, G. W. (w), and A. Alphona (a). 2014a-e. *Ms. Marvel* #1–5.

Kamala Khan's Superhero Burkini:
Negotiating an Autonomous Position between
Patriarchal Islamism, French Secularism, and Feminism

Chris Reyns-Chikuma and Désirée Lorenz

ONLY ONE YEAR after the initial publication of *Ms. Marvel: No Normal* in the U.S. – and only one month after the *Charlie Hebdo* massacre in Paris on January 7, 2015 – its French translation, *Ms. Marvel: Métamorphose*, came out. The book was displayed on tables and in shop windows in many general and specialized comic book stores in France, as well as in bigger chains of bookstores, and sales suggest that it has been relatively successful. What is particularly innovative about this new Ms. Marvel is that she is Muslim.

Why and how a Muslim superheroine can be successful in France, a country that has had troubled and tense relations with Muslim culture for at least several decades, is the main questions we will try to answer in this chapter. To answer this question, we proceed in three stages. First, in order to contextualize the publication and the reception of an Muslim American superheroine in France, we briefly present the specific cultural history of superhero comics in France and an overview of what in France is called *bandes dessinées* (BDs) by women and minorities. Second, we outline the tense and complex relationship between Muslim culture and French republicanism and secularism, which creates an unwelcoming climate for the publication of a book like *Ms. Marvel*. Here, we also present a content analysis of the text, finding that the ideological content is built on accepted and shared representations that can appeal to a large but diverse audience. This partly explains how, in spite of an ambiguous context, *Ms. Marvel*'s sales are still comparatively high. Finally, we will see how its success in France (like in the U.S.) seems to be mainly due to the fact that, within the didactic frame chosen by her creators (the writer G. Willow Wilson and the editor Sana Amanat), Kamala is represented as courageously choosing the Muslim feminist option, after several unsatisfactory trials and errors.

French Context:
Multilayered and Complex

Superheroes in France

American superheroes have never really been popular in France, for a variety of reasons.[1] First, a 1949 law protecting children against violence and indecency, seen as a postwar reaffirmation of national values against what was perceived as American imperialism, prevented superhero comics from gaining a foothold in France. Second, the absence of a vigilantist tradition in France (partly as a reaction against the many summary executions of Nazi collaborators at the end of World War II in France) made any French connection with Batman and other superheroes less obvious. Third, there were also large differences between editorial and artistic traditions. With very rare exceptions,[2] since the end of World War II, the only and relatively successful superheroes in France were French parodies, such as Superdupont (1972).[3] If there were readers of superheroes in France, strangely enough, they were either young readers or some very rare intellectuals. That said, interest in the superhero genre was boosted in the 1980s by the Hollywood blockbusters (beginning with Richard Donner's *Superman* in 1978), in a context of the globalization of culture. Meanwhile, U.S. superhero comics were aiming more and more at an adult audience with, for example, *The Dark Knight Returns* (1986) and *Watchmen* (1986), two high-profile revisions of the genre. These comics were quickly crowned as masterpieces by fans, ordinary readers, and critics, both in the U.S. and in France.[4] At the same time, companies other than the "Big Two" superhero publishers (i.e. DC & Marvel) were producing material in the new "graphic novel" category in the U.S., often in a format closer to the alternative French-European album.

However, since the turn of the twenty-first century, the figure of the superhero has become omnipresent through arts and media worldwide. In the past decade, several intellectuals, critics, writers, and artists in France and Europe have started to connect with the superhero tradition.[5] For instance, Serge Lehman, essayist, writer, and comics scripter specializing in science fiction, has co-published (with Fabrice Colin, Gess, and Céline Bessonneau) superhero stories explaining why French superheroes died in France during

---

1. See Vessels 2012; Lorenz 2015.
2. There were French superheroes, such as Fantax (1946–1959), but they were relatively unknown. See Fournier 2014.
3. See Vessels 2012, 188–189.
4. For example, *Watchmen* received the prize for best foreign album at the Angoulême festival in 1989.
5. See Fournier 2014.

World War II in his BD *La Brigade chimérique* (2012). Inspired by this re-invented tradition, he has also created *Masqué* (2012–2013), about a French superhero working in a futuristic Paris.[6] It is important to note that all of the superheroes are male and white and that nothing in these recent series alludes to a multiculturalist perspective. Of course, American comics are in a very similar misogynistic situation.[7] Take Wonder Woman for example, who, in spite of being presented as an extraordinary feminist icon, is still sexualized through her scantily-clad patriotic dress, or similarly, the various versions of former Ms. Marvel, Carol Danvers. In general, superheroines have been represented for a long time, and until recently, in ambivalent ways, since they were either portrayed as female hyper-masculine or hyper-sexualized icons, or both.[8]

Women and Minorities in French Comics

As has been pointed out time and time again, women have not been common in French BD, either as producers (authors, editors, publishers) or as characters (main or secondary).[9] When women are represented, their roles are often not positive, and they are presented as stupid and/or ugly, old, hypersexualized, and/or employed in subordinate jobs.[10] Interestingly, one of France's most famous female comics authors, Iranian-born Marjane Satrapi, is, at least partly, credited for the surge of BD by women with her globally successful graphic novel *Persépolis* (2000–2003). Ironically, although her narrative is by no means anti-Islamic, her story of a girl growing up and trying to adapt in various revolutionary social and political contexts could inadvertently confirm Islamophobic feelings for some readers, since she primarily describes crimes committed by the Iranian government during and after the Iranian Revolution of 1979. For instance, while the very first chapter, entitled "Le voile" ("The Veil"), could be read as a playful critique of the headscarf as imposed by the new Islamic government,[11] it can also be interpreted more simplistically as a plain criticism of the veil, which continues to be a hot issue within the contemporary French context.[12]

6. See Lorenz 2016.

7. See Deman 2015.

8. See Deman 2015.

9. Katha Pollitt (1991) has labeled the fact that in many stories and specifically comics one could find only one woman character among many male characters as the Smurf syndrome, since in the comics there is only one Smurfette in the Smurfs' village.

10. See Pilloy 1994; Reyns-Chikuma 2016.

11. It is also the only title that is repeated twice in *Persepolis* (see Chapter 34). In the English translation, see "The Veil," pg. 3 and 233; see also Richards and Williams 2012.

12. An interview with the author of a similar successful BD (*L'Arabe du futur*, 2012 [*The Arab of the Future*, 2013] by Riad Satouf) reinforces this sentiment (Shatz 2015).

In the past two decades, a growing number of BDs by women and by minorities have been published.[13] Although there is still a long way to go before reaching equal representation of women and minorities, the French BD world is slowly becoming a more favorable environment for a more diverse array of producers and protagonists.[14] Since 2000, the number of female artists has increased significantly, leading to more and more complex female BD protagonists, new collections, and the Artemisia prize created in 2007 for women BD artists. However, this progressive evolution is not linear, as the scandal over the all-male list of nominees for the grand prize presented at the Angoulême Festival in early 2016 showed.[15]

Conversely, minorities are not in as comparatively favorable a position; they have been marginalized for decades as second-class citizens or stood at the peripheries of the empire for centuries as non-citizens. French scholar Mark McKinney has concluded that

> colonialism and imperialism left an imprint on French comics, generally in the form of unsavory imagery and colonialist narratives. There are, of course, still both republished and brand new works that perpetuate the tradition of colonialist ideology and imagery, so there is much that remains to be done to reconfigure the field of comics.[16]

However, McKinney also recognizes that "post-colonial, ethnic minority cartoonists who have returned to the history of French colonialism and imperialism in their comics, as well as cartoonists from other groups who are sympathetic to anti-colonialism and the viewpoint of the [formerly] colonized, have made significant progress toward reconfiguring comics production."[17] McKinney has also noted how, in the past two decades, things have been changing for minorities, through BD artists such as Yvan Alagbé, Clément Baloup, Farid Boudjellal, Jacques Ferrandez, and Joann Sfar, many of whom come from a minority background. We see more minorities as agents of their own stories and histories told in a positive manner. However, on the one hand, these minority BD artists are not read by large audiences, and, on the other hand, the mainstream public is still bombarded by a stream of BDs that include few minority characters and are particularly void of minority

13. See Reyns-Chikuma 2016.

14. Another main factor for this positive change for women in comics is the Internet with no gatekeepers to prevent, consciously or not, women from entering the field; see Reyns-Chikuma 2016.

15. See also the collective of women BD creators against sexism in bdegalite.org; see *Le Monde*, Jan. 8 2016.

16. McKinney 2011b, 164. See also McKinney 2008.

17. McKinney 2011, 164.

women. Hence, mainstream France is still not receiving a lot of positive images of and from minorities.

Muslim Superheroes in France

It is also important to emphasize that several other relatively successful attempts with non-white, non-Western (including Muslim) superheroes have been made before, although mostly coming from outside of France. The most famous and recent case of Muslim superheroes is *The 99*, published in 2006 in Arabic and in 2007 in English. Although welcomed by some critics,[18] *The 99* cannot be characterized as successful in France (unlike in the U.S.). First, it has not been translated into French. Second, the left-wing newspaper *Libération* (Dec. 29, 2007), which is traditionally open to non-mainstream ideas and people but also very anchored within a secularist tradition, was not positive about it, as indicated by the title of its article: "Des comics koweitiens pour la promo d'Allah" ("Kuwaiti Comics for Promoting Allah"). However, more recently, other Muslim comics, such as *Paasban,* were reviewed rather positively in the conservative *Le Figaro* (June 8, 2015) with an enticing title: "Quand la bande dessinée part en guerre contre les djihadistes" ("When BD Goes to War against Jihadists").

At the same time, some recent attempts at French translations of non-white superheroes have been successful in France and are, therefore, more traceable. This is especially the case of *Batman, Inc.*, where, in November 2010, protagonist Bruce Wayne decides that his war against crime cannot be limited to Gotham City and therefore gives a franchise to local superheroes (local "Batmen") in other big cities. Although created by the British author David Hine, one Batman "franchisee," the Nightrunner (le Parkoureur), is French. More specifically, he is from Clichy-sous-Bois, one of the Paris *banlieues* (French suburbs),[19] and, like many inhabitants of that area, he is French-Algerian and Muslim. Interestingly, Olivier Delcroix, who regularly writes about comics/BD in the centrist and right-wing *Le Figaro* (Jan. 7, 2011), is quite positive about the idea of Nightrunner and the character's result. Similarly, the left-leaning *Slate.fr* published a relatively long and positive article, followed by a lengthy string of very diverse but positive comments on this new French superhero.[20] Interestingly, both articles and series of comments actually seem to enjoy citing and quoting the negative reactions from conservative American blogs about the notion that a Batman could be Muslim. Their French point of view is, therefore, proudly pitted

18. Editors' note: see the articles by Fredrik Strömberg and Ken Chitwood in this volume.
19. French suburbs are equivalent to inner cities in the U.S..
20. Karaboudjan 2011.

more against American conservatism, often deeply disliked in France, than against the fact that Batman was now represented as Muslim. As noticed by some commentators, these adventures not only represent the French realities of the *banlieues* but also the BD tradition. For example, they noticed that the Nightrunner's name, Bilal Asselah, could be interpreted as an allusion to the famous French-Serbian BD author Bilal. This knowledge and acknowledgment of the local French culture might be a key element to the success of this character in France.[21]

Published for the first time in *Detective Comics Annual* #12 in February 2011, the first story of Nightrunner has not been translated into French yet. However, other later issues were translated, for example, "Nyktomorph" (*Batman Incorporated* #6) was translated in *Batman Showcase* #1 in March 2012, and "The Dark Knight and the Devil's Daughter" (*Batman Incorporated* #13) was translated in *Grant Morrison Présente* #8 in May 2014. In addition, French publishers have also published translated stories featuring minority superheroes such as Sooraya Qadi/Dust,[22] Simon Baz/Green Lantern,[23] and even the earliest Black Panther stories.[24] Therefore, Kamala's French publication can be interpreted as a continuation rather than a breakthrough. As demonstrated by some studies, comics are now transnational and often bypass the national(ist) gatekeepers.[25] While some publishers did postpone their publications or promotion campaigns of more mainstream products such as novels because of the *Charlie Hebdo* massacre,[26] Marvel-Panini did not delay publication of the first volume of *Ms. Marvel*. This shows that the audiences of the two media (novels and comics) may be different, but also that comics publishers follow their own logic, which is primarily commercial.

However, neither fans' reception nor commercial logic might be the most salient way to evaluate the reception of these Muslim superheroes in the specific post-*Charlie* context which is exacerbating old tensions. Mainstream attitudes toward Muslim culture and religion do not seem to have

---

21. Faure and Garcia 2005.

22. "Dust," *X-Men Legacy* #133 (December 2002), was translated for the first time in 2003 in *X-Men* #81 "Poussière" (Panini Comics).

23. "The New Normal," *Green Lantern* #5 (November 2012), was translated in *Green Lantern Saga* #13 in June 2013.

24. In *L'Inattendu* published by Arémit/Artima from 1979 to 1980.

25. Bieloch and Bitar 2013: 113–117.

26. About the suspension of the promotion of Michel Houellebecq's novel *Soumission* (*Submission*), see Leyris 2015. *Soumission* (translated in English in Sept. 2015) is a political satire representing a situation where a Muslim party is able to form a government with the support of the left-wing party against the extreme right party. See also the nuanced book review by Knausgaard 2015.

changed very much in the last decades in mainstream France. Hence, in the general context, France cannot be described as especially welcoming to a Muslim superheroine. Although the legal and psychological French context can be described as secular (that is, 'neutral' towards religion[s]), the general atmosphere in France is quite ambivalent towards Muslim culture, due to various factors (some specific to France, and others owing to globalization). As we will see below, since we believe that *Ms. Marvel* is marketed not only to a fan audience but also to a wider audience with a strong secularist belief, the "secularist" factor is important to keep in mind in order to gauge its relative success.

Muslim(s) in France

The most obvious example of how Muslim culture is perceived in France is that of the "affaire du foulard" (headscarf affair). This "affair" started in 1989 and led to the expulsion of three Muslim girls who, after challenging the school several times, refused to remove their headscarves on school premises. School officials who made that decision cited the 1905 Laïc Law, that is a law that consecrated the separation of state and religion.[27] The affair escalated with a few more expulsions to be finally "settled" legally in 2004 with the promulgation of a new law forbidding any religious paraphernalia, such as the headscarf, in schools. However, the "affair" is still very much ongoing, as intense public debates in all media show. As European studies scholar Bronwyn Winter notes:

> The peculiarity of the French hijab debate is necessarily entwined, first with the peculiarity of French secularism and its links with the ideas of nation, state, and citizenship; second, with the history of France's pre-colonial, colonial, postcolonial, and noncolonial relationship with the Arab and Muslim worlds, particularly the Maghrib [North Africa]; and third, with the rise of Islamism and its implantation in Europe. It is also necessarily, from a feminist point of view, tied up with the peculiarities of French feminist and anti-racist activism and their relationship both with each other and with the State.[28]

Thus, the headscarf debate is also a symbol of the numerous tensions emanating from both real events and fantasies about the Other. And since, as we will see, *Ms. Marvel* is partly about issues of what is interpreted as Muslim

27. See Laborde 2010 for an introduction to how the concept of "laïcité" is understood dogmatically by some in France.
28. Winter 2008, 5.

clothing (i.e. the headscarf), the debate is therefore relevant to the understanding of the reception of this BD/comic. The debate deeply divides secularists, feminists, and anti-racist groups,[29] since the expulsion of these girls and the new law were interpreted simply as a strict application of the 1905 Laïc Law by some and as discriminatory by others. To some feminists, the expulsion was seen as a typical product of patriarchy, since it denied any agency to Muslim women and emphasized the problems they encounter, further hiding the continuing sexist discriminations and violence against women in France and the West.[30] The difficulty for some French feminists has been to conceptualize and implement "intersectionality," or the cross domination of victims of sex, race, and class discrimination, beyond colonial heritage and republican secularism.[31] However, the expulsion has also been interpreted by others as discriminatory towards Muslims and minorities who were already marginalized.[32] Indeed, some French feminists defend the veil, which for them becomes a symbol of the fight against discrimination. In a context where the veil is regarded as a cultural symbol rather than a religious one, the defense refers to the right of women to control their bodies as they wish.[33] The debate goes on as some scholars, such as sociologist Zahra Ali through her book *Féminismes islamiques* [*Islamic Feminisms*]), reach a broader audience and explain the possibility of a Muslim feminism outside and inside France/the West.[34]

This already-complex and tense situation was made even more so after the *Charlie Hebdo* massacre. Occurring one month before the publication of *Ms. Marvel*, the massacre's massive impact owed not only to its being one of the biggest terrorist mass executions to ever take place in French territory – 17 people were killed – but also that it became world news right away and remained present for weeks. Although obviously different, the 9/11 attacks were often mentioned as a precedent, to explain (and to an extent, excuse) a certain paranoia in Europe and, in particular, in France about Islam. The massacre's potential to negatively influence reception of *Ms. Marvel* is tied to *Charlie Hebdo*'s being a magazine essentially based on cartoons, and the massacre occurred because the magazine had published some caricatures of

---

29. Winter 2008, 7.

30. The debate went much beyond feminists' circles, see Badiou 2004, and Duroux and Sinapi 2004. For the complexity, intricacies, and tricks of the debates, see Norton 2013.

31. For example, Garcia 2012; Dot-Pouillard 2015.

32. See the petition "Un voile sur les discriminations," *Le Monde*, December 7, 2003.

33. See Delphy 2008; Guénif-Souilamas and Macé 2004.

34. For the French context, see also Saida Kada, president of the association Femmes Françaises et Musulmanes, Engagées (Engaged French Muslim Women) and Malika Hamidi's publications.

Muhammad. Such anti-Islamic caricatures were not new in Europe. A similar outrage had occurred over Danish caricatures in 2006. It led to hundreds dying during protests in some countries with a significant Muslim population (such as Nigeria) and then, reactively, to some acts of violence in Denmark and the West. Both incidents led to Muslim and anti-Muslim demonstrations, all of which were small, but widely reported.[35]

The impact of the *Charlie Hebdo* massacre was also large, with over one million people marching through the streets of Paris and numerous other cities and towns in France four days later. In itself, this massive demonstration is a remarkable event, a peaceful response to the massacre seemingly showing that tolerant attitudes prevailed over emotional reactions. The "Je suis Charlie" march was first and foremost presented as a healthy reaction of a united France in support of freedom of the press and against intolerance. But slowly, some started to disagree with the "Je suis Charlie" slogan and then questioned the motivations of the participants of the event.[36] Historian and sociologist Emmanuel Todd synthesizes most of these critiques in his book, *Qui est Charlie? Sociologie d'une crise religieuse* [*Who Is Charlie? Sociology of a Religious Crisis*], published in May 2015.[37] Todd contends that the marchers' motivations were not as positive as often projected in the French media, which presented these demonstrations as defending freedom of the press and as standing up for tolerance.[38] Using maps of participation in the "Je suis Charlie" demonstrations and maps of religious affiliations and socioeconomic status, he argues that the majority of demonstrators were older, white, and middle-class. Because most of these demonstrators may no longer be practicing their religion, Todd uses the term "zombie Catholics" to describe them, i.e. to present them as Catholics infused with all the social conservatism of that religion, its hierarchies, and inequality, and usually living in the French peripheral regions.[39] The book sold well but has not been positively received by some critics and many scholars, apparently because its methodology and conclusions are problematic.[40]

Even if one accepts that *Charlie Hebdo*'s journalists had the right to ex-

---

35. Some of these Danish caricatures were republished by some Western newspapers and magazines, including by *Charlie Hebdo*. See Klausen 2009; Sniderman, Petersen, Slothuus, and Stubager 2014.

36. Regarding *Charlie Hebdo*, see Ory et al. 2015.

37. Translated as *Xenophobia and the New Middle Class*. See Todd 2015.

38. These demonstrations have inspired a publishing boom; see Lamothe 2015.

39. Todd 2015.

40. For example, see Tiberj 2015. According to the author, Todd uses for example monocausal explanations of a complex event and other simplifications such as transforming the right to free speech into the obligation to blaspheme.

press their atheist "faith," or secularist mentality, or anarchistic celebratory attitude – towards beliefs like Islam as well as towards other religions – one has to recognize that they ignored the feelings of colonial and marginalized Muslims in France. However, one cannot conflate the various issues involved in these debates, such as racism, anti-Islamism, anti-veil, secularisms, freedom of expression, feminisms, and the reading of a Muslim superheroine comic book. One can find people supporting *Charlie Hebdo* and "Je suis Charlie," opposing the veil, and approvingly reading *Ms. Marvel*. As our textual analysis will show, the series is framed in ways that many French readers can understand as fitting within a national consensus on matters religious while also smoothly referring to a critical knowledge of the contemporary condition of Muslim women in France and Western countries.

"Text": Westernization and Covering Kamala

The Covering-Up and Kamala's Double Audience

The first collected volume of *Ms. Marvel*, titled "No Normal," came out in February 2014, after its heroine's first brief appearance in *Captain Marvel #14* in August 2013. The comic book was translated into French by Nicole Duclos and Jeremy Manesse· and published in February 2015, in a collected hardcover format (more associated with the French-European album) under the subtitle: "Métamorphose" ("Metamorphosis"). Changing the title right on the front cover is already significant since it seems to reveal that the literal translation of "No Normal" might not be easily presented to a French audience. Because "No Normal" are words thought and said by the protagonist Kamala when expressing her uneasiness towards assimilation,[41] they had to be replaced by terms that put less emphasis on her uneasy feelings towards the French mainstream support of assimilation. The French translators may have had to cover up issues that might have been detrimental for the French reception and switch in a consensual title. The rest of the French front cover is very similar to the U.S. one: picture, colors, sizes, and paratext (titles, authors, publishers, etc.) are more or less the same.

    In both versions of the cover, one can see a woman's body whose face is cut off above the nose, with brown hair hanging along the face down to the shoulders. And she is wearing a bright, colorful, reddish scarf on her shoulders, as well as sporting the stylized bright yellow lightning bolt of Ms. Marvel on her black shirt. It is worth mentioning that this is a far cry from traditional representations of superheroines on a front cover, includ-

41. Wilson and Alphona 2013, 8

ing previous iterations of Ms. Marvel, which are either more action-oriented or more sexually alluring or both.

Moreover, the current Ms. Marvel is presented as an ordinary student carrying three books in her left hand. These could be interpreted as signs revealing (parts of) her identity. It is worth noting that even in the French version, these book titles are all kept in English, but the cognates remain easily readable for French audiences. On the spine of the most visible book, one can read *U.S. History*. For the American and French audience, this is a reassuring sign that prepares audiences to more easily accept the second book, titled *Hadith to Live By*. This title might not be understandable for many non-Muslim or less educated readers, but it should be readable as "foreign" by most readers, and maybe as "Muslim" by some.[42] The third title, *Illust[ration] & Design*, is only partly visible, but is sufficient to hint at her intellectual and professional interest, perhaps interpretable as a sign of both (artistic) self-reflexivity and autobiography, where the protagonist is seen as a projection of the author and creative team.[43] She also wears several rings and bracelets on her right arm and hand, which is closed in a fist, connoting both fashion and determination.

Hence, in contrast to most representations of Carol Danvers and other superheroines, first, Kamala is not represented right away as a superhero, and, second, she is not sexualized; conversely, she is intellectualized. This inaugural volume is therefore presented in many ways as something closer to a "graphic novel," which is to say as more "mature" than a comic book. Moreover, the translated French version reinforces this aspect by choosing to emphasize the story of a "real" woman rather than the superhero aspects, and this emphasis might appeal to non-fans and broader audiences. Of course, if they have not yet heard about the book or the superheroine from their networks, superhero fans will find usual clues for their genre through the Marvel logo, which reminds readers of the prestigious publisher and of all its symbolic capital. Nevertheless, except for one of the three books (*Hadith to Live By*) that might be understood by some, nothing on the front cover reveals the "Muslimness" of the heroine and her adventures. Furthermore, the front cover also features the two authors' Western-sound-

42. In Islamic terminology, a *hadith* is a traditional account of the speeches or actions attributed to the prophet Muhammad. By extension, it refers to the collection of reports claiming to quote what the prophet said.

43. If the story is a fiction, it partly reflects the reality told by Marvel editor Sana Amanat. Amanat is herself Pakistani-American and Muslim, and the author of this Ms. Marvel, Willow Wilson, converted to Islam in 2004. Moreover, Wilson is now also famous for writing several books connected to Islamic culture: one memoir (*The Butterfly Mosque*, 2010) and one novel (*Alif the Unseen*, 2012), quickly translated into French in 2013 (*Alif l'invisible*).

ing names (Wilson, Alphona), and it is therefore not going to be bought as a "surreptitious" Muslim "promotion," as other superhero stories have sometimes been perceived by some French critics and journalists.[44]

The French back cover is different from the U.S. one. While the U.S. back cover represents what seems to be the same character as the one on the front cover (but in a jumping-flying superheroine position), the one in French represents some of these same elements, but in a less action-oriented way and within a more mysterious atmosphere. One can see the same young woman as on the front cover, but this time she is dressed in a superhero costume and in a static, hands-on-hips, determined, waiting pose. She is illuminated by an eight-pointed, star-shaped light that comes from behind and keeps her face invisible – almost masked (or veiled?) – with her bright eyes glowing. Her scarf is now drawn as a typical wind-blown superhero cape.

Somewhat surprisingly, the French text on the back-cover is more explicit than the U.S. back-cover paratext (our emphasis):

> Kamala Khan, une jeune fille *de confession musulmane*, se découvre du jour au lendemain d'extraordinaires pouvoirs. Grande admiratrice de Carol Danvers, cette adolescente va s'apercevoir qu'être une superheroïne s'avère plus difficile qu'il n'y paraît...

> [Kamala Khan, a young adult *of Muslim faith*, suddenly discovers that she has extraordinary powers. Very fond of Carol Danvers, this teenager is going to realize that to be a superheroine is more difficult than it seems ...]

The American text mentions Kamala Khan's Muslimness, but only after mentioning that she "is an ordinary girl from Jersey City" and by making it part of a longer list of possible identities: "But who truly is the new Ms. Marvel? Teenager? Muslim? Inhuman [a group of superpowered individuals in the Marvel Universe]?" The French text mentions "musulmane" (Muslim) in a way that could be read as very respectful, using the higher-level language phrase "de confession musulmane" (of Muslim faith-denomination). However, in both versions, the cover-text also emphasizes Kamala' connection to the Western/American, non-explicitly-religious Carol Danvers, and to the theme of the story: a teenager's struggles to be an adult, or a "coming-of-age" narrative. This will reassure any non-religious and moreover non-Muslim reader that this book is not a religious propaganda tool.

Finally, the French version contains a foreword by none other than Stan Lee (creator of, among many other characters and titles, The Fantastic Four

---

44. See the article from *Libération* (Dec. 29, 2007), cited above.

and Spider-Man), an author that any superhero fan, even in France, would immediately recognize. Surprisingly, his name is not mentioned on the front cover, reinforcing the idea that this BD was not only aimed at superhero fans. Lee's Western(-ized) name might reassure both fans and non-fans alike, since, as noted by McKinney, for comics and BD the inclusion of a non-minority as a collaborator might reassure readers from the majority that it is also for them.[45] Similarly, the brief introduction addresses the two audiences, since for fans the content resituates Kamala within a superhero tradition, and as a preface, it gives symbolic capital to the book for French broader audiences not accustomed to comics. All this packaging would reinforce the idea that the book addresses a broader audience and not only superhero readers. It also supports the idea still prevailing in many non-fan circles in France and the U.S. that a graphic novel is more intellectual than most comics.

Furthermore, the foreword is preceded by two images. The first one is a photo-like representation of a cool, self-confident teenage Kamala on a roof top, in the same costume; the billowing scarf remains, but now she is popping bubblegum. Again, this picture could be interpreted in two ways: as a superhero (a typical representation of Superman, Batman, Spider-Man on top of a building) and as a daring and funny teenager. The second image is much more cartoonish and presents all the main dramatis personae, aligned along a row of school lockers. In the center, we can see an embarrassed Kamala, who has just slammed the door of her locker. One can still see the end of a red scarf, a picture of the famous World War II-era American Westinghouse "We Can Do It!" illustration[46] (now featuring Carol Danvers), and a bright light shining through the crack of the locker-door. Shorter than the other characters, but with a superhumanly long arm, Kamala appears rather clumsy and uncomfortable, standing next to three other characters: her male Italian-American friend Bruno, her female Turkish-American friend Nakia, and the white American bully, Zoe. The three do not seem to notice anything, since all three are in their own way totally self-absorbed.

To summarize, except for the brief mention of the word "Muslim/ musulmane," everything else presented on the covers or in the paratext of this first volume is reassuring for an audience that is suspicious of religion in general and of Muslim religion in particular. In many ways, then, the story of this first volume seems to try to reassure the French mainstream

---

45. McKinney 2004, 203–204. Many French readers might not know that Stan Lee is the penname of Jewish American writer-editor Stanley Martin Lieber.

46. The picture was produced by J. Howard Miller in 1943.

audience, still not comfortable with signs of Muslimness in the public space, American or French.

Yet, the first *Ms. Marvel* volume might be a difficult comic to sell in France, since its main issue is more directly connected to "Muslim-ness" than are the following volumes. The first volume, well summarized in its title and its translation, "No Normal"/"Métamorphose," tells the story of a 16-year-old American-Pakistani youth who does not feel normal because of her minority habitus and habits compared to those of her peers. After a special event that we discuss below, she realizes that she can metamorphose into a superhero. She has special powers such as shape- and size-shifting. This power can easily be read as a typical metaphor of the changes that a teenage body and mind encounters. On top of other typical characteristics of the superhero (e.g. a double identity, a mentor, a sidekick, and an evil enemy), she is also going to need a costume, and the first volume concerns what type of costume and appearance she must choose if she wants to be faithful to the sources of her identity.

The Story In Between

Kamala can be read ideologically and visually as being in between two poles, between a certain kind of traditionalism and modernity. The first pages are clear about this in-betweenness when seen in an American multicultural-ist context. The second (central) frame of the first page presents the three main characters; in front and center, Kamala is hanging over the sandwich counter, defiantly and playfully challenging a Muslim rule about pork – she longingly smells the "delicious infidel meat" of a BLT.[47] On the reader's left, Bruno, her Italian-American friend (and future, often involuntary, ally or sidekick), is telling her that she has to choose: "Either eat the bacon or stick to your principles." And, on the reader's right is Kamala's other peer, Na-kia, an American but "proud Turkish" woman, who wears a dark *hijab* and does not need an "'Amreeki' [American] nickname." For both of her friends, although mutually tolerant, Kamala has to choose one or the other: eating the pork *or* respecting one's principles. If these two characters differ in their choices, they still respect each other, and the three might be presented as a multicultural group. Further, they are all pitched against the negative rep-resentation of two stereotypical, insensitive white people. The next page introduces Caucasian "concern troll[s]" Zoe Zimmer and her boyfriend Josh, both presented as overly self-confident and arrogant, and saying rac-ist things in a way they deem funny. Ambiguously, Kamala is fascinated by

---

47. Later (p. 4), Kamala also politely challenges the imam.

this girl, Zoe, who is tall and blond, and somewhat resembles Carol Danvers. Hence, even after Zoe's multiple offensive remarks, Kamala defends her ("But she is so nice.").

These representations of Kamala and her antagonists may, again, be reassuring to French mainstream readers. If Kamala is looking for an identity as a teenager, she is immediately presented as open-minded since she is able to distance herself from religious rules (i.e. pork taboo), and, importantly for the French audience, she is presented in contrast to the overly serious, headscarved Nakia, while still friendly to Zoe and Josh in spite of their stigmatizing reactions.

However, the *Ms. Marvel* creative team's open-minded views of Islam quickly challenge this French majority's belief in various ways. First, Nakia replies to Zoe's arrogant jokes and beliefs about her headscarf that "actually, [her] dad wants [her] to take it off. He thinks it's a *phase*" (page 3). The "veil" is here affirmed as a choice. It is not imposed by a male family member as it may be done in traditional Muslim families and as it is too systematically represented in the West. If Nakia's choice is accepted by many in the Anglo-Saxon world, even if it is progressively changing in France, fewer French people and movements are comfortable with Nakia's point of view.[48] In the name of equality between girls and boys, and in the name of secularism, French law forbids the headscarf on school property until the end of high school (i.e. ages 17-18). As argued by Winter, to explain the position held by the majority in France on that topic, free choice is a difficult position to defend for the 12-year-old girls who were expelled from their schools for refusing to take off their veil, since studies claim that the "choice" of the headscarf results most of the time from adults' and peers' pressure. However, since Nakia, like Kamala, is about 16-17, and lives in a country that promotes gender equality in various ways, how can one argue against her choice? Actually, many French citizens are growing more and more aware and accepting of this complexity, even if many still think that a law is necessary for protecting girls and women from their male counterparts, who are seen as actively participating in a patriarchal and even macho culture.[49]

Male figures in this *Ms. Marvel* volume are similarly not stereotyped, and they certainly do not fit the common French anti-Muslim model. First, while the father figure is strict – and, through a radical feminist lens, could still be seen as patriarchal when he forbids his daughter to go out because she is a girl – he is also a very caring figure. Second, though her brother Aamir is pictured as very conservative (a Salafist), their own father sheds a doubt on his

48. See Winter 2008, 262–264.
49. Winter, 260.

son's motivation, hinting that he only prays so much in order to avoid real responsibilities, such as finding a "real" job. Also in his relationship with his sister, Aamir is presented more as a competitive, teasing sibling than as a model "Islamofascist." He has more of a teen's phlegmatic attitude than the ideological dogmatism of a "barbu" (bearded one). Finally, the third male Muslim figure in the early *Ms. Marvel* stories, the imam, is similar to the father, even respecting Kamala's choice of not revealing what is going on in her life, whether it is about her superpowers or her difficulty in choosing what type of superheroine she wants to be. Beyond Zoe's jockish boyfriend, the only negative representations of males are the members of the "sect," a group of Ms. Marvel's adversaries led by antagonists Edison and the Inventor. The sect is not a religious group per se, but a group based on scientific research with the goal, at the expense of youths' lives, of contributing to a more efficient society.

The word "sect" has a stronger negative connotation in France than it has in the U.S., because in the former, the word was and still is mostly used and understood in reaction against centuries-old Catholic control and religious obscurantism. Therefore, France has a stricter secularist attitude and stricter laws against "dérives sectariennes" (sectarian driftings/excesses).[50] With regard to the sectarian adversary, the challenge for French readers comes from the fact that the leaders of the "sect" are not Muslim, not even religious (in a primary sense of the word), but are Westerners and scientists. This part of the story is only just hinted at in the end of the first volume and is developed in volume two, *Generation Why* (same title in French). But it is important to underline that it is two Westerners, the "Inventor" and Edison,[51] who kidnap teenaged boys and girls to use them as slaves to serve their own experimental, scientific, and economic purposes.

Therefore, the team of comics creators challenges the conventional French understanding of sects as religious groups that kidnap disoriented

---

50. "In English, it is a term that designates a religiously separated group, but in its historical usage in Christendom it carried a distinctly pejorative connotation. A sect was a movement committed to heretical beliefs and often to ritual acts and practices like isolation that departed from orthodox religious procedures" (Wilson 1982, 89). Because of the multiplication of dangerous sectarian Islamic groups, some people in France and in the U.S. might still consider Islam a sect.

51. The name "Edison" resonates much more in the U.S., and especially in New Jersey, where the story takes place, than in France, since Thomas Alva Edison was American and the popular history of sciences is still studied within national[ist] lines; the authors of *Ms. Marvel* play with a lot of references to that history-made-myth in the U.S., also associated with the other character/name called Knox (19th-c. scientist who first "kidnapped" corpses in cemeteries and then was found guilty of being an accomplice in the killing of homeless people to use their bodies in his experiments).

youth and, through psychological techniques, indoctrinate them through brainwashing. This story challenges such mainstream perceptions by making the bad guys Western scientists and the hero a Muslim.[52] Here, then, we have what amounts to a critique of the conventional model, that imposes a Western, rational, progressive, modern view of what a hero should be and how the hero should act. This is particularly challenging for French mainstream majority audiences, since they tend to automatically associate religion (of whatever denomination, but even more Islam) with obscurantism, and secularism with science. However, *Ms. Marvel*'s clearly non-conventional, non-mainstream interpretation might also, in various ways and to various degrees, please more and more French people. Over the past decade, more French people have come to criticize what they perceive as non-democratic decisions made by technocrats in the name of globalization, capitalism, Europeanization, and French centralization, through which they often feel as if they have been deprived of agency.[53]

Agency, Powers, and Identity

One could argue that agency is actually the most revolutionary aspect of *Ms. Marvel*. Since agency is also a key concept in feminist studies,[54] it is important to emphasize its role in this *Ms. Marvel*. In some ways, some might dismiss this supposedly silly teenage superhero story since it could be read as a simple version of the Cinderella myth: a girl turning 16 wakes up and realizes that she is becoming an adult. However, a main difference is that the comics story emphasizes Kamala's agency, while in traditional fairy tales agency is only given to the patriarchy (e.g. the father, the charming prince).

Moreover, readers follow Kamala struggling not only to become an adult but more specifically to become a singular person who assumes and fights for her difference. Readers follow Kamala in her quest for identity.[55] Caught between what is represented as an excessively liberal society and as a conservative Muslim family, Kamala is presented as struggling to find a way to be acceptable and accepted by both. She first tends to reject her parents' rules and, partly under peer pressure (represented by her schoolmates, especially Zoe and Josh), disobeys her parents. She goes to a party in the middle of what seems to be a public park where alcohol is served. Most French and American parents might not frame such a prohibition within

52. Moreover, she is allied with a non-Muslim, Western, white sidekick, Bruno.
53. This can be seen, for example, in the rise of populism in France and the growing support of the National Front led by Marine Le Pen; cf. Grunberg 2008.
54. For the concept of agency, see Judith Butler.
55. See co-creator Sana Amanat's talk for TEDxTeen 2014.

a gender framework like Kamala's parents do. The rule of forbidding a 16-year-old to go out late and to a place where alcohol is served might seem reasonable to many middle-class parents, American or French. The issue in this story is then: who is going to decide between what is right or wrong? Is it the parents preventively or the teenager spontaneously?

In this story, like in most Western societies, more and more often the market tends to pressure parents and institutions to grant teens and kids more autonomy. This also implies more vulnerability to the "invisible hands," both the one of the market (see Adam Smith) and the one still dominating and dominated by old patriarchal views, as some feminist studies would suggest.[56] In French society, even if the state is still struggling to retain some power within the market economy, it is less and less effective when facing both global and patriarchal forces. In Muslim societies or, more generally, in more traditional communities (including secularist or Christian ones), the family decides, as long as the decision follows the patriarchal rules. This is something we can see in this comic. Tricked, Kamala is served a drink with alcohol but spits it out, apparently before swallowing. She runs away from the party, mad at Bruno for what she feels is his patronizing attitude when he tries to help her, and she faints. She wakes up under a ray of light, welcomed by a vision of her heroes, three Avengers: Captain America, Iron Man, and her "idol" Captain Marvel, Carol Danvers. This is when she is granted her wish to be like Captain Marvel and gains her superpowers.

Like Nakia and her headscarf, Kamala makes decisions for herself in several key situations. First, she goes out to a party against her parents' decision. She does this partly to push back against a prejudice against women that does not trust them to choose when faced with some men's bad intentions. Then, she refuses alcohol, which could be seen both as simply mature and/or as Islamic. The most difficult choice for Kamala is choosing with which models/ideals to identify. First, we have seen that she ambivalently supports the white blond Zoe in spite of her meanness. More importantly, she also wants to identify with Carol Danvers, saying that "my chances of becoming an intergalactic superhero are even slimmer than my chances of becoming blond and popular" (page 4). However, Kamala progressively transforms into what moderate Muslims and other non-Muslim groups would see as a "decent" multicultural Muslim American woman.

Asked by a hallucination of her idol Carol Danvers what she wants, Ka-

---

56. See for example Nancy Fraser's edited volume, *Fortunes of Feminism*. Such patriarchal views defend, for instance, positions like "if you are a woman outside at night, it means you want it." On this particular claim, see Debbie Schlussel's outrageous negative comments about Lara Logan's assault in Egypt, in Norton 2013, 69.

mala replies that she wants to be like Danvers (page 17). With what is perhaps the extraterrestrial mist that is at that moment released over New York, and which is the actual cause of Kamala's transformation, in the background, she then transforms into Ms. Marvel: blond, scantily dressed, and white-skinned (page 19). She proceeds to save Zoe, who falls into water after her drunk boyfriend's overbearing insistence for intimacy, confirming Kamala's parents' predictions about boys (page 6–7). Kamala then goes through some difficulties in adapting to her new disguise: "I always thought that if I had amazing hair, if I could pull off great boots, if I could fly ... That would make me feel strong. That would make me happy. But the hair gets in my face, the boots pinch ... and this leotard is giving me an epic wedgie" (page 12). On her way back home, Kamala is addressed by an otherwise wise homeless person (another stereotype countered). He comments on her "beautiful nice knees" (page 13), adding: "maybe you outghtta think about puttin' on some pants". She realizes that something is wrong, that being "undressed" like Carol Danvers is not what makes a superhero, and that all "[t]his is rapidly becoming no fun." She runs home and, spontaneously reverting back to her original form, is welcomed by her conservative brother and her parents, who strictly but kindly scold and ground her for sneaking out. In the third episode of the story arc, as announced visually by the reprinted cover from the original comic book, she transforms again to save her friend Bruno, but this time she is fully dressed (page 17), yet still blond and white.

Kamala's transformation is complete only in the next chapter (4), where she appears fully dressed and with her brown hair and her regular skin color (page 16). Interestingly, her dress code is much closer to a Muslim one, since she repurposed her burkini as her superhero costume. A burkini is a portmanteau referring to a combined *burqa* and bikini – a swimsuit recommended by many liberal and moderately conservative Muslims, but still rejected by the more conservative. Similarly, as reported in the conservative newspaper *Le Figaro* (Aug. 2009), some French local officials rejected the burkini, basing their decision on the general rule that one cannot bathe fully clothed in a public pool for reasons of hygiene and safety. They even cynically added that such an outfit cannot be Islamic since it is not in the Qur'an.[57]

Although it would have to be proven that the burkini is not hygienic and safe, since other countries such as Sweden have accepted it in their public pools, all these arguments miss the point that the burkini is a remarkable compromise between cultures. Additionally, the same pools that forbid the burkini allow string bikinis, a decision that could be interpreted as fitting

57. See Kovacs 2009a; 2009b.

one step further towards the hypersexualization of women in public space.[58] The French ban of the burkini excludes minorities, and Muslims in particular. Hence, when Kamala says that she does not feel "normal" since she is "signed out of health class" (gym class), it reinforces the secularist perspective (page 12). However, the burkini invites parents to reconsider their attitude towards gym classes (as women soccer players are now allowed to play wearing headscarves by FIFA in Europe, and also in the U.S. and Canada). Muslim girls and women can do whatever other girls/women and boys/men do (i.e. play soccer or be a "superhero"). That is certainly an idea that Kamala in her superhero burkini promotes, and one that challenges anti-Muslim attitudes in France and in the U.S.

Kamala's transforming into a superheroine who is fully herself, and not a copy of someone else (i.e. a blond, white, scantily-dressed Carol Danvers), addresses the issue of assimilation. Therefore, Kamala's new perspective on her identity includes the more general question of how far to assimilate, especially to "rules" that are seen by some, Muslim or not, as degrading for women: the veil for some French/Western people or quasi-nudity for Muslims (and other conservative groups). Within the didactic frame chosen by Wilson, readers can see that, after some trials and errors, Kamala is represented as courageously choosing the Muslim feminist option, which is also a multicultural one. This choice might be the most important one she makes, since it summarizes her decisions: it is a hybridized version of the superheroine, where she can still be a strong woman using a superhero costume, but in line with Islamic codes that resist hypersexualization. If this choice pleases most other French religious conservatives (Catholics, Jews, etc.), it could also appeal to secularists who believe that we should not simply accept market-oriented choices that tend towards hypersexualizing women's bodies, but it also should be satisfying to French multiculturalists, including most feminists.

Ms. Marvel represents an extraordinarily positive multicultural agenda and one possible solution, if not for all feminists and all women, then at least for people who accept that some women want to wear the headscarf and a burkini. In many ways, Kamala could be a model for a Muslim feminism that could challenge negative or skeptical French views of Islam as necessarily patriarchal and in desperate need of Western help. She could also be a model for open-minded, flexible French people who submit to

---

58. However, it is not clear if the burkini has been tolerated in most pools and on beaches in France, since surprisingly no article on the topic has been published in the main press since that incident; the debate is still raging, see Jamain-Samson 2011, 45–71. [Editors' note: New controversies were sparked in 2016.]

the French national(ist) patriarchal secularist state agenda, itself more and more submissive to the patriarchal market agenda. Contrary to the belief in one essentialist way of representing identity, Kamala presents an extraordinary flexibility, with several simultaneous and equal identities (American, Muslim, woman), reflective of her shapeshifting powers. She adapts to the context: in the mosque, for example, she uses her scarf as a head covering (pages 3 and 5); in the streets, she wears it as a fashion accessory, as shown on the front cover of vol. 1; and finally, when "working," doing her duty as a superheroine, she uses it as a cape.

Brief and Provisional Conclusion: Beyond a Traditional Progressive-Conservative Opposition?

Although Kamala is inscribed within what tends to be a conservative ideology, that is, the vigilantist, moralist, and individualist U.S. superhero tradition, we have seen that she can be perceived positively in a French context. In an American context, it might be because her costume could be interpreted as a continuation of the superhero tradition, while having successfully integrated an intersectional multicultural feminism. In France, it seems that in spite of a social climate much less sensitive to multiculturalism understood in an Anglo-Saxon way,[59] this positive view of Kamala stems mainly from the fact that she does not wear the veil (in contrast to her friend, Nakia) and is not overly religious in public spaces. Hence, she is quite easy to accept for French readers, be they Muslim mainstream or non-Muslim citizens. One has to add that this initial success was recently boosted, since *Ms. Marvel* was selected as the best series of the year at the Angoulême Festival.[60] One can hope that the terrorist acts of November 2015 in Paris and of March 2016 in Brussels will not stop this smart and generous series from further publication in France. At least the publisher Marvel-Panini seems convinced that it will not stop in spite of the difficult context, since they published the third volume in French in December 2015, and had, at the time of writing, slated the following volumes for publication in 2016.

59. For a discussion of the different ways of perceiving multiculturalism in Anglo-Saxon countries and in France, see Laborde 2010.
60. Alverson 2016.

Works Cited

Ali, Z. 2012. *Féminismes islamiques*. Paris.

Alverson, B. 2016. "'Miss Marvel' wins best series at Angouleme." *Comics Book Resources*, Jan.31. http://www.cbr.com/ms-marvel-wins-best-series-at-angouleme/.

Anonymous. 2015. "Nadine Morano évoque la 'race blanche' de la France." *Le monde.fr*, September 27. http://www.lemonde.fr/politique/article/2015/09/27/nadine-morano-evoque-la-race-blanche-de-la-france_4773927_823448.html.

Anonymous. 2011. "Une photographie d'art controversée vandalisée à Avignon." *Le monde.fr*, April 17. http://www.lemonde.fr/culture/article/2011/04/17/une-photographie-d-art-polemique-detruite-a-avignon_1509023_3246.html.

Anonymous. 2007. "Des comics koweïtiens pour la promo d'Allah." *Libération.fr*, December 29. http://archive.li/2fba.

Anonymous. 2003. "Un voile sur les discriminations." *Le Monde*, December 17, 2003.

Bacholle-Boskovic, M. 2010. "Des minorités plus visibles: Réflexions d'auteurs de jeunesse." *Raison Publique* 13: 351–365.

Badiou, A. 2004. "Derrière la Loi foulardière, la peur." *Le Monde.fr*, March 22.

Bieloch, K., and S. Bitar. 2013. "Batman goes Transnational: The Global Appropriation and Distribution of an American Hero." In *Transnational Perspectives on Graphic Narratives: Comics at the Crossroads*, edited by D. Stein, S. Denson, and C. Meyer, 113–126. London and New York: Bloomsbury.

Carletti, S., and J.-M. Lainé. 2011. *Nos années Strange, 1970-1996*. Paris.

Delcroix, O. 2011. "Le partenaire français musulman de Batman crée la polémique." *Le Figaro.fr*, January 7. http://blog.lefigaro.fr/bd/2011/01/le-partenaire-francais-musulma.html.

Deman, J. A. 2005. *The Margins of Comics: The Construction of Women, Minorities, and the Geek*. Toronto.

Delphy, C. 2008. *Classer, dominer: qui sont les autres?* Paris: La Fabrique.

Dot-Pouillard, N. 2007. "Les recompositions politiques du mouvement féministe français au regard du *hijab*." *SociologieS*, http://sociologies.revues.org/246.

Faure, S., and M.-C. Garcia. 2005. *Culture hip-hop, jeunes des cités et politiques publiques*. Paris.

Fournier, X. 2014. *Super-Héros. Une histoire française*. Paris.

Garcia, M.-C. 2012. "Des féminismes aux prises avec 'l'intersectionnalité': le mouvement Ni Putes Ni Soumises et le Collectif féministe du Mouvement des Indigènes de la République." *Recherches féministes* 25 (1): 111–165.

Grunberg, G. 2008. "Euroscepticism in France: 1992–2002." In *Opposing Europe? The Comparative Party Politics of Euroscepticism*, edited by Paul Taggart, vol. 1: 38–57.

Jamain-Samson, S. 2011. "La 'Lolita' et la 'sex bomb': Figures de la socialisation des jeunes filles." *Sociologie et sociétés* 43 (1): 45–71.

Karaboudjan, L. 2011. "Le batman français est un musulman du 9-3." *Slate.fr*, January 6. http://blog.slate.fr/des-bulles-carrees/2011/01/06/le-batman-francais-est-un-musulman-du-9-3/.

Klausen, J. 2009. *The Cartoons That Shook the World*. New Haven.

Knausgaard, K. O. 2015. "Michel Houellebecq's 'Submission'." *The New York Times*, November 2. https://www.nytimes.com/2015/11/08/books/review/michel-houellebecqs-submission.html

Kovacs, S. 2009a. "IDF: le 'burkini' interdit à la piscine." *Le Figaro*, Aug. 12.

———. 2009b. "Du burkini au voile: l'Europe cherche la réponse." *Le Figaro*, Sept. 9. http://www.lefigaro.fr/international/2009/09/07/01003-20090907ARTFIG00339-du-burkini-au-voile-l-europe-cherche-la-reponse-.php.

Laborde, C. 2010. *Français, encore un effort pour être républicains!* Paris: S.

Lamothe, J. 2015. "Le 11 janvier est aussi devenu un phénomène d'édition." *Le Monde.fr*, May 13. http://www.lemonde.fr/livres/article/2015/05/13/le-11-janvier-est-aussi-devenu-un-phenomene-d-edition_4633065_3260.html.

Lehman, S., F. Colin, C. Bessonneau, and Gess. 2012. *La Brigade chimérique. Intégrale*. Nantes.

Lehman, S., and S. Créty. 2012–2013. *Masqué. Tomes 1 à 4*. Paris.

Leyris, R. 2015. "Le frappant téléscopage entre la sortie du livre de Houellebecq et l'attentat contre 'Charlie Hebdo'." *Le Monde.fr*, January 9. http://www.lemonde.fr/livres/article/2015/01/09/le-frappant-telescopage-entre-la-sortie-du-livre-de-houellebecq-et-l-attentat-contre-charlie-hebdo_4552323_3260.html.

Lorenz, D. 2015. "Mythe et idéologie des comics de super-héros." In *Les personnages mythiques dans la littérature de jeunesse*, edited by N. Prince, and S. Servoise, 149–160. Rennes.

———. Forthcoming 2016a. "Généalogie d'une poétique hypermédiale à l'ère des industries culturelles. Le cas de la transmédiation du récit des origines de Spider-Man." In *La bande dessinée au miroir: bande dessinée et réflexivité*, edited by D. Mellier. Toronto.

———. 2016b. "Modalités et enjeux de la réappropriation culturelle de la figure du super-héros dans *La Brigade chimérique* et *Masqué* de Serge

Lehman." In *La « BD » américaine vue par l'Europe. Réception et réappropria-tions*, edited by A. Boillat, and M. Atallah. Gollion.

McKinney, M. 2000. "The Representations of Ethnic Minority Women in Comic Books." In *Women, Immigration and Identities in France*, edited by J. Freedman, and C. Tarr, 85–102. New York.

———. 2004. "Histoire et critique sociale dans les bandes dessinées afric-aines-américaines et franco-africaines." In *Minorités postcoloniales et francophones: Etudes culturelles comparées*, edited by A. G. Hargreaves, 199–218. Paris.

———. 2008. *History and Politics in French-language Comics and Graphic Novels.* Jackson, MS.

———. 2011. *The Colonial Heritage of French Comics.* Liverpool.

———. 2013. *Redrawing French Empire in Comics.* Columbus, OH.

Miller, F. 1986. *The Dark Knight Returns.* Burbank, CA.

Norton A. 2013. *On the Muslim Question.* Princeton, NJ.

Ory, P., C. Delporte, B. Tillier, L. Bihl, and E. Pierrat. 2015. *La caricature...et si c'était sérieux? Décryptage de la violence satirique.* Paris.

Paulet, A. 2015. "Quand la bande dessinée part en guerre con-tre les djihadistes?" *Le Figaro.fr*, June 8. http://www.lefigaro.fr/bd/2015/06/08/03014-20150608ARTFIG00125-quand-la-bande-des-sinee-part-en-guerre-contre-les-djihadistes.php.

Pilloy, A. 1994. *Les Compagnes des héros de BD: des femmes et des bulles.* Paris.

Pollitt, K. 1991. "Hers: The Smurfette Principle." *New York Times*, April 7. http://www.nytimes.com/1991/04/07/magazine/hers-the-smurfette-principle.html.

Reyns-Chikuma, C. 2016. "La BD au féminin." Special issue of *Alternative francophone* (March 2016).

Richards, J., and C. M. Williams. 2012. "Performing the Veil: Gender and Resistance in Marjane Satrapi's *Persepolis* and Shirin Neshat's Photogra-phy." In *Teaching Comics and Graphic Narratives: Essays on Theory, Strategy and Practice*, edited by L. Dong, 130–144. Jefferson, NC.

Satrapi, M. 2000–2003. *Persepolis. Tomes 1 à 4.* Paris.

Sattouf, R. 2014. *L'Arabe du futur. Une jeunesse au Moyen-Orient (1978–1984).* Paris.

Shatz, A. 2015. "Drawing Blood: A French novelists' shocking memoir of the Middle East." *New Yorker*, October 19. http://www.newyorker.com/magazine/2015/10/19/drawing-blood.

Sniderman, P. M., M. B. Petersen, R. Slothuus, and R. Stubager. 2014. *Para-doxes of Liberal Democracy: Islam, Western Europe, and the Danish Cartoon Crisis.* Princeton, NJ.

Tiberj, V. 2015. "Le simplisme d'Emmanuel Todd démonté par la sociologie des 'Je suis Charlie'." *Le Monde.fr*, May 19. http://www.lemonde.fr/idees/article/2015/05/19/le-simplisme-d-emmanuel-todd-demonte-par-la-sociologie-des-je-suis-charlie_4635826_3232.html.

Todd, E. 2015. *Who is Charlie? Xenophobia and the New Middle Class.* Cambridge.

Vessels, J. E. 2012. *Drawing France: French Comic and the Republic.* Jackson, MS.

Wilson, G. W., and A. Alphona. 2014. *Ms. Marvel Volume 1: No Normal.* New York.

———. 2015. *Ms. Marvel: Métamorphose (Tome 1).* Translated by N. Duclos, and J. Manesse. Nice.

Winter B. 2008. *Hijab and the Republic: Uncovering the French Headscarf Debate.* Syracuse, NY.

The Comics That Hate Produced: Representing the African-American Muslim Experience in DC Comics

Dwain C. Pruitt

IN FRAMING HIS 2011 STUDY of post-9/11 representations of Muslims in American superhero comics, comics scholar Fredrik Strömberg aptly notes that superhero comics are "very much an American preoccupation [...] a mirror of the political and socioeconomic climate in the United States."[1] Drawing on Edward Said, Strömberg focuses on comics' presentation of Arabs and Muslims as "Oriental," fundamentally Othered characters who, even when portrayed sympathetically, tend most often to be "stereotypical."[2] Muslim blogger Jehanzeb Dar arrives at similar conclusions in "Holy Islamophobia, Batman!: Demonization of Muslims and Arabs in Mainstream American Comic Books," lamenting superhero comics' "almost" complete lack of "realistic portraits of Muslims and Arabs" and arguing that Hollywood has portrayed Muslims as "completely antithetical to Western Judeo-Christian values." As a result, these comic book Muslims cannot be heroes or heroines as Batman or Superman are. Cast as "threats and polar opposites" to "truth, justice, liberty, and equality," they are necessarily villains.[3]

These scholars' considerations of U.S. comics' fraught efforts to portray Islam and persons of Middle Eastern origin offer important insights; however, the scholarly focus heretofore on Arabs, the Middle East, and post-9/11 geopolitics in comics' Othering of Muslims, while understandable, underplays an important aspect of the "American-ness" of superhero comics. The Silver and Bronze Ages of comics, roughly the period between 1959 and 1975, were impacted by the cultural and racial politics of the 1960s and 1970s. During this time period, American Islam's face in the news and popular media was black. Islam as a religion was inextricably linked with the Nation of Islam

1. Strömberg 2011, 574.
2. Strömberg 2011, 574, 577.
3. Dar 2010, 100–101.

(NOI) and the nascent Black Power Movement. According to sociologist C. Eric Lincoln's famous study of the Black Muslim movement, membership in the NOI doubled from approximately 25,000 to approximately 50,000 during the summer of 1959 and had grown to possibly as many as 100,000 persons by 1964, heightening fears that the Black Muslims were a radical insurgency that "purvey[ed] cold black hatred."[4] This fear of blackness and Islam impacted how a generation of African-American superheroes, particularly DC Comics's first African-American superheroes introduced between 1971 and 1976, were characterized. These characters were not represented as practicing Muslims and professed no religious creed; rather, these crypto-Muslims were introduced as the nation's politics grew darker in the mid-1960s and conservative elements sought to criticize the Black Muslim movement by creating a series of angry black radicals who needed to be introduced to "real American values" to be set on the right path. These characterizations, inspired by Malcolm X and Muhammad Ali, the Nation of Islam's two best-known and most controversial members, defined DC Comics's African-American superheroes until the publication of *Superman vs Muhammad Ali*, the result of a major shift in popular perception of both the boxer and the Nation of Islam as it reorganized as a more orthodox Islamic organization.

With the cultural tensions of the 1960s and 1970s past, DC Comics's Black Muslims disappeared until 1993, when Milestone Comics, an African-American-led imprint distributed by DC Comics, introduced Wise Son of *Blood Syndicate*, whose journey towards an authentic Muslim identity reflects what anthropologist Robert Dannin describes as the "typical [African-American] conversion narrative."[5] Unfortunately, the Milestone experiment ended in failure and, by 2002, DC Comics's writers were drawing from a very familiar well in their creation of African-American Muslim characters.

African Americans and Islam

Islam has been a part of the African-American experience since the arrival of enslaved Muslims from West Africa. Scholars suggest that "at least one fifth" of slaves brought to the Americas were Muslims.[6] Scholar of religion Aminah Beverly McCloud identifies Islamic cultural retentions and naming practices as one of four major factors in Islam's rising popularity among African Americans at the turn of the twentieth century.[7] Islam spread into black communities in the urban North through the Great Migration. Afri-

4. Lincoln 1994, 103, 218.
5. Dannin 2002, 7.
6. Lincoln 1994, 255.
7. McCloud 1995, 9.

cans fleeing the South for new opportunities often found conditions in the North to be harsh physically and economically, spreading dissatisfaction. American racism, bad economic and social conditions, as well as Muslim immigration and Islamic cultural retentions helped to popularize Islam in certain African-American communities.[8] Early African-American Islam was dominated by heterodox sects. These movements adopted a heady mix of mysticism, racial consciousness, anti-colonialism, and gangsterism. Early African-American Islam emphasized African Americans as the true Israel of God, to be redeemed from its Gentile tormentors.[9] Islam was "a holy protest against [anti-black] racism" and a call to Allah's chosen people to reclaim their true cultural and historical role.[10] As such, the movements were separatist in nature and shared "a disdain for the West and Christianity."[11] The most important of these heterodox African-American Muslim movements, the Nation of Islam, was founded by Wallace D. Fard in Detroit in 1930. In 1934, control of the organization was passed to Elijah Muhammad under whose direction the Nation of Islam grew to have a significant presence in urban centers, particularly Chicago, Detroit, and New York City. During that same time period, African-American radicalization intensified as those who fought for others' freedom in World War II only to return to racial inequality at home "introduced the possibilities of social, cultural, and political revolution at home."[12]

The spread of this Black Nationalist Islam was largely confined to the urban North. As historian Peniel Joseph notes, New York City, and particularly Harlem, was the epicenter for militant African-American Islam and its challenges to discrimination and injustice. Long before the rest of America knew of the Nation of Islam's existence, New York was "a battleground" as the Black Muslims demanded reform and attacked police brutality. Muslims' bold 1957 challenge to police violence when a Black Muslim known as Johnson X was brutally beaten, jailed, and refused medical treatment, won them popular admiration and converts in the African-American community.[13] As Malcolm X's syndicated newspaper column would later call them, they were "God's Angry Men."[14] While many blacks responded favorably to the Nation of Islam's inflammatory rhetoric and message of racial pride and uplift, the white community responded with worry. The Nation of Islam's insistence

8. McCloud 1995, 9.
9. Dannin 2002, 26.
10. Jackson 2005, 29–30.
11. McCloud 1995, 51.
12. Joseph 2006, 3.
13. Joseph 2006, 10–14.
14. Joseph 2006, 3, 10.

on racial separation, virulent anti-white and anti-Christian rhetoric, call for reparations, and willingness to disobey laws that it deemed unjust seemed harbingers of racial warfare.[15]

During the week of July 13, 1959, CBS News introduced America to New York's Muslim "problem" with its *News Beat* story "The Hate that Hate Produced," an exposé of the Nation of Islam by Louis Lomax, a black reporter, and Mike Wallace. Historian Dawn-Marie Gibson writes of the documentary:

> The five-part series was ingeniously edited to increase its shock appeal [...] Every feature of the production is tailored to portray the NOI as a radical, Black supremacist cult. Through the lens of Lomax and Wallace, the NOI was projected to the American public as an entity that was detrimental to the Civil Rights Movement and the wider African-American community [...] The American public's reaction to the production was uniform. Both Wallace and Lomax were applauded for their work in the series. Wallace was commended for "laying before the public gaze an ugly and terrifying sickness loose in our society."[16]

Peniel Joseph offers additional insight into the documentary's unprecedented cultural impact:

> The program boiled down the Nation of Islam's mix of religious evangelism and racial militancy to hate mongering. Descending into homes of white Americans via a new medium, television, whose power was largely untested, the Nation of Islam received a dramatic, if not entirely unflattering debut. More than simply putting the Nation of Islam and other black militants on the radar of ordinary Americans, the documentary ushered in the first intraracial political controversy of the civil rights era, pitting black separatists against integrationists. *News Beat*'s coverage also served as a coronation of sorts – marking Malcolm X as a new breed of black militant. [17]

The large Nation of Islam presence in New York City is important for explaining some of what happens in comics publishing in the 1960s and 1970s. Both of the major superhero comics publishers of the day, DC Comics and Marvel Comics, were based in New York City. Black activist movements have been led by and/or inspired by African-American Muslims in New York City

15. Bracey et al. 1970, 404–405.
16. Gibson 2012, 44–45.
17. Joseph 2006, 22.

at least since the 1940s.[18] Due to the city's large African-American Muslim population, the Nation of Islam received "important coverage" in the *New York Amsterdam News*, an African-American newspaper.[19] The artists, editors, and writers who were creating mainstream superhero comics experienced metro New York's unique cultural and racial politics, which, arguably, impacted the types of stories they chose to tell and how they understood what black Islam was.

Between 1959 and 1963, paranoia about African-American Islam increased significantly. While Black Muslim leaders like Wallace Fard and Elijah Muhammad had provoked concerns in some governmental circles, Malcolm X's rise to prominence as the Nation of Islam's spokesperson heightened national awareness of the movement. Cassius Clay's conversion to Islam further inflamed popular Islamophobia in the mid-1960s. J. Edgar Hoover's FBI had surveilled the Nation of Islam and its leaders since the early 1950s, convinced that the organization was a threat to national security. In 1959, Hoover sought to have the NOI's leaders prosecuted for subversion, a request that the Justice Department denied as baseless and, perhaps more importantly, unnecessary. The Nation of Islam, the Justice Department reasoned, had no national profile and was easily contained to urban ghettoes. Clay's conversion and subsequent adoption of the name Muhammad Ali forced the federal government to rethink its strategy.[20] After his success in the 1960 Olympics, Clay returned to the United States and began his march towards a heavyweight title bout. A loud, flamboyant and gregarious young man, Clay was commonly viewed as a "lovable clown" generally popular with sports writers.[21] As his championship bout with Sonny Liston approached, Clay's ties with the Nation of Islam and the possibility of his conversion became fodder for intense media speculation. After he had become world champion in 1964 and had publicly confirmed that he was a member of the Nation of Islam, the sports media turned on him, "elevat[ing] his Muslim ties to the level of a catastrophe for America" and, as did New York boxing writer Jimmy Cannon, denouncing the new heavyweight champion as "an instrument of mass hate" and a "weapon of wickedness."[22]

Renamed Muhammad Ali, the world heavyweight champion now was arguably the world's most visible Muslim and a powerful recruiting tool. Sportswriter Jerry Izenberg commented that Ali was attempting to "become

18. Lazerow and Williams 2006, 25, 28, 40.
19. Lincoln 1994, 138.
20. Bingham and Wallace 2000, 61–62.
21. Bingham and Wallace 2000, 53.
22. Bingham and Wallace 2000, 82–83; Hauser 1991, 120–121.

Super Muslim at that stage of his life," to show his appreciation and dedication to the Nation of Islam.[23] His efforts paid off. Minister Jeremiah Shabazz, who introduced Ali to the Nation of Islam, suggested that the organization's following increased "maybe a hundred percent" after Ali joined and became a featured speaker.[24] Ali was Hoover's worst nightmare come to life: a Black Muslim who galvanized support nationally and internationally. When Ali traveled to Africa in May–June 1964, his celebrity preceded him.[25] As Dawn-Marie Gibson writes, Ali "heightened the Nation's profile both at home and abroad. Ali played the key role in upholding the Nation's image and proved useful in brokering loans from international donors."[26] As Ali's prominence in the Nation of Islam increased, so, too, did the criticisms aimed at him and his new faith, culminating in his protracted legal battle with the federal government over his conscientious objector status and refusal to serve in Vietnam. Ali ultimately lost three years of his boxing career, but, more than that, he earned scorn from the majority of Americans across the political spectrum, even after Dr. Martin Luther King, Jr. endorsed his principled opposition to the war.[27] Ali's refusal to serve in the military at a time when most Americans still supported the campaign in Vietnam underscored prevailing opinion that the Black Muslims were angry, irrational, and unpatriotic.

In 1966, another black political movement emerged: the Black Power Movement. The movement first emerged among younger African Americans who had grown disenchanted with the mainstream Civil Rights Movement and Dr. Martin Luther King, Jr.'s nonviolence crusade. During the March Against Fear, Stokely Carmichael articulated a vision for black politics and engagement that drew heavily upon the rhetoric of Malcolm X.[28] Inextricably linked to African-American Islam in the popular imagination, Black Power soon came to be associated with political radicalism and violence, due largely to negative portrayals of the Black Panther Party for Self-Defense and the FBI's systematic efforts to infiltrate and destroy it and similar organizations through COINTELPRO, its covert 1956–1971 counterintelligence program to infiltrate and destroy radical movements. So thoroughly did the FBI convince Americans of Black Power's seditious intentions that, even in the twenty-first century, "Black Power is most often remembered as a tragedy, a wrong turn from Martin Luther King, Jr.'s, hopeful rhetoric toward the polemics of black nationalists who blamed whites for the worsening urban

23. Hauser 1991, 122.
24. Hauser 1991, 135.
25. Bingham and Wallace 2000, 110.
26. Gibson 2012, 50.
27. Bingham and Wallace 2000, 167.
28. van Deburg 1992, 1–10.

crisis, on the one hand, and, on the other, gun-toting Black Panthers who vowed to lead a political revolution with an army of the black underclass."[29]

The Super Crypto-Muslims

What do the Nation of Islam, Muhammad Ali, and the Black Power Movement have to do with DC superhero comics? Mainstream American comic books first introduced a black superhero in 1966 with Marvel Comics' Black Panther. The character had been created in 1965 and developed under the name the Coal Tiger. According to journalist Ronin Ro, Jack Kirby created the character over a weekend, inspired by the realization that his comics had African-American readers and that those readers would appreciate a black hero. His collaborator Stan Lee similarly locates the character's introduction as responding to readers' desires and having no significant political motivation.[30] Journalist Sean Howe's history of Marvel Comics points out, however, that there may have been some second guessing about debuting a black character since the costume was altered before his first appearance, completely concealing his black skin.[31] The character's name had nothing to do with the Black Panther Party; in fact, the Black Panther's name was later temporarily changed to the Black Leopard to disassociate him from Black Nationalists.[32] But Marvel's project to introduce African-American characters, even if it was often hampered by "white-liberal-cluelessness," resulted from Lee and Kirby's desire to populate the Marvel Universe with black characters through what Howe describes as "casual representation." Black characters appeared and, in the cases of black heroes introduced prior to 1968 like the Black Panther and Black Goliath, were scientists just like Reed Richards and Tony Stark, or, in the case of Gabriel Jones, were World War II heroes who had fought alongside Captain America and Nick Fury.[33] When DC Comics moved to introduce black characters, it did not do so casually; rather, it acted in the maelstrom of late 1960s-early 1970s politics. As Peniel Joseph astutely observes, by this time the "blunt speaking, rough-hewn, at times riotously vulgar cadences of northern black activists and race leaders," key among them being the Nation of Islam, were rejected in favor of "the dignified, frequently mesmerizing oratory of southern black preachers." As a result, the African-American campaigns in the South took

29. Joseph 2006, xiii.
30. Ro 2008, 98–99; McLaughlin 2007, 191; Howe 2012, 97.
31. Howe 2012, 70
32. Howe 2012, 133.
33. Howe 2012, 97.

on a moral legitimacy never popularly afforded to northern activism.[34] In short, Marvel was creating southern black ministers and Third World Cold War allies while DC's editors and writers, drawing from the day's headlines and imbibing free-floating racial anxieties, created and re-created the same character: a two-dimensional Malcolm X circa 1960 or Muhammad Ali defined by misplaced rage and hostility. After all, as historian William Van DeBurg states, "angry blacks always had made good copy."[35]

DC Comics introduced its first African-American superhero in the December 1971–January 1972 issue of *Green Lantern/Green Arrow*, a series made remarkable by its direct engagement with political and social controversies at a time when superhero comics generally reflected conservative values. In this issue, the reader is introduced to John Stewart. Immediately upon viewing the cover, the reader knew that Stewart would represent a significant departure from the norm. Dressed in the Green Lantern's uniform, Stewart is dragging the fallen Green Lantern towards him as he brandishes his power ring at an unseen foe and, therefore, at the reader, and screams a furious warning to the onlooker that he would not be "whipped" as the Green Lantern had been. As the cover's title blurb indicated, John Stewart "really means it when he warns" that the reader should "beware my power."[36] This blurb was a coded reworking of the classic Green Lantern oath, which ends, "let those who worship evil's might / beware my power / Green Lantern's light." Previously, thematic emphasis fell on the last line, the hero's shining light. This new Green Lantern's focus fell on his power and its potential menace, an artistic choice made all the more interesting by the fact that the events portrayed on the cover never occur in the interior story.

American studies scholar Adilifu Nama describes John Stewart's first appearance as "buried under a mound of racial rhetoric and anxiety concerning the type of Black Power politics John Stewart symbolized in the beginning of the story."[37] In the Green Lantern mythos, earth's Green Lantern is a member of an intergalactic police force, the Green Lantern Corps, assigned a sector of space to protect by the Guardians of the Universe. In the story, Earth's prime Green Lantern, Hal Jordan, must train a replacement, who is found in a "certain urban ghetto." Stewart is introduced to the readers through this exchange with a racist police officer hassling black children playing dominos on the street:

34. Joseph 2006, 50–51.
35. van DeBurg 1992, 13.
36. O'Neill and Adams 1971, cover.
37. Nama 2011, 19.

Police officer:	You want trouble?
John Stewart:	I don't want it, but I am not about to run from it, either! And anyway, I kinda doubt you're man enough to give it even with your nightstick! [38]

The scene is provocative for its day, since the comics industry's self-censoring Comics Code forbade negative portrayals of police officers.[39] Hal Jordan is appalled that the Guardians would entrust a power ring to a man with "a chip on his shoulder the size of Gibraltar," a fear that seems warranted when Stewart, an out-of-work architect, describes the oath as "corny ... except for the part that says, 'Beware my power'! Mmm-hum, I do dig those words!"[40] "Beware My Power's" main plot involves Senator Clutcher, a racist running for President who attempts to stage a shooting for which Black Nationalists will be blamed, the aftermath of which will push him into the Oval Office. Hal Jordan tells John Stewart that he must prove his worthiness to be a Green Lantern by protecting the senator, after Stewart intentionally uses his power ring to cause him to be sprayed with oil. The drama, however, is in the two Green Lanterns' differing world views. Stewart seeks to use his newfound power for personal vengeance and to punish racists like Senator Clutcher who seek to exploit racial prejudice. Jordan responds with platitudes, reminding Stewart that he has not been appointed a judge and that the rights of men like Clutcher must be protected if the U.S. is to have free speech. Jordan also implicitly describes Stewart as a racist after the latter man refers to him as "whitey":

Hal Jordan:	One last thing! Don't call me whitey! Something in that reminds me of that bit about "he who is without sin" casting "the first stone."[41]

Rhetorically, John Stewart has been described just as the mainstream press described Black Muslims: he is an angry, power-hungry racist who does not appreciate American values. Chastised, Stewart is redeemed when he foils the senator's plot. He and Jordan make amends as Stewart states that "style" and "color" are not important, which Adilifu Nama rightly describes as a "change of heart [that] is clearly an ideological nod toward Dr. Martin Luther King's axiom that people should be judged by the quality of their character and not the color of their skin."[42]

John Stewart was followed by the introduction of Nubia, Wonder Wom-

---

38. O'Neill and Adams 1971, 5.
39. Nyberg 1998, 170–175.
40. O'Neill and Adams 1971, 5, 7.
41. O'Neil and Adams 1971, 9.
42. Nama 2011, 19.

an's black half-sister, in February 1972's *Wonder Woman #204*. This landmark issue represented the end of "the New Wonder Woman," a short-lived attempt to embrace 1970s feminism that alienated readers and editors who longed for the original series dynamic to be reestablished. In the issue, an amnesiac Wonder Woman returns to Paradise Island to have her memory restored and to reclaim her mantle as the Amazons' ambassador to the outside world. Diana is suddenly challenged by a heavily-armored woman insisting that she, not Diana, is Wonder Woman. Combat between the two ends in a stalemate, and the armored warrior removes her helmet to reveal that she is a black woman named Nubia. Nubia departs to her Floating Island, an analog to Paradise Island, promising to return so that one day she and Diana may determine who is the rightful Wonder Woman. Diana's adventures continue along another path in issue #205 with Nubia returning to the main feature in issue #206, "War of the Wonder Women." In this tale, writer Cary Bates reveals Nubia's true origin: she is Queen Hippolyta's long-lost daughter. The traditional Wonder Woman origin story established that Hippolyta made her daughter from clay and that Diana sprang to life after receiving Aphrodite's blessing. "War of the Wonder Women" adds the creation of a second child, one made of dark clay instead. Aphrodite blessed both girls, but the god of war, Ares, absconded with the dark child, raising her to be his weapon of vengeance, on a segregated island populated only by black men.[43] In the course of the inevitable battle between Wonder Woman and Nubia, Wonder Woman is able to remove Ares' ring from her sister's finger, severing his control over her mind. She joins with her half-sister and, together, they foil Ares' plot. In the crisis's denouement, Nubia has the same moment of moral clarity that John Stewart experiences, telling the beaten Ares that:

> Nubia: Princess Diana and the Amazons aren't all evil! All those years, you lied to me ... trained me for a combat ... groomed me to fight your war![44]

Embracing Amazonian love and the sisterhood of all women, Nubia realizes that she has been duped by warmongers too afraid to fight their own battles. Rejecting war, she vows to lead her black male warriors "into ways of peace."[45]

DC Comics creators continued their attack on Black Nationalism and Black Power with the introduction of Tyroc in 1976. According to artist Mike Grell, he wanted to introduce a black character into the thirtieth- and thirty-first-century superhero team, the Legion of Super-Heroes, arguing

43. Bates and Heck 1973, 6–8.
44. Bates and Heck 1973, 22.
45. Bates and Heck 1973, 23.

that it made little sense that the team featured green-skinned androids but no black characters. Previous series writer Jim Shooter had also wanted to introduce a black Legionnaire, but he, too, was forbidden to do so by series editor Murray Boltinoff. Grell recalls that Boltinoff put him off for months by assuring him that DC was developing another black character to debut in the series. That promised character never materialized. Finally, plans were made to introduce Tyroc in April 1976's *Superboy #216*. Grell was horrified:

> They might as well have called him Tyrone. Their explanation for why
> there were no black people ever featured in *The Legion of Super-Heroes*
> up until this point was that all the black people had gone to live on an
> island [...] It's possibly the most racist concept I ever heard in my life. I
> mean, it's a segregationist's dream.[46]

"The Hero Who Hated the Legion" covers familiar ground. Tyroc is the protector of Marzal, "an independent, totally self-sufficient community populated entirely by a black race that wants nothing to do with the outside world!"[47] Tyroc's voice gives him creative and destructive powers. When the Legionnaires first encounter Tyroc, they are so impressed with his powers that they instantly wish to offer him a position among them. Tyroc, however, immediately teleports away and sends a message to his people directing them "not to offer them [the Legion] friendship" because the Legion had never before shown concern for Marzal's problems due to the population's skin color.[48] The Legionnaires describe Tyroc as "bitter" and accuse him of brainwashing his people to the point that they are unable to "express gratitude" when the Legionnaires save their lives. At the story's end, however, Tyroc repents of his "hatred and contempt" of the Legion after its members save Marzal from a poisoned satellite. The Legionnaires tell him that "[w]hen it comes to race, we're color-blind! Blue skin, yellow skin, green skin, we're brothers and sisters united in the name of justice everywhere."[49] The story is hardly thematically subtle: ardent black separatism and contempt for the outside world, long held to define the Nation of Islam and the entire Black Nationalist movement, were the problem, not a response to another, larger social problem, and it was blacks whose racial ideology made them latecomers to genuine multicultural community.

Ironically, DC Comics's portrayal of both African Americans and genuine African-American Muslims transformed thanks to one of the greatest victims of 1960s Islamophobia, Muhammad Ali, and the publication of 1978's

46. Cadigan 2003, 90.
47. Bates and Grell 1976a, 4.
48. Bates and Grell 1976a, 7.
49. Bates and Grell 1976a, 12.

Superman vs Muhammad Ali. During the years of his ban from boxing, Ali traveled extensively on the college lecture circuit. In the process, he became a counter-cultural hero. By 1968, Ali's stand resonated with the growing numbers of young Americans opposed to the war and seemed prescient after the Tet Offensive proved that the campaign was not going as well as Americans had been led to believe. Through his personal trials, Ali was evolving into a new, "ideological" heavyweight champion "fighting for millions of people in the United States against the government of the United States."[50] On June 28, 1971, the Supreme Court decided in his favor in *Cassius Clay vs the United State of America*, ending his long exile from boxing. Popular interest in seeing the aging Ali regain the title he had never lost swelled. When Ali finally regained the belt from George Foreman in 1974's "Rumble in the Jungle" bout, his journey to international folk hero status was complete, earning him an invitation to the White House and multiple honors from a boxing press that ten years earlier had vilified him as a cowardly draft-dodger duped by racial charlatans.[51]

The new Ali sought out opportunities to engage with the public in a manner that Elijah Muhammad had always disapproved. As Elijah Muhammad's health declined, his son and successor, Wallace, took greater control of the organization and began shifting towards orthodox Islam. After Elijah Muhammad died in February 1975, the Nation of Islam's transformation began in earnest, ultimately becoming in 1980 the World Community of al-Islam in the West. Highlighting its new engagement with the outsiders and rejection of a racially-defined Islam, boxing promoter Don King was given permission to throw a party at its Chicago headquarters for Ali and his manager, Herbert Muhammad, to which several Hollywood celebrities were invited.[52] *Superman vs Muhammad Ali* seems to have grown out of the Nation of Islam's new openness as former DC Publisher Jenette Kahn relates that it was Don King who brought the proposal to DC Comics.[53] As Adilifu Nama comments, this story is "best framed as marking the beginning of the complete transformation of Muhammad Ali from one of the most despised black athletes in America to one of the most beloved icons in American pop culture."[54]

Superman vs Muhammad Ali is the story of two American heroes banding together to stop the Scrubb, an alien race convinced that humanity is too dangerous to the galaxy to be allowed to live. Muhammad Ali is in Metropolis's ghetto playing basketball with the local youth when Clark Kent,

50. Bingham and Wallace 2000, 213.
51. Hauser 1991, 280–281.
52. Marsh 1996, 104.
53. Adams and O'Neill 2015, 79–80.
54. Nama 2011, 23.

Lois Lane, and Jimmy Olsen – at this time in *Superman*'s history working as television reporters instead of print journalists – arrive to interview Ali. The Scrubb emissary arrives and proposes a boxing match between Ali and their champion for the fate of the world. This prompts Clark, who by this time has performed a quick change and appears as Superman, to insist that he should face this extraterrestrial threat. The Scrubb leader demands that they choose one champion within twenty-four hours, prompting Superman to fly Ali to his Fortress of Solitude, where, using a device to slow time, Super-man is trained to box by Ali himself. When the two champions are forced to square off or see earth obliterated, they fight under a red sun, which negates Superman's super powers. The two engage in a grueling contest. Superman is outclassed by the champion but refuses to fall. At the end, Ali refuses to continue, winning the bout by decision. With Superman seemingly defeated, Ali must battle to save the world against a larger, more powerful foe. Though outmatched, Ali stands toe-to-toe with his opponent and triumphs, winning the respect of both the crowd and his opponent. Meanwhile, Superman has been working behind the scenes to foil the Scrubb leader's plot to destroy the Earth regardless of the fight's outcome. Faced with the leader's treach-ery and awed by Muhammad Ali and Superman, the Scrubb overthrow their leader and pledge themselves to peaceful relations with the earth. The world is saved by "fair play" and integrity:

> Lois: That's what did it, fair play? Fair play saved the Earth?
>
> Ali: When you come right down to it, fair play is what it's all about! If more people tried to live by the simple rules of fair play, my people ... all people would get a fair shake. [55]

The story famously closes with Ali and Superman shaking hands, the cham-pion showing uncharacteristic modesty in proclaiming, "Superman, we are the greatest!"[56]

Muhammad Ali was DC Comics's first genuine African-American Muslim superhero and the first character to portray Muslim humanity. Following Ali's comic book debut, DC introduced a new generation of black superhe-roes. DC's next African-American superhero, Black Lightning, also debuted in 1977. Jefferson Pierce is a former Olympian who returns to Metropolis's slums to teach at the local high school. When his intervention in a drug deal results in the murder of one of his students, Pierce adopts the Black Lightning persona to fight crime. Black Lightning, then, has a decidedly tra-ditional superhero origin that, while tied to inner-city crime, does not link him to a stereotypical representation of black life.

55. Adams and O'Neill 2015, 70.
56. Adams and O'Neill 2015, 72.

Milestone Comics and the
African-American Muslim Experience

DC Comics introduced a number of black characters beginning in the 1980s, most notably Cyborg, but the next African-American Muslim characters to appear in DC Comics did not appear until 1993. In 1993, a group of African-American comics veterans launched Milestone Comics, an imprint to be distributed by DC that pledged to offer greater diversity than traditionally seen in superhero comics. The Milestone Universe was centered in the fictional city of Dakota. Dakota has a serious gang problem, so the chief of police approves a risky plan to use what she believes to be experimental tear gas on a crowd of gangsters gathered for a major brawl. The tear gas is supposed to contain a radioactive tracer that will allow the police to hunt down and arrest everyone in attendance, effectively ending crime in the city; instead, it provokes something called "the Big Bang." Hundreds are killed, but those who survive it, the "Bang Babies," are endowed with strange new powers.

Debuting in 1993, *Blood Syndicate* is the story of a multiethnic, superpowered gang formed by teenaged gangsters transformed by the Big Bang. With their powers, they effectively control Paris Island, Dakota's crime-ridden slum, and survive by raiding crack houses for money. Blood Syndicate is led by a Puerto Rican gangster called Tech-9 and his de facto second-in-command is Wise Son, an invulnerable, super-strong African-American Muslim also known as Hannibal White. Wise Son's Muslim identity is visually identified through his apparel, a Force of Islam hat like those worn by the Nation of Islam's security teams, and dialogue. Wise Son's early dialogue is forced and clichéd, requiring the character to say things like "I got no respect for the white man's media."[57] He is vulgar, quick-tempered, misogynistic, and ruthless, casually hurling sexist epithets and using machine guns to reduce a drug dealer's hands to pulp.[58] Wise Son's only redeeming characteristic in the first issue is his steadfast insistence that the drugs seized in the Blood Syndicate's raids be destroyed to prevent them from poisoning the community. Wise Son's portrayal is disappointingly stereotypical. Series writer Ivan Velez, Jr., addressed this in a second-issue feature, noting that Wise Son is an African American "learning to live according to the ways of Islam."[59]

Six issues later, Wise Son's characterization was still a source of reader frustration. A Muslim reader, Brother Joe, was prompted to address the character's shortcomings in a letter that appeared in the eighth issue:

57. McDuffie and Velez, Jr. et al., 1993, #1, 8.
58. McDuffie and Velez, Jr. et al., 1993, #1, 7–8, 16.
59. McDuffie and Velez, Jr. et al., 1993, #2, 28.

I just want to tell you and your staff that Blood Syndicate is a great comic and has a very good story. But I must tell you that I am angry and offended with the portrayal of the brother that follows Islam. On page 3 of BLOOD SYNDICATE #5 you have him drinking alcohol. Sirs, I know you know no man of Islam will drink alcohol of any kind. You also have him cursing in the comic.

This is a disappointment to me and is very close to an attack on Muslims all over the United States [...] Sirs, you created him and you should portray him with the strict teaching and strong mind of a real Muslim.[60]

The editorial response again acknowledged that Wise Son was only beginning to walk as a Muslim. "For now," the editors responded, "he adheres more to the TRAPPINGS of Islam than to its teachings. As Wise matures, this will change."[61] The editors announced that Wise Son's substantive evolution as a Muslim would be represented in the *Wise Son: The White Wolf* mini-series, during which Wise Son would finally interact with other Muslims. Unfortunately, the mini-series did not appear until 1996, three years after Brother Joe's letter. This makes following the narrative of the main *Blood Syndicate* series somewhat complicated because character developments reflected in the ongoing title were shown out of chronological order.

Tech-9 is killed in issue #4, throwing the team into disarray. Wise Son steps into the leadership vacuum, struggling to win his teammates' respect as their leader, since he was shown them little evidence of depth or substance of character beyond Black Nationalist platitudes. Beginning with Tech-9's death, then, Wise Son's primary story arc is not about superheroism; rather, his story is about his development of an authentic Muslim faith. His growth is uneven, but dedicating a character arc to his spiritual journey was revolutionary at this time in comics. In issue #7, the reader sees Wise Son struggling to assume Tech-9's role. He contemplates forsaking the gang and the responsibility for keeping everyone safe, knowing full well that he can retreat to his own home and family. He realizes, however, that the Blood Syndicate is now also his family and that, if they can become disciplined, they can serve a greater good. Interestingly, the sequence in which Wise Son is contemplating these options is visually constructed so that he is gazing at his FOI hat, a cue that he has obligations that he must honor according to the beliefs to which he claims to ascribe.[62]

Wise Son's dilemma seems to be in keeping with common aspects of Af-

60. McDuffie and Velez, Jr. et al., 1993, #8, 25.
61. McDuffie and Velez, Jr. et al., 1993, #8, 25.
62. McDuffie and Velez, Jr., et al. 1993, #7, 24.

rican-American Islam. Amirah Beverly McCloud and Robert Dannin describe the unique aspects of the African-American conversion to Islam. McCloud traces the history of African-American Islam as one in which emphasis has shifted from "the development of a historically grounded national identity outside of mainstream American society" to one focused on the *ummah* and a deeper spiritual engagement.[63] Dannin identifies the themes of *The Autobiography of Malcolm X* – "symbolic death and rebirth, heroism, sacrifice and commitment" – as being central to African-American converts' spiritual pursuits.[64] For African Americans converting to Islam,

> The typical conversion narrative is a ritual act depicting an individual's pilgrimage from the chaos of unbelief ... toward salvation. The ritual and also the narrative theme resolve the historical tension of African-American society by concluding that liberation from racial domination and spiritual redemption are one and the same. The end goals require an indefatigable dedication to transform one's self and one's fellows. "Verily, Allah does not change the state of a people until they change themselves inwardly" (Quran 13:12) is by far the most frequently quoted scriptural passage among African-American Muslims. [65]

Wise Son may not be a good Muslim, but his experience is authentic to that of many African-American converts to Islam.

This experience as a convert is fully fleshed out in the 1996 *Wise Son: The White Wolf* mini-series. The series' plot focuses on a string of attacks on black Muslim ministers by white supremacists. The series is richest, however, in its treatment of Wise Son's slow maturation as Muslim and as man. The first issue begins on Wise Son's twentieth birthday. The character's every vice is on display from his first appearance: he is drunk, profane, and despondent. The reader later learns that Wise Son has effectively abandoned his family, his children, and the mother of his children. Wise Son's demons are metaphorically represented by a white wolf that hunts him in his dreams. He leaves his own birthday party and ends up in a Paris Island neighborhood, engaging with a Muslim minister and an elderly Muslim couple that owns a bookstore called Third World Books. They encourage him both to read about Islam and to answer some fundamental questions about himself in the process.

In the second issue, for example, the elderly male store owner challenges the authenticity of Wise Son's conversion: "Well, you talk the talk.

---

63. McCloud 1995, 5.
64. Dannin 2002, 6.
65. Dannin 2002, 7.

You wear the Star and Crescent. What do you think they mean? Or is it just a fashion statement to you?"[66] Throughout the series, Wise Son gravitates back to Third World Books, both seeking and rejecting the advice of the Muslim couple. By the third issue, Wise Son's life is an even greater mess. He learns that he has a second child coming and, in the face of all of his life's chaos, he has an emotional breakdown at the bookstore, lamenting his life's pointlessness and seeking direction:

Wise Son: What's the point of all of this when I know I could go tomorrow and no one would even care that I was ever here?

owner: Well, no one knows the answer to that question. Certainly I don't. I believe one can, I don't know, purify oneself, if he wants to. Maybe coming here tonight was your first step. If you're ready to change, maybe. I can help you, but you have to be ready. Are you ready, Hannibal?

Wise Son: I'm ready.[67]

With Wise Son's decision to purify himself, he finally escapes the White Wolf chasing him in his dreams.

The final issue opens with Wise Son having shaved his head and preparing to cleanse himself physically and spiritually. He removes his Star and Crescent, stating that it did not "feel right" for him to wear them.[68] For the first time since this character appeared, his dialogue is free of profanity and he seeks to live a normal life helping out around the bookstore and trying to reconcile with his baby's mother and his son. He congratulates a Muslim minister on his service to the community and rejects his former lifestyle when a gun dealer approaches him trying to sell him stolen handguns. Just as Wise Son seems poised to start a new path, his temper provokes him to headbutt the white nationalist responsible for the deaths of the murdered Muslim ministers. That evening, Third World Books is firebombed, killing the owners and sending Wise Son into a murderous spiral to avenge his surrogate parents and to save his pregnant girlfriend. Wise Son returns to the Blood Syndicate and, as the series closes with him holding another bottle of alcohol in his hands, the White Wolf returns. Wise Son's failure to adhere to a truer path as a Muslim is lamentable, but the conversion experience portrayed is realistic, particularly for a character so burdened by vices. That

66. Anderson 1996, #2, 4.
67. Anderson 1996, #3, 25.
68. Anderson 1996, #4, 3.

the reader experiences this with Wise Son and mourns at his failure demonstrates how remarkable this tale is in comics history.

Wise Son's spiritual progression reached its summit in the 1995 "Long, Hot Summer" Milestone event. Stated simply, "Long, Hot Summer" is the story of a riot encouraged, in part, by the Blood Syndicate, after a real estate developer builds a giant theme park on Paris Island, displacing locals and disrupting the local economy. Popular sentiment against the park boils over and, on its opening day, a riot ensues. Seeing the chaos that he has helped to unleash, Wise Son assumes responsibility for his actions and his community, renouncing the despair and violence born of urban frustration:

> Wise Son: We are men and women and all we can think about is pain and anger and sorrow and fire and death, being cheated and striking back and ... God. It's just not right. So ... we made the world we know today ... all of us ... right or wrong ... we did this. We have to own this thing and we have to stop. Stop it now. Stop it cold. We can't let this anger, this outrage get the best of us. We can't let anyone else get hurt now. Because we are human ... because we are men and women ... we have to stop now. [69]

As scripter D. G. Chichester writes, this is the day that Wise Son earns his name.[70]

When Milestone ceased publication in 1997, most of its characters disappeared from the DC Universe. Since the 1990s, the majority of Muslim characters introduced into the DC Universe have been Arabs. One notable exception is the 2002 introduction of Muhammad X in *Superman* #179. It is not clear that X is actually a Muslim; rather, he explains to Superman that he "took the names of my two heroes" to show respect for "men who have done more for the black cause than I could ever hope to."[71] One assumes he means Muhammad Ali, but he could equally mean Elijah Muhammad, and the story never clarifies the object of his devotion. The story is tonally strange and could easily have been published in the 1970s. Leaving a therapy appointment in New York City, Superman overhears a robbery in Harlem being reported on a police scanner. He intervenes to stop the robber, only to be chastised by Muhammad X for daring to be in Harlem. Superman criticizes his unwarranted hostility and leaves. The remainder of the issue sees Superman wondering about whether white heroes can serve black communities' emotional needs. He is assured by Lois Lane and the Martian

69. Chichester and Cowan 1995, 15–16.
70. Chichester and Cowan 1995, 17.
71. Loeb and Olivetti 2002, 10.

Manhunter that he is "color-blind" and that he is bothered by Muhammad X's comments "not because you don't care, but because you do care so deeply about doing the right thing."[72] Superman then returns to Harlem to speak to Muhammad X again, telling him that his ultimate goal is "to be a human being. And hopefully, someday, we'll see each other only in that way." As Superman flies out of the frame, his body streaking away from a balled-up black fist, Muhammad X replies, "Yeah, well, I guess that's how you sleep at night."[73] Muhammad X may simply be a throwaway character introduced to engage with a popular debate about diversity in comics. This issue appeared shortly after 9/11, however, so perhaps Muhammad X serves as a stand-in for perceived Islamic hostility to America. The creators' intent is unclear, but harkening back to this sort of representation of African-American Islam is an unfortunate step backwards.

Conclusion

Efforts at presenting African-American Muslims in DC Comics have effectively disappeared in the wake of 9/11 and the War on Terror. Muhammad X seems to be the last African-American Muslim introduced in one of the company's titles. This is unfortunate for several reasons. According to Pew Research, African Americans made up 23% of American Muslims in 2011, and the native-born American Muslim population "contains a higher proportion of blacks, and lower proportions of whites and Asians, than the foreign-born population." In fact, 59% of third-generation Muslims are African Americans.[74] Even though comics creators have attempted to diversify their representations of Muslims, focusing on Muslims from the Middle East or Western Europe reinforces the notion of the Muslim as Other. Exploring the African-American Muslim experience could offer skilled creators the opportunity to show an underrepresented aspect of the African-American experience. Moreover, the limited representations of African-American Muslims are still largely defined by harmful, decades-old stereotypes. Because a comic book can take place literally anywhere and during any time period, comics have remarkable educational potential. One can only hope that future comics will take advantage of these possibilities.

72. Loeb and Olivetti 2002, 13, 17.
73. Loeb and Olivetti 2002, 22.
74. Pew Research Center 2011, 16.

Works Cited

Adams, N., and D. O'Neil. 2015. *Superman vs Muhammad Ali: Deluxe Edition.* New York.

Anderson, H. C. 1996–97. *Wise Son: The White Wolf.* #1–4. New York.

Bates, C., and M. Grell. 1976. "The Hero Who Hated the Legion." *Superboy,* Vol. 28, No. 216, April 1976. New York.

———. 1976. "The Secret Villain the World Never Knew." *Superboy,* Vol. 28, #218, July 1976. New York.

———. 1976. "This Legionnaire is Condemned." *Superboy,* Vol. 28, #222, December 1976. New York.

Bates, C., and D. Heck. 1973. "War of the Wonder Women!" *Wonder Woman,* Vol. 32, #206, June–July, 1973. New York.

Bingham, H. L., and M. Wallace. 2000. *Muhammad Ali's Greatest Fight: Cassius Clay vs The United States of America.* New York.

Bracey, J. H., A. Meier, and E. Rudwick, eds. 1970. *Black Nationalism in America.* New York.

Cadigan, G. 2003. *The Legion Companion.* Raleigh, NC.

Chichester, D. G., and D. Cowan. 1995. *Long Hot Summer.* #1–3. New York.

Dannin, R. 2002. *Black Pilgrimage to Islam.* New York.

Dar, J. 2010. "Holy Islamophobia, Batman!: Demonization of Muslims and Arabs in Mainstream American Comic Books." *Counterpoints* 346 (2010): 99–110.

Gibson, D.-M. 2012. *A History of the Nation of Islam: Race, Islam and the Quest for Freedom.* Santa Barbara, CA.

Hauser, T. 1991. *Muhammad Ali: His Life and Times.* New York.

Howe, S. 2012. *Marvel Comics: The Untold Story.* New York.

Jackson, S. 2005. *Islam and the Blackamerican: Looking toward the Third Resurrection.* New York.

Joseph, P. 2006. *Waiting til the Midnight Hour: A Narrative History of Black Power in America.* New York.

Lazerow, J., and Y. Williams, eds. 2006. *In Search of the Black Panther Party: New Perspectives on a Revolutionary Movement.* Durham, NC.

Lincoln, C. E. 1994. *The Black Muslims in America.* Third edition. Trenton, NJ.

Loeb, J., and A. Olivetti. 2002. "What Can One Icon Do?" *Superman* 179, April 2002. New York.

Marsh, C. E. 1996. *From Black Muslims to Muslims: The Resurrection, Transformation, and Change of the Lost-Found Nation of Islam in America, 1930-1995.* Second edition. Lanham, MD.

McCloud, A. B. 1995. *African American Islam.* New York.

McDuffie, D., I. Velez, Jr., et. al. 1993–1996. *Blood Syndicate.* #1–35. New York.

McLaughlin, J., ed. 2007. *Stan Lee Conversations.* Jackson, MS.

Nama, A. 2011. *Super Black: American Pop Culture and Black Superheroes.* Austin, TX.

Nyberg, A. K. 1998. *Seal of Approval: The History of the Comics Code.* Jackson, MS.

O'Neill, D., and N. Adams. 1971. "Beware My Power!" *Green Lantern/Green Arrow* Vol. 2, #87, December 1971/January 1972. New York.

Pew Research Center. 2011. *Mainstream and Moderate Attitudes: Muslim Americans: No Signs of Growth in Alienation or Support for Extremism.* Washington, DC.

Ro, R. 2008. *Tales to Astonish: Jack Kirby, Stan Lee and the American Comic Book Revolution.* New York.

Strömberg, F. 2003. *Black Images in the Comics: A Visual History.* New York.

———. 2011. "Yo, rag-head!": Arab and Muslim Superheroes in American Comic Books after 9/11." *Amerikastudien/American Studies* 56: 4: 573–601.

van Deburg, W. L. 1992. *New Day in Babylon: The Black Power Movement in American Culture, 1965–1975.* Chicago.

Additional Suggested Readings

Bagby, I. 2011. *The American Mosque 2011: Report Number One: Characteristics of the American Mosque. Attitudes of Mosque Leaders.* Washington, DC.

Barboza, S. 1993. *American Jihad: Islam after Malcolm X.* New York.

Berg, H. L. 2005. "Mythmaking in the African American Muslim Context: The Moorish Science Temple, the Nation of Islam, and the American Society of Muslims." *Journal of the American Academy of Religion* 73 (3): 685–703.

Brown, J. A. 1999. "Comic Book Masculinity and the New Black Superhero," *African American Review* 33 (1): 25–42.

———. 2001. *Black Superheroes, Milestone Comics, and Their Fans.* Jackson, MS.

Cowsill, A., et. al. 2010. *DC Comics Year by Year: A Visual Chronicle.* New York.

Griffin, R. 2016. "Black Power or Blaxploitation?: On Black Lightning's Afro Wig and Black Heroes in Comics." Fanzing.com/mag/fanzing32/feature4.shtml. Accessed 30 March 2016.

Howard, S. C., and R. I. Jackson II, eds. 2011. *Black Comics: Politics of Race and Representation.* New York.

Kanigher, R., and D. Heck. 1972. "The Second Life of the Original Wonder Woman." *Wonder Woman,* Vol. 32, #204, January–February 1973. New York.

———. 1973. "The Mystery of Nubia." *Wonder Woman*, Vol. 32, #205, March–April 1973. New York.

Schumer, A. 2013. "The Greatest!: Neal Adams and *Superman vs Muhammad Ali*," *Comic Book Artist Special Edition* 1 (2013): 36–39, 52–54.

Singer, M. 2002. "'Black Skins' and White Masks: Comic Books and the Secret of Race." *African American Review* 36 (1): 107–119.

Washington III, R. L. and J. P. Leon. 1993. "Louder Than a Bomb: Megablast!" *Static* 5, October 1993. New York.

———. 1993. "Louder Than a Bomb: War at 30 Frames Per Second." *Static* 6, November 1993. New York.

———. 1993. "Louder Than a Bomb: You're Gonna Get Yours." *Static* 7, December 1993. New York.

Wells, J. 2016. "The Racial Justice Experience: Diversity in the DC Universe: 1961–1979." Fanzing.com/mag/fanzing32/feature2.shtml. Accessed 30 March 2016.

Marked by Foreign Policy:
Muslim Superheroes and their Quest for Authenticity

Mercedes Yanora

SCROLLING THROUGH *TV GUIDE*, browsing for movies on Netflix, or perusing a book in a Barnes and Noble store can reveal the intimate relationship between America's popular culture and its foreign policy. War-themed movies, books, and even comic books abound. Created during World War II, Captain America is perhaps one of the most iconic superheroes to ever embody U.S. foreign policy. Yet he is not alone: throughout the genre's history, both minor and major superheroes have dueled against the U.S.'s many foes; Nazis, communists, and foreign terrorists have all had their time as antagonists in the superheroic spotlight.

Unsurprisingly, Muslim characters have figured predominantly as villains in comics.[1] *Batman: A Death in the Family* (1988) is but one example. One scene conflates Arabs with Persians by depicting the Joker in Arab headdress while he angrily addresses the United Nations as an Iranian Ambassador. For Jehanzeb Dar, a scholar and independent filmmaker, this is a prime example of a comic book paralleling U.S. foreign policy; both foreign policy and this particular comic erroneously group Arab, Iranian, and Muslim identities as one uniform identity exhibiting a radical hatred of the West.[2] Furthermore, this scene is a specific example of the conflation of Persians with Arabs, which still exists within the larger framework of portraying all Muslims as Arabs. But do Muslim superheroes similarly mirror U.S. foreign policy? This chapter will answer that question, and show that, like their villainous counterparts, Muslim superheroes do, in fact, appear when regions heavily populated by Muslims are of strategic importance in real-world U.S. foreign policy. It will do so by presenting close readings of three texts: *Psi-Force #32* (1989); "The Sinbad Contract" (1990); and *Ms. Marvel Volume 1: No Normal* (2014).

While it is true that some Muslim superheroes, such as the Arabian

1. See Dar 2010; Shaheen 1991.
2. Dar, 2010, 102.

Knight and Black Raazer, appeared in comics during the Cold War, Sedara Bakut, a female mujahideen fighter appearing in the *Psi-Force* series, represents a shift in the previous decades' portrayal of Muslim superheroes, as she was the first to appear in an explicitly politicized context. The ideological clash between the U.S. and the Soviet Union from the mid-1940s until the late 1980s explains the absence of politically significant Muslim superheroes from 1944's Kismet, Man of Fate, until 1989's Sedara Bakut. Though the Middle East was undoubtedly important to U.S. foreign policy, as evidenced by the Suez Crisis of 1956, the Arab-Israeli Wars of 1967 and 1973, and the OPEC Oil Embargo of 1973–1974, the battle of ideologies between the U.S. and the U.S.S.R. was the primary referent for the era's comics. The Soviet Union was America's primary enemy during the Cold War; therefore, once the Soviet Union was directly involved in the Middle East, during the Soviet Afghan War (1979–1989), the Muslim superhero gained particular political currency.

While prior work has addressed the frequent portrayal of Muslim villains,[3] my chapter expands on previous scholarship by examining the correlation between the U.S.'s involvement in the Middle East and the comic book industry's increased depiction of Muslim superheroes. Linking the fiction to reality – Muslim superheroes to U.S. foreign policy – is not this chapter's ultimate goal, however. Instead, these three case studies confront a number of issues including representations of gender, Otherness, and authenticity. In addition, analysis of these case studies touches upon both the developing normalization of Muslim superheroes and the space in which Muslim superheroes operate. Yet, all of these issues must be viewed against the backdrop of U.S. foreign relations, because the political climate invariably influences how Muslims and non-Muslims alike view Muslims, both real and fictional.

Foreign Policy, Muslim Representation, and American Popular Culture

Communications scholar Jack Shaheen is perhaps the first scholar to systematically engage with the representation of Muslims, more specifically Arabs, in modern U.S. popular culture. His work, although sometimes perpetuating the conflation of Arabs, Persians, and Muslims, is a useful starting point for our reading of Muslim superheroes, because it provides a foundation for understanding the kind of stereotypes that permeate popular culture and, more specifically, comic books. One particular stereotype, the representa-

---

3. See Dar 2010, 101–105; Strömberg 2011.

tion of Arabs as terrorists, is especially significant because it is often applied to all Muslims, not just Arabs. This stereotype thus indicates a shift from a public (mis)perception based on ethnicity/nationality to one founded on religious identity.[4]

Both print culture and the movie industry have contributed to the proliferation of these negative stereotypes; for example, as early as 1888, *National Geographic* portrayed Muslims as savage, unclean, dark, and culturally underdeveloped, while many movies, from *The Fire and the Sword* (1914) through *Protocol* (1984), depicted Muslims as overly violent hook-nosed men with mockingly exaggerated voices.[5] These stereotypes are not based in empirical fact but, instead, arise from an embedded practice where American identity is constructed in opposition to an Other.[6] Although written about nineteenth-century "racial science," the following also reflects how Muslims are pitted against Americans today: "Racist scientists [or, in this case, the news media and popular culture] maintain a vision of identity that becomes a procrustean scheme determinedly cropping reality to fit their preconceptions [...] they rigorously maintain repressions and exclusions from representations [...] that might trouble the integrity of their categorized hierarchies."[7]

American studies scholar Waleed Mahdi argues that the colonial construct of the West as virtuous, intelligent, and modern as opposed to that of the East – synonymous here with vice and the state of being *nonhuman* – is a main contributor to such stereotypes. One of the most humiliating stereotypes is the association of Muslims with animals: Muslims are placed side-by-side with goats, donkeys, dogs, chickens, and sheep. Yet these associations are dwarfed by that of the Muslim in relation to his camel; "'camel-brother,' 'sons of she camels,' 'sons of a flea bitten camel,' and 'camel farts' are all popular media insults directed at Muslims."[8] Stereotypes such as these are not only offensive but harmful to one's individual identity; stereotyping affiliates each group with a common group mindset, thus denying the individual autonomous and rational thought.[9]

By the 1980s, in the wake of the OPEC Oil Embargo and the Iranian Revolution, Muslims were increasingly represented as terrorists armed with radical ideologies and bent on spreading holy war. This representation was

4. Thank you A. David Lewis for helping me to draw out this point.

5. See Mahdi 2014, 153, 169. Mahdi relies heavily on Said 1979. See also Shaheen 2001, 5, 14, 16, 25; Shaheen 1991.

6. Michael 2008, 207.

7. Michael 2008, 208.

8. Mahdi 2014, 150, 155, 156, 158. An example of a film featuring such insults is *Things Are Tough All Over* (1982).

9. Gottschalk and Greenberg 2008, 71.

not based in reality but instead on "neoconservative dogma," which was further exacerbated by Samuel Huntington's clash-of-civilizations framework during the 1990s.[10] The American public's view of both Islam and the Middle East was far more nuanced; however, a fear of radical Islam, or as policy scholar and journalist Leon Hadar puts it, the "Green Peril," was born and still persists today.[11] In light of this supposed Green Peril, films, such as 1998's *The Siege*, linked languages such as Arabic with terrorism, violence, and clandestine mosque operations. The lack of subtitles in films such as *The Siege* further generated misrepresentation of Muslims, by portraying them as speaking only Arabic, which was structured as a gibberish and fanatical language.[12] Comics, too, reflected a political climate overwhelmed with the growing threat of terrorism; in his study of 208 Muslim characters, Shaheen reports that only thirty are depicted in a positive light, while many more are terrorist villains.[13] After the September 11th attacks, terrorism became a concrete and pervading reality in both the real world and the comic book world. The two leading superhero publishers, DC Comics and Marvel Comics, fashioned storyworlds permeated by fear and isolation where superheroes, like the U.S. government, "advised readers to trust no one, not even themselves."[14] In a world overrun by terrorism, superhero crossover episodes proliferated, while increased militancy and secret wars flourished and were justified by the omnipresent threat of terrorism.[15]

Although international developments and crises did occur in Muslim-majority regions during the Cold War, Muslim superheroes were virtually absent from comic books until 1989.[16] It was not until the end of the Cold War, when the Soviet Union and the U.S.-backed mujahideen faced off in a bloody and costly war, that the Middle East gained even greater visibility in the minds of Americans, thus calling for the portrayal of explicitly political Muslim superheroes.

Although the Soviet Union was the U.S.'s chief adversary, it was not its

10. Hadar 2008.

11. Hadar 2008.

12. Said 1997, 6, as cited in Bayoumi 2014, 109 and Mingant 2014, 170, 172, 173, 174, 179. Some post-9/11 films, however, attempt a more nuanced depiction of Muslims by using language that accurately reflects the geographic region in which the film takes place. Additionally, these languages are now subtitled, offering Muslims an actual voice and platform to express their thoughts.

13. Shaheen 1991, 10.

14. Johnson 2011.

15. Lewis 2012, 225, 226, 232.

16. Some notable exceptions are the Arabian Knight first appearing in 1980 under Marvel, Desert Hawk from Marvel's *Sergeant Fury and his Howling Commandos* (1963), and Black Raazer from Marvel's *Alpha Flight #32* (1986). Yet none of these superheroes are as intimately tied to U.S. foreign policy as Sedara Bakut.

sole enemy. In fact, the two never engaged in direct combat. They indirectly fought each other through regional proxy wars (e.g. Korea, Vietnam, and Afghanistan), and the Middle East and Central Asia, though not focal points, did factor into U.S. Cold War policy. These regions were conceptualized as a green belt along "the arc of Islam," a potential barrier for containing the Soviet Union's southern flank.[17] During the 1950s and 1960s, the U.S.'s main concern was the rise of left-wing nationalisms, resulting in its regional alliances with monarchies and fundamentalist groups (so-called "Islamists"). The U.S. often supported coups in nations where left-wing nationalism was perceived as a threat. By the 1980s, U.S. support of Islamism was at its zenith, with billions spent on aiding the mujahideen during the Soviet-Afghan War.[18]

As previously noted, U.S. foreign policy makers treated Muslim-majority countries (and Islam for that matter) as a barrier to the expansion of communism. Following the establishment of the Afghan Republic under Muhammad Daoud in 1973, the CIA began funding anti-communist Islamic groups as part of a shift in policy, under which the notion of "Islam-as-bulwark" gave way to "Islam-as-sword."[19] Islamic fundamentalist groups were now an active and increasingly significant Cold War weapon. The U.S.'s lengthy involvement with Afghanistan's religious militias marks the beginning of the Middle East and Central Asia's migration from the fringes of U.S. foreign policy to its core. In this context, it is unsurprising that Muslim superheroes closely aligned to policy development would once again surface in U.S. comic books. The end of the Cold War ushered in an era where Muslim superheroes, like their countries of origin, were gaining more prominence and greater visibility in American comic books.

Superheroes: Who Are They and What Do They Represent?

Before turning to the case studies, we must ask the following questions: what exactly are superheroes; what do they look like; where do they come from; and who is worthy of becoming one? All of these questions require a response because their answers establish a normative framework against which to measure the Muslim superhero, and it is this construct that helps determine whether or not a Muslim superhero is justly depicted. We have established *why* Muslim superheroes are increasingly present in comic books – as reflections of U.S. foreign policy. Yet this chapter supplements this issue by examining *how* they are depicted in comic books, in light of

17. Dreyfuss 2005, 2.
18. Dreyfuss 2005, 2–4.
19. Dreyfuss 2005, 245, 246, 260.

foreign policy and its influence on popular culture and perception. Comics scholar Peter Coogan defines the superhero genre according to three core elements: altruistic missions, special powers, and secret identities.[20] Furthermore, political scientist Matthew Costello claims that the superhero genre can offer, in terms of the West, "an avenue through which one can access the core values of a society, the ideals that give that society an identity, and the 'other' that society fears."[21] The superhero genre is thus restricted to a societal ideal and is therefore built on hegemonic power structures and institutions, often at the exclusion of certain marginal groups.[22] By the early 1940s, superhero comics depicted many of their characters as muscular men and women dressing in bright-colored tights, defeating their foes, and performing superhuman feats. Their costumes were, and still are, extremely significant for a number of reasons: they highlight the hero's physicality, are a key marker of identity, may be source of his or her power, and, for men at least, convey virility.[23]

Superheroes are more than their set of powers and flashy costumes. Many, but not all, are characterized by emotional hang-ups and very human aspirations as well as anxieties; for example, they are plagued by mysterious origins and lost parents; are confronted with problematic personal and emotional relationships; and are invested both in justice and the use of their powers in politics. Conversely, many superheroes are identified by uncommon identity markers such as man-god traits; the desire to remain unknown; and powers gained through freak accidents. As this set of criteria is not absolute, superheroes can generally be divided into two basic categories, according to literary critic John Cawelti: "as a superhero with exceptional strength or ability or as 'one of us' – a figure marked, at least at the beginning of the story by flawed abilities and attitudes presumably shared by the audience."[24] Furthermore, superheroes often, though not always, uphold a dualistic and unsophisticated morality – they lack the ability to evaluate complex personalities or situations; only good and bad exist, gray areas are non-existent.[25]

Another crucial aspect in the superhero plot is the hero overcoming obstacles and dangers in order to accomplish a moral mission, what Coogan terms "the pro-social mission."[26] Though the overall formula is repetitive,

20. Coogan 2006, as cited in Dittmer 2013, 6.
21. Costello 2009, 15, as cited in Miettinen 2011, 5.
22. Murray 2000, 143. Cited in Miettinen 2001.
23. Bongco 2000, 86, 104.
24. Cawelti 1976, 34, as cited in Bongco 2000, 91; Bongco 2000, 102, 103.
25. Strömberg 2011, 597.
26. Coogan 2006, 30.

comics still draw in their audience because of innovation within the story, as will be seen in our case studies.[27]

The essence of the superhero is easy to understand, yet can just anyone be considered a superhero? Are all superheroes created equal? To start with, superheroes must predominantly *look* heroic, which is to say they must possess a "hypermasculine physique" and fight crime in a way that favors heterosexuality.[28] This requirement is unsurprising since the comic book world mirrors the real world – both are structured to favor the white and heterosexual male.[29] The male superhero's body is one of the ultimate testimonies to his heteronormativity; his toned and virile body becomes the canvas on which masculinity is painted.

Hypermasculinity is perhaps one of the most desired traits for superheroes; that is, for white superheroes. Black superheroes are stereotyped as too masculine and too physical. Their bodies, difficult to restrain, are linked with crime and therefore incapable of representing an altruistic crime-fighting superhero.[30] The media only adds to this misconception by overrepresenting blacks as criminals and under-representing them as respectable citizens. The same is true of Muslim superheroes. Though not necessarily conflated with street crime, select media outlets are so effective in painting Muslims as terrorists that their audiences take this as fact; therefore, a Muslim superhero protecting American society and institutions, as opposed to destroying them, is for many very unrealistic.[31] A specific example of "inauthentic" Muslim superheroes are those appearing in Naif al-Mutawa's *The 99.* Communications scholar Avi Santo, discussing the reception of the animated *The 99* television series by American audiences, notes the staunch resistance launched by conservative organizations. While it is true that al-Mutawa's comic and animated series are steeped in both Islamic and Western values, his Muslim superheroes are dubbed inauthentic by conservative groups, because in their view Islam is violent, oppressive, and hateful by nature.[32] That being said, some Americans are misled by these erroneous assumptions and are therefore unable to contextualize Muslims as superheroes.

The female superhero is also effectively Othered because she, too, fails to measure up to the industry's hypermasculine demands. Although women are depicted as superheroes, they are often represented as sex objects because of the dominance of the male gaze. Citing feminist film theorist Laura Mulvey, Dar explains that the male gaze demands the portrayal of the female

27. Cawelti 1976, 34.
28. Phillips and Strobl 2013, 171.
29. Phillips and Strobl 2013, 169–170.
30. Phillips and Strobl 2013, 171; Brown 1999, 28, 30.
31. Philips and Strobl 2013, 166, 170, 171, 172.
32. Santo 2014, 689.

superhero in ways that her male heterosexual writers, artists, and audiences would like to see her.[33] Female representation in superhero comics became increasingly violent and hypersexual during the late 1980s into the 1990s, paralleling the rising popularity and accessibility of plastic surgery and pornography. The "pornification" of female superheroes was evident as their hips became more accentuated and their breasts outgrew their skimpy costumes. Relying on Michel Foucault's theory of discipline, American studies scholar Nickie Phillips and criminal justice scholar Staci Strobl claim that "contemporary men and women reproduce cultural hegemony by disciplining their own bodies."[34] Just as the male superhero's body is treated as a canvas for depicting masculinity, the female superhero's body is representative of a disciplined, idealized, and hypersexual femininity. Both female and male bodies are acted on, albeit in different and gendered ways. Continuing this line of thought, both female and male superheroes are sexualized; however, male readers are invited to both view male superheroes as role models to emulate and female superheroes as objects to enjoy.[35] According to gender theorist Judith Butler, gender does not consist of identities, but is instead performative, possible only through actions.[36] Female superheroes perform their gender within a patriarchal context; thus the female superhero straddles both her masculine superhero identity as well as her traditional and feminine identity, because acting too much like a man or woman would effectively undermine her credibility as both a desirable woman and legitimate superhero.[37]

The male-dominated comic book industry essentially responds to the question of who can be the classic superhero: the white heterosexual man. Yet the increase in various minority superheroes, during the late twentieth and early twenty-first century, has challenged the genre and forced it to somewhat amend its heteronormative framework. As Muslim superheroes, Sedara Bakut, Davood Nassur, and Kamala Khan all question the hierarchy that both American society and the superhero genre have set in place.

Psi-Force: American Interventions

Psi-Force was a comic book published by Marvel Comics between 1986 and 1989, under their New Universe imprint. It originally featured a group of five paranormal teenagers who used their telepathy, astral projection, telekinesis, and psionic detonation to battle various government operatives and

33. Mulvey 1975, 6–18, as cited in Dar 2010, 106.
34. Phillips and Strobl 2013, 163; 162.
35. Phillips and Strobl 2013, 164.
36. Butler 2006.
37. Phillips and Strobl 2013, 147–148.

rogue superhumans. Issue #32, the last in the series before its cancellation, is extremely important because of its portrayal of gender and Otherness as well as its function as an allegory both reflecting and critiquing U.S. foreign policy.

Before delving into a full analysis, however, the real-life historical context in which this story is based must be examined in brief. In 1973, Afghani politician Muhammad Daoud, with the help of pro-Soviet military and political factions, overthrew King Zahir and established the Republic of Afghanistan. On April 28, 1978, the Khalqis, a faction of the Marxist People's Democratic Party of Afghanistan, murdered Daoud. The Khalqi leader, Noor Taraki, assumed Daoud's role as Prime Minister. Taraki signed a friendship treaty with the Soviet Union that permitted direct intervention should the insurgence (i.e. mujahideen) threaten his government's stability. Many Islamic insurgent groups openly rejected and rebelled against Taraki's communist government. On December 24, 1979 the Soviet invasion of Afghanistan commenced. The U.S. responded by increasing its aid to the mujahideen and by establishing training schools both in Pakistan and at home. The Soviets eventually withdrew in February of 1989, leaving a power vacuum ripe for civil war between the various mujahideen factions and government forces.[38] Although the U.S. was allied with the mujahideen, it did not view these fundamentalists as equals; rather, the mujahideen were only pawns to be disposed of once they were no longer needed.

The final *Psi-Force* issue, titled "The Fist of Love," opens on a hill overlooking a Soviet supply camp near Herat, Afghanistan, on May 13, 1989. As the date indicates, the story is situated in an alternate reality where the Soviet Union has won the war and looks to consolidate its power in Iran – a far cry from historical reality.[39] Sedara Bakut, a young female mujahid dressed in army clothing and wearing a red *hijab*, partners with a group of American mercenaries and fellow mujahid. Their mission, to raid a Soviet supply camp, fails miserably and they are forced to flee through one of Sedara's telekinetic portals. Sedara returns alone to the same Soviet camp with the intent of destroying her enemies and of locating information proving that American mercenary Lincoln Stryker betrayed the mujahideen. Sedara then meets and teams up with Psi-Force (composed of team members Thomas Boyd; Johnny, Boyd's adopted son; Wayne Tucker; and Lindsey, Tucker's love

38. Dreyfuss 2005, 260; Office of the Historian 2013.

39. Whether or not this alternate reality was intended is debatable. As A. David Lewis and Martin Lund have suggested, the issue could have been written and prepared prior to Soviets withdrawing from Afghanistan, therefore making the alternate reality unintended. However, the New Universe imprint is also known for creating events that distinctly mark its reality from that of the reader (for example, the White Event).

interest); the group successfully blows up the camp. Back at the mujahideen camp, Sedara discovers that her father is, in fact, the traitor working with the Soviets. She shoots him in the head before he can even finish explaining his motives. The epilogue depicts all the members of Psi-Force happily enjoying their last day in Afghanistan, while Sedara mourns over the graves of her mother, brother, and father. After saying her final goodbyes, Sedara and the rest of the force head to Switzerland through one of her portals.

Although Sedara is eventually accepted into Psi-Force, both she and the Soviets are portrayed as inferior Others. Sedara and the rest of Psi-Force utterly dehumanize their Soviet enemies. Returning to the Soviet camp alone, Sedara thinks to herself while pulling a knife from her bag: "This requires a more personal touch ... a more enjoyable one!"[40] Although violent, her intent to fling a knife into a Russian's neck is not enough. Instead, Thomas Boyd, a Psi-Force member, stops her and comments, "You're a pretty fast draw, little girl. Cold, too, using a blade like that ... but sometimes, it pays to see their eyes ... kind of gives you this feeling of power ... it's more fun than pinning his neck with a knife at thirty feet."[41] As Boyd speaks these lines, he uses a rope as a lasso and chokes/electrocutes the Russian, while dragging him through the sand by his feet.

While death is a natural part of combat, the pleasure that Sedara and Boyd derive from killing Russians, especially in overtly gruesome ways, is indicative of a hyper-patriotic Cold War mentality. As the U.S. and mujahideen's ideological foes, Russians were often depicted as lesser humans deserving brutal deaths. Though not treated as sub-human, Sedara is viewed through an Orientalist lens, thus marking her, too, as inferior. In the above quote, Boyd belittles her when he calls her "little girl." Yet this implicit insult is nothing compared to another Psi-Force member's explicit remarks. Before the group sets up a bomb, Tucker turns to Sedara and leers, "We do *more than just blow things up* and we do more than *fight for revenge*."[42] Following this jeer, we see one side of Sedara's face: it emits annoyance as her mouth grimaces in a frown and her eyebrows arch inwards. The dialogue clearly demonstrates a framework in which the mujahideen are figured as an incompetent and overly emotional Other, led by their desire for revenge, while Sedara's facial expression challenges this assumption.

Yet, Sedara remains Other until the very last scene of the comic. While kneeling in front of her family's gravesite, Sedara is in a way tamed because she forsakes her troubled past and quest for vengeance. Interestingly

---

40. Nicieza et al. 1989, 12.
41. Nicieza et al. 1989, 13.
42. Nicieza et al. 1989, 15.

enough, Sedara fits the superhero ideal in that she is plagued by the loss of her family, yet she engages with this loss in a way that promotes the selfish use of her powers; in other words, she originally uses her powers for revenge. However, she is capable of joining Psi-Force as a rational member once she abandons this misuse of power. Psi-Force is composed of prototypical super-heroes because it is defined by its altruistic mission: the destruction of the bad guys for the greater good – in this case, the Soviets. Sedara, conversely, possesses superpowers, but initially lacks altruism because she is primarily motivated by revenge. By abandoning her desire for revenge, Sedara accepts the call to altruism, allowing her to fully accept the title of superhero.

Psi-Force's altruistic mission can represent American exceptionalism while Sedara (for the majority of the comic) and the rest of the mujahideen for, that matter, are stand-ins for the emotion-driven Oriental. In other words, Psi-Force fights for loftier and rational goals, such as the preservation of democracy, while Sedara acts according to emotion and is thus marked as irrational. The dialogue is explicit; it makes its presence readily known while Sedara's unspoken reaction is subtler and in need of deconstruction. This deconstruction reveals an underlying theme of this work: the questioning of the U.S.'s presence in Afghanistan. Sedara's apparent disapproval, during her above encounter with Tucker, counters Tucker's insinuations; the reader should take Sedara's reaction as a cue to not readily accept accusations and labels that belittle the mujahideen.

Sedara's depiction as the Other both strengthens and dismantles Orien-talist rhetoric. In addition, her status as Other is also representative of how the U.S. viewed itself in relation to the mujahideen. Upon first encountering Psi-Force, Sedara asks them why they are in the Soviet camp. Boyd responds: "Same reason as you, but we're here to *do it right*" (my emphasis).[43] This is a loaded sentence because it possibly points to the U.S. public's perception of the mujahideen as incapable of battling the Russians on their own, thus war-ranting American intervention. Aspects of the story also mirror the U.S.'s radical use of propaganda during the war. Sedara, discovering her father is a traitor, shoots him point blank. She, like many superheroes, operates on a moral binary – her father has defied the mujahideen and allied himself with the Soviets, committing the ultimate wrong. This betrayal is inexcus-able for Sedara, thus justifying her decision to execute him. Before he is shot, her father desperately explains his actions: "We were going to lose – to die – we have lost so much already – I – I was thinking of your welfare."[44] Yet Sedara is unable to fully evaluate the complexity of her father's actions. She is incapable of viewing the situation in shades of gray – her father is simply

43. Nicieza et al. 1989, 14.
44. Nicieza et al. 1989, 21.

a traitor. This scene also resonates with the radical propaganda found in a USAID-funded textbook produced by the University of Nebraska for Afghan children:

> The speed of a Kalashnikov bullet is 800 meters per second. If a Russian is at a distance of 3200 meters from a mujahid, and that mujahid aims at the Russian's head, calculate how many seconds it will take for the bullet to strike the Russian in the forehead.[45]

This unsettling math problem demonstrates just how pervasive foreign policy can be during times of conflict; education textbooks and comic books are not immune to sadistic propaganda.

Psi-Force #32 is not unequivocally propagandistic nor are its female characters utterly sexualized. Both Sedara and Psi-Force's only female character, Lindsey, wear *hijabs* and outfits that cover their entire bodies. Their clothing is significant because it carries multiple meanings: it effectively desexualizes them which simultaneously heightens their value as superheroes in their own right – they are forces to be reckoned with, not because of their physical attractiveness, but because of their powers. Lindsey's *hijab* also reveals Psi-Force's attempt to respect the religion of its allies. Lindsey, a non-Muslim, could have easily been depicted without the *hijab*, yet she wears it throughout the entire story (except when swimming) without commenting on its presence or her reason for wearing it, thus making it a non-issue.

In the scene where Sedara shoots her father, there is a departure from Cold War propaganda and, instead, a sense of realism; believing that the mercenary and mujahideen ally, Lincoln Stryker, is the traitor, she aims her gun at him and calls him an "American Pig." Tucker deflects her arm and states, "No, Stryker's been profittin' from the arms and drug traffickin', but he's not the traitor."[46] The U.S.-could-do-no-wrong ideology is broken because Tucker's jibe unearths the selfish reasons behind Stryker's (and by extension U.S.'s) presence in Afghanistan; however, writer Fabian Nicieza achieves this by relying on a verbal rather than visual critique. In other words, Sedara's previous criticism is more implicit because it is depicted visually through facial cues and often in the background of the panel, while Tucker's disdain is explicitly verbalized and at the panel's foreground. Perhaps Nicieza imbues Tucker with this assertive right to critique because he is both American and a member of Psi-Force? Though in a way representative of the U.S., Psi-Force is at times quite critical of authority figures, including the U.S. government and those allied to questionable causes, a theme prevalent throughout the entire series. It is, therefore, unsurprising that one of its members, rather

45. Mamdani 2004, 137.
46. Nicieza et al. 1989, 21.

than Sedara, is the first to explicitly state what was previously only implied through imagery; Tucker's words are not muddled by ambiguity and interpretation, but instead forcefully clear.

Perhaps the most jarring, yet honest, scene is the epilogue. Boyd and his adopted son are playing football while Tucker and Lindsey get engaged. Sedara, however, is in stark contrast to the others as she crouches over her family's graves, all notably marked by wooden crosses despite their Muslim heritage, as the setting sun shines in the background. Her words cut into the prior, frivolous scene: "Thank you for all you have given me ... hope and misery, guilt and innocence. I've had enough of your way, father. I think for mother and brother's sake, I will forsake the past."[47] This scene can act as an allegory. Sedara represents Afghanistan, a nation in which foreigners have intervened and wrought havoc, a nation left for dead. Psi-Force, on the other hand, may be seen to represent the ease with which America intervenes in the affairs of others while often suffering only comparatively minor losses and disregarding the long-term consequences its policies may have. Stryker embodies this glaring policy flaw as he departs for the Persian Gulf: "Lots of money to be made, lots of wrongs to be righted."[48] He also personifies the U.S.'s disingenuous support of Islamic groups such as the mujahideen. He calls to Sedara, while holding his fist to his heart, "Sedara ... may Allah be with you wherever your path may lead you, child of the fury [... M]ake peace with God on the strength of your convictions alone."[49] The melodramatic dialogue is perhaps indicative of yet another critique of the U.S.'s involvement not only with Muslim-majority countries, but with the religion of Islam. Stryker's invocation of Allah, along with the phrase, "child of the fury," comes off as farce. That being said, his words are both ludicrous and disingenuous; Stryker invokes Allah as he abandons Sedara for the bountiful Persian Gulf. Stryker's insincere remarks can therefore be equated with the U.S.'s hypocritical and temporary involvement with militant Islam. Both the U.S. and Stryker engage with militant Islam as a way to advance their own material interests.

The comic's creators use *Psi-Force* #32 to reveal some moral and political reservations surrounding the U.S.'s involvement in Afghanistan. They achieve this through the use of dialogue as well as the juxtaposition between Sedara Bakut, the members of Psi-Force, and Lincoln Stryker. A cursory glance at the comic may reveal propaganda as well as action-packed scenes and intense dialogue, each providing excitement while moving the plot for-

47. Nicieza et al. 1989, 25.
48. Nicieza et al. 1989, 26.
49. Nicieza et al 1989, 26–7.

ward. Yet a closer look at the dialogue, and the ways in which it is delivered and received by each character, reveals a striking reality – the mujahideen fighters in Afghanistan were mere pawns in America's game for political and economic dominance.

"The Sinbad Contract":
A Superhero both Muslim and American?

"The Sinbad Contract," published in the titles *Superman* #48, *The Adventures of Superman* #471, and *Superman in Action Comics* #658, was released during the Persian Gulf War (1990–1991).[50] The plot, succinctly stated, is as follows: Davood Nassur is an immigrant from the fictional state of Qurac, which is often associated with terrorism. One day, his latent meta-human powers are amplified by a mysterious belt. The villainous Lex Luthor, needing the belt to kill Superman, tries to frame Davood as a terrorist. The trilogy ends with Davood and Superman saving Metropolis from a giant saucer-shaped bomb, which disables the belt, thus diminishing Davood's powers. Despite using the freighted moniker "Sinbad," "The Sinbad Contract" does, in fact, depict its Muslim superhero, Davood Nassur, in a rather progressive manner, and it goes beyond *Psi-Force* #32 by confronting in greater detail issues of gender and belonging.

At the beginning of the trilogy, we are introduced to a Quraci-American family. One highly visible marker of this identity is clothing. In fact, Davood's whole family, including his mother, wear Western clothing and leave their heads uncovered. The family, though speaking Quraci at home, is portrayed as an average American family. Davood does not perform his religion overtly, either; instead, his main identity is that of a teenager, one who fights with his sister, Soraya, or goofs off with the neighborhood kids.

Although Davood's family appears Americanized, they are highly conscious of their otherness and are not fully integrated into American society; perhaps they will never be because complete integration could compromise their religious and national identities.[51] One evening during dinner, Davood's Uncle Jahir exclaims: "The police don't care! The costumes don't care! No one outside gives a damn about us [residents of Little Qurac]! We have to be strong! Otherwise, we'll be destroyed!"[52] It is worth citing the next few panels at length:

50. Messner-Loebs 1990a-c.
51. I would like to thank A. David Lewis for calling to mind the near-impossibility of fully integrating into a culture not one's own.
52. Messner-Loebs 1990a, 5.

Davood's cousin:	And they whisper "terrorist, terrorist" behind our backs!
Davood:	That's why I let the kids call me "David" rather than "Davood." It's easier.
Uncle Jahir:	You pretend you're not an Arab, not Quraci? That is very bad!
Davood:	Aww, to them, "Arab" means Sinbad the Sailor or Ali Baba and the Forty Thieves! Or somebody who blows up air planes!"[53]

This is a far cry from propaganda. Instead of generalizing an entire population, this comic is sensitive to the challenges of being simultaneously American, Arab, and Muslim, thus facilitating further dialogue on the broader narrative of immigration and belonging. For one, it recognizes the social and psychological tensions that are exacerbated when "one's culture is hijacked by terrorists, and when one's new country marks you as suspect."[54] These tensions often result in a double consciousness of sorts. The term, coined by W.E.B. Dubois, is applied to those with multiple and conflicting identities.[55] To quote Dubois, "It is a peculiar sensation, this double-consciousness, this sense of always looking at one's self through the eyes of others, of measuring one's soul by the tape of a world that looks on in amused contempt and pity."[56] Davood, an American, Quraci, and Muslim, is acutely aware of his multilayered identity and, as demonstrated above, oscillates between his identities given the situation. Although not adhering to his peers' beliefs, he does, in fact, look at his own identity through the lenses of prejudice and misinformation. Instead of attempting to educate his peers, he modifies his own identity because it is, as he says, easier.

In seeming contrast to the above conversation between Davood and his family, the dialogue at times offers glaring examples of anti-Muslim sentiment. This, however, is done with the intent of critique; as comics scholar and journalist Fredrik Strömberg's work notes, comics sometimes use stereotypes specifically for the purpose of overturning them.[57] Clark Kent's coworker, Timmons, has the following to say about Little Qurac: "We all know that neighborhood breeds terrorists and crime. What we need is someone like Gotham has a Batman – to wipe it out!" Kent responds: "The Batman's not a racist or a fool, Timmons, and that puts him miles ahead of you."[58]

53. Messner-Loebs 1990a, 6.
54. Sirin and Fine 2007, 11: 152.
55. DuBoseopedia, "Double Consciousness."
56. Dubois 1903, 16–17.
57. Strömberg 2011, 585.
58. Messner-Loebs 1990a, 8.

Luthor, in the midst of framing Davood, describes the young superhero to the police with the following: "The leader is a savage young fanatic with meta-human powers [...] he threatened to blow up bridges and schools and factories all over the city."[59] Outlandish stereotypes are used once again as a way to condemn racial and religious profiling. By linking the act of stereotyping to a villain, the behavior gains a negative association.

The comic continues to counteract stereotypes while simultaneously portraying Davood as an authentic superhero. Both *Psi-Force* #32 and "The Sinbad Contract" conclude with Sedara and Davood, respectively, embracing the concept of the altruistic mission. Sedara abandons her quest for revenge while Davood risks his life for the sake of Metropolis. Yet there is a major division in each superhero's respective trajectory toward altruism. Sedara initially uses her superpowers in the name of revenge while Davood initially uses his superpowers in the name of good fun (i.e. using his powers to mess around with his neighborhood friends). In other words, both superheroes eventually subscribe to the altruistic mission, yet Davood's original use of his powers is far more benevolent and rational than Sedara's. Perhaps this difference is rooted in gendered stereotypes. Female characters are often depicted as irrational beings predisposed to acting on impulse. Regardless, "The Sinbad Contract" is a noticeable improvement in comparison to *Psi-Force* #32, because Davood is portrayed as less irrational and violent than Sedara, thus making for a smoother and more authentic transition to altruistic superhero.

Unlike Davood, Luthor and his henchmen are far from altruistic. In fact, they purposely frame Davood, and by extension the Quraci community, with acts of terrorism. Luthor's henchmen dress up as highly caricatured Arabs, each with matching white turbans, and impersonate Davood while blowing up buildings. Once again, the comic pushes the message that stereotyping is reprehensible, while simultaneously revealing the comic's major flaw; by painting non-Western (turban-wearing) looking Arabs as terrorists, the comic inadvertently sends the message that only a certain kind of Muslim can integrate into American society. The superhero genre is known for its ability to mirror both the real world and the sentiments of its readers. "The Sinbad Contract" is no exception because it reaffirms societal beliefs about the Muslim community, despite its attempt to present American audiences with an authentic Muslim superhero. Those who appear "Islamic" and those who perform Islamic rituals are associated with a violent form of Islam.[60] Davood's Americanized and non-overtly religious family, however, are associated with a secular and thus non-violent branch of Islam. That being said,

59. Messner-Loebs 1990a, 17.
60. Gottschalk and Greenberg 2008, 63.

"The Sinbad Contract" counters the stereotype that all Muslims are terrorists while inadvertently promoting another stereotype – that "Islamic" Muslims are still capable of committing acts of terrorism. While the comic offers an attempt at an authentic Muslim superhero, it simultaneously marginalizes other Muslims – the overtly religious and non-Westernized. The solidification of this stereotype excludes certain Muslims from the superhero genre and, by extension, from society, which in a way threatens Davood's status as an authentic superhero, thus undermining the comic's overall goal.

To end our analysis of "The Sinbad Contract," let us instead focus on gender, more specifically the portrayal of the masculine superhero's body. Recall that the normative male superhero bears a hypermasculine physique. Though the image of a tall and well-toned superhero is not necessarily sexualized, it is idealized. Davood deviates from this construct because he is neither exceptionally tall nor muscular, yet he is just as much a superhero, or perhaps even more so, as his chiseled counterpart, Superman. It is Davood, and not Superman, who ultimately saves Metropolis from destruction. Upon realizing that the saucer-shaped bomb is seconds from exploding, Superman grasps the bomb with his hands and flies as far away from Metropolis as possible. Yet his failure is apparent as an entire page is dedicated to the image of the bomb exploding over Metropolis. Davood, however, risks his life by flying toward the explosion and creating a shield large enough to protect the entire city from incineration.

This scene suggests a purposeful deviation from the standard depiction of the male form. Davood is able to transcend bodily expectations and therefore represents an alternate superhero form. Davood, dark-skinned, short, and wearing the clothes of a normal teenager – jeans and a t-shirt as opposed to a colorful, skintight costume – maintains his super strength and ability to fight crime. While Davood's body lacks a hypermasculine physicality and the virility that accompanies it, his ability to achieve superhuman feats is hardly constrained. To invoke John Cawleti's categorization of superheroes, Davood is both hero and one of us.

Ms. Marvel Volume 1: No Normal:
A Divergent yet Authentic Superhero

Ms. Marvel Volume 1: No Normal (2014) succeeds where "The Sinbad Contract" fails. Like Davood, Kamala Khan, from Jersey City, is first and foremost a teenager, struggling to fight villains while also navigating her life at home and at school. Yet Kamala's world differs from Davood's because hers is more inclusive, in that multiple categories of Muslim identity can exist without one being labeled a terrorist (e.g. most prominently her brother, Aamir, who dresses in a *kurta pajama* and is a self-described Salafi). The comic also actively depicts an authentic use of a non-English language, Urdu. Words such as *ami* (mom), *abu* (dad), *beta/i* (son/daughter), and *shaytani* (devilish) abound.

No Normal chronicles Kamala's initial adventures as Ms. Marvel. Kamala and her two friends, Nakia and Bruno, are invited to a waterfront party by Zoe Zimmer, the All-American queen-bee type, and her boyfriend, Josh, the stereotypical jock. Kamala sneaks out of her house and attends the party only to get trapped by the Terrigen Mists, a mutagen cloud released by the Inhumans, that imbues her with superpowers. Kamala is forced to use her newfound powers to save Zoe after she drunkenly falls into the Hudson River. Yet Kamala's primary adventure, besides learning how to accept both her powers and herself, is rescuing Bruno's younger brother, Vick, from a gang ruled by a mysterious and tech-savvy villain called the Inventor.

Anti-Muslim stereotypes and misconceptions abound in Jersey City, despite its status as a diverse city. Akin to the "The Sinbad Contract," stereotypes are used in *No Normal* as a strategic method of eradicating these very misconceptions. For example, Zoe fawns over Nakia: "Your headscarf is so pretty, Kiki. I love that color. But I mean ... nobody pressured you to start wearing it, right? Your father or somebody? Nobody's going to like honor kill you? I'm just concerned."[61] Nakia, visibly annoyed, responds that, "Actually, my dad wants me to take it off. He thinks it's a phase."[62] Like Clark Kent in "The Sinbad Contract," Nakia successfully turns a stereotype on its head. The day after Kamala gains her powers, Bruno questions his brother: "Where were you last night, Vick? Mom and Pop freaked out when that mist was everywhere and you weren't answering your phone. They thought it was, like, terrorists or something."[63] This is unsurprising as today's foreign policy is still very much centered on containing terrorism, which is largely viewed as a Muslim problem.

Ms. Marvel attempts to disaggregate both Islam as a religion and Muslim as an identity. What Strömberg writes about another superhero, G.W. Bridge, member of the intelligence agency SHIELD and convert to Islam, is also applicable to Kamala: "[She] is a Muslim, but [her] personality is not dictated by [her] religion alone."[64] Like Americans from other religious denominations, Kamala's identity is multifarious, and she even questions her religion. At Sheikh Abdullah's Saturday youth lecture, she questions the separation of the sexes by stating that the Prophet's Mosque in Medina originally al-

61. Wilson and Alphona 2014, 2.
62. Wilson and Alphona 2014, 3.
63. Wilson and Alphona 2014, 44.
64. Strömberg 2011, 589.

lowed mixed-sex congregations.[65] Through her characterizations, Kamala undermines two stereotypes: first, that a Muslim's core identity is his or her religious identity and second, that Muslims never question their faith or practices.

Like "The Sinbad Contract," *Ms. Marvel* presents us with a superhero who is both Muslim and American. *Ms. Marvel*'s attempt at creating an authentic Muslim superhero, however, surpasses that of its predecessor. Like many superheroes, Kamala is plagued by emotional hang-ups. Most telling, and perhaps most mundane, is her strained relationship with her parents. A number of panels are devoted to Kamala and her parents arguing over her curfew, boys, and school detention, to name but a few points of contention. Adolescence, as a time of personal turmoil, is easily understood by most readers, regardless of race, religion, or gender. By focusing on familial strife, so typical of the life of an American teenager, the comic ensures that Kamala is viewed as a genuine American teenager.

Problematic relationships are not reserved for Kamala and her parents. From the comic's beginning, Kamala is patronized by Zoe and her boyfriend, Josh. Zoe's interaction with Kamala and her friends is marked by its insincerity – there is an obvious tension between the teenagers. When Zoe falls into the Hudson River, mere minutes after Kamala gains her superpowers, Kamala is confronted by the superhero's altruistic mission, which she eagerly accepts. In other words, Kamala's instinct is to save Zoe despite her incessant bullying. Unlike Sedara and Davood, Kamala neither experiences a superpower "trial-run" nor abuses her newfound powers. Kamala immediately subscribes to the altruistic mission so common to the superhero world. In light of Sedara and Davood, Kamala is the end point in an evolving process. With each comic, the Muslim superhero adopts the altruistic mission – and, for that matter, authenticity – quicker than his or her predecessor. Yet Kamala's acceptance of the altruistic mission is framed by the following Qur'an verse, "Whoever kills one person, it is as if he has killed all mankind – and whoever saves one person, it is as if he has saved all of mankind."[66] Kamala's adoption of the altruistic mission is unhindered by Islam; in fact, Islam facilitates her choice to accept the altruistic mission and her status as a superhero, thus giving her an authenticity unlike that of Sedara and Davood.

No Normal's attempt to dismantle rigid biases is not restricted to religion alone. Kamala is, in fact, a trailblazer not only for Muslim superheroes but for female superheroes as well. Another Marvel superhero, both Muslim and

65. Wilson and Alphona 2014, 46.
66. Wilson and Alphona 2014.

female, is the character Dust. Unlike Kamala, Dust is a victim of post-colonial and gendered thought because she is presented as a Muslim woman who needs to be saved by a white man.[67] Kamala, however, is largely a reversal of Dust. It is Kamala who saves Zoe, while Josh, the strong heterosexual male, is rendered useless. Furthermore, when Bruno discovers Kamala's superhero identity, he expresses great concern for her safety and the following conversation ensues:

> Kamala: You protect me from stuff all the time. You have since we were kids. But now I'm the stronger one, and I'm gonna protect you, and that totally freaks you out.
>
> Bruno: You're right. It totally freaks me out.[68]

Kamala and Bruno's relationship experiences an inversion where the female, Kamala, is responsible for the safety of the male; the woman character is no longer the damsel in distress nor the highly sexualized female girlfriend and/or sidekick.

Kamala also defies conventional standards of beauty. Her initial encounter with the Terrigen Mists transforms her into a replica of her favorite superhero, Ms. Marvel. Kamala, realizing that she now sports blond hair, white skin, and a highly sexualized costume, looks uncertain when she asks, "Ummm ... is it too late to change my mind?"[69] Throughout the initial phases of her transformation, Kamala repeatedly questions the relationship between her own self-image, her Ms. Marvel image, and her perception of beauty and self-confidence. While toying with her blond hair and hiked up skirt, Kamala thinks to herself: "I always thought that if I had amazing hair, if I could pull off great boots, if I could fly – that would make me feel strong, that would make me happy. But the hair gets in my face, the boots pinch, and this leotard is giving me an epic wedgie."[70] Kamala's return (before her first battle at the Inventor's lair) from a pale-skinned blond to that of her own physical self defies the white standard of beauty upheld by many in real-life society and in the comic book world. Kamala stands tall in front of the Inventor's lair and says to herself: "Who am I? It seems like an easy question. And then I realize [... M]aybe the name belongs to whoever has the courage to fight. And so I tell them," speaking the last words aloud, "You can call me Ms. Marvel."[71] This scene is especially poignant because it paints

---

67. Strömberg 2011, 583. [Editors' note: See also the article by Nicholaus Pumphrey in this volume.]

68. Wilson and Alphona 2014, 70.

69. Wilson and Alphona 2014, 20.

70. Wilson and Alphona 2014, 33.

71. Wilson and Alphona 2014, 76.

Kamala as a figure initially marked by a flawed attitude, a theme common to the superhero genre. Kamala's attitude is originally flawed because she subscribes to conventional ideas of beauty, which negatively affect her own sense of worth. Her struggle with self-acceptance is undoubtedly shared by many of her readers. This emotional tie between Kamala and the reader only heightens Kamala's eventual self-acceptance.

Kamala continues to challenge conventional beauty standards after losing her first battle against the Inventor's cronies. Kamala vents to Bruno: "So I can take my clothes with me when I embiggen [grow bigger] and stuff, but it's distracting. I was slow at that house in Greenville. I need a costume I can forget about. Which means it has to be really, really stretchy."[72] Kamala's perfected costume, fashioned from a burkini – a modest swimsuit for Muslim women – covers her entire body from the neck down, yet her costume is by no means ugly. Kamala is willing to sacrifice a flesh-revealing costume that captures the male gaze for one that ensures her ability to fight crime like a legitimate superhero. Kamala, unlike many of her predecessors, breaks from the notion that female superheroes must straddle two forms of gender. Kamala is a competent superhero, defined by her ability, not her sexuality – a welcome change for female readers, Muslim and non-Muslim alike.

For much of the Cold War, Muslim superheroes were largely absent from comic books. Their villainous counterparts, however, flew widely through comic book panels, be it on magic carpets or in doomed airplanes. Although developments in Muslim-majority countries, most tellingly the OPEC Oil Embargo of 1973–1974, did impact both American foreign policy and consciousness, such nations were not as acutely significant to U.S. foreign policy and imagination until the Soviet-Afghan War. As the Soviet Union faltered in its final years, Muslim-majority countries started assuming a central position in U.S. foreign policy. It was this foreign policy shift that led to the introduction of a Muslim superhero, Sedara Bakut in *Psi-Force* #32. Despite its overall use of propaganda, the comic is somewhat progressive because it is conscious of the drawbacks in U.S. foreign policy. *Psi-Force* #32 not only marks a shift in the Middle East's strategic importance, but it also criticizes the U.S.'s interventionist policies while also foreshadowing the U.S.'s entrenchment in the region.

"The Sinbad Contract" is both underrated and well before its time. Although it suffers some shortcomings, such as narrowly defining the Muslim community, it is progressive in its depiction of Muslims. The introduction of Kamala Khan was a watershed moment because she was the first American-

72. Wilson and Alphona 2014, 94.

created Muslim superheroine to gain her own series. The number of Muslim superheroes has steadily increased since 2001 because of non-Muslim curiosity and the need to provide an image counter to the one found in popular media.[73] Yet *Ms. Marvel* is unique because it presents Muslims in a more nuanced manner when compared to its predecessors. Kamala neither conforms to the male gaze nor is she a subsidiary character, as is often the case for many minority superheroes. While Kamala is unique in her ability to subvert traditional representations of minority and female superheroes, she subscribes to the altruistic mission as much, or perhaps more so, than her non-Muslim counterparts. Kamala is undoubtedly an authentic superhero.

73. Strömberg 2011, 595.

Works Cited

Bayoumi, M. (2014). "The Race is On: Muslims and Arabs in the American Imagination." In *Muslims and American Popular Culture,* edited by I. Omidvar, and A. Richards. Santa Barbara.

Bongco, M. 2000. *Reading Comics: Language, Culture, and the Concept of the Superhero in Comic Books.* New York.

Brown, J. 1999. "Comic Book Masculinity and the New Black Superhero." *African American Review* 33: 25–42.

Butler, J. 2006. *Gender Trouble: Feminism and the Subversion of Identity.* Tenth anniversary edition. New York.

Cawelti, J. 1976. "Notes Toward a Typology of Literary Form." *Journal of Popular Culture* 10 (1).

Coogan, P.. 2006. *Superhero: The Secret Origin of a Genre.* Austin.

Costello, M. 2009. *Secret Identity Crisis: Comic Books and the Unmasking of Cold War America.* New York.

Dar, J. 2010. "Holy Islamophobia, Batman! Demonization of Muslims and Arabs in Mainstream American Comic Books." *Counterpoints* 346: 99–110.

Dittmer, J. 2013, *Captain America and the Nationalist Superhero: Metaphors, Narratives, and Geopolitics.* Philadelphia.

Dreyfuss, R. 2005. *Devil's Game: How the United States Helped Unleash Fundamentalist Islam.* New York.

Dubois, W. E. B. 1903. *The Souls of Black Folk,* Chicago.

DuBoiseopedia. 2013 "Double Consciousness." *DuBoiseopedia.* http://scua.library.umass.edu/duboisopedia/doku.php?id=about:double_consciousness.

Gottschalk, P., and G. Greenberg. 2008. *Islamophobia: Making Muslims the Enemy.* Lanham.

Hadar, L. 2008. "Islam and the West: The Myth of the Green Peril." *Anti-war. com.* http://antiwar.com/hadar/?articleid=13718.

Johnson, J. 2011. "Terrified Protectors: The Early Twenty-First Century Fear Narrative in Comic Book Superhero Stories." *Americana: The Journal of American Popular Culture (1900-Present)* 10. http://www.americanpopularculture.com/journal/articles/fall_2011/johnson.htm.

Lewis, A. D. 2012. "The Militarism of American Superheroes after 9/11." In *Comic Books And American Cultural History: An Anthology,* edited by M. Pustz. New York.

Mahdi, W. 2014. "Marked Off: Hollywood's Untold Story of Arabs, Muslims, and Camels." In *Muslims and American Popular Culture,* edited by I. Omidvar, and A. Richards. Santa Barbara.

Mamdani, M. 2004. *Good Muslim, Bad Muslim: America, the Cold War, and the Roots of Terror.* New York.

Michael, J. 2008. "Douglass's Cosmopolitanism: American Empire and the Failure of Diplomatic Representation." In *Identity and the Failure of America: From Thomas Jefferson to the War on Terror,* edited by J. Michael. Minneapolis.

Miettinen, M. 2001. "Superhero Comics and the Popular Geopolitics of American Identity." PhD dissertation, University of Tampere.

Messner-Loebs, W., C. Swan, and D. Janke. 1990a. "The Sinbad Contract: Part One." *Superman* vol. 2 #48, October. New York

———. 1990b. "The Sinbad Contract Part Two." *The Adventures of Superman.* #471, October. New York.

———. 1990c. "The Sinbad Contract Part Two." *The Adventures of Superman #658,* October. New York.

Mingant, N. 2014. "Beyond Muezzins and Mujahideen: Middle-Eastern Voices in Post-9/11 Hollywood Movies." In *Muslims and American Popular Culture,* edited by I. Omidvar, and A. Richards. Santa Barbara.

Mulvey, L. 1975. "Visual Pleasure and Narrative Cinema." *Screen* 16: 6–18.

Murray, Chris. 2000. "Popaganda: Superhero Comics and Propaganda." In *Comics and Culture. Analytical and Theoretical Approaches to Comics,* edited by A. Magnussen, and H.-C. Christansen. Copenhagen.

Nicieza, F., R. Ramos, and C. Ivey. 1989 "The Fist of Love." *Psi-Force* #32. New York.

Office of the Historian. 2013. "The Soviet Invasion of Afghanistan and the U.S. Response, 1978–1980." *Office of the Historian.* https://history.state.gov/milestones/1977-1980/soviet-invasion-afghanistan.

Phillips, N., and S. Strobl. 2013. *Comic Book Crime: Truth, Justice, and the American Way.* New York.

Said, E. 1997. *Covering Islam.* New York.

Santo, A. 2014. "'Is It a Camel? Is It a Turban? No, It's *The 99*': Branding Islamic Superheroes as Authentic Global Cultural Commodities," *Television and News Media* 15: 679–695.

Shaheen, J. 1991. "The Comic Book Arab." *The Link* 24: 1–11.

———. 2001. *Reel Bad Arabs.* Northampton.

Sirin, S., and M. Fine. 2007. "Hyphenated Selves: Muslim American Youth Negotiating Identities on the Fault Lines of Global Conflict." *Applied Development Science* 11, no. 3: 151–163.

Strömberg, F. 2011. "'Yo, rag-head!': Arab and Muslim Superheroes in American Comic Books after 9/11." *American Studies* 56: 573–601.

Wilson, G. W., and Adrian Alphona. 2014. *Ms. Marvel Volume 1: No Normal.* New York.

Superhero Comics from the Middle East:
Tyranny of Genre?

Fredrik Strömberg

WHAT HAPPENS IF A CULTURALLY SPECIFIC GENRE travels geographically and/or culturally? Will it retain its core conventions or be transformed, through adaptation, into something else? More specifically, is the superhero genre so rooted in its original American culture that it is problematic to adapt it to a Middle Eastern setting?

Superhero comics are intimately associated with the United States. The genre emerged in the U.S. in the late 1930s and is still popular in its native country. Despite American superhero comics having been exported for more than seven decades, there have been few commercially successful comics created in that genre in the rest of the world. Given that there have been several violent conflicts between the U.S. and Arab or Muslim-majority nations since the beginning of the twenty-first century, it is intriguing that attempts at establishing a line of original superhero comics were made in the first decade of the twenty-first century by two different publishing houses in the Middle East: AK Comics in Egypt and Teshkeel Media Group in Kuwait.

I will in this chapter analyze these publishers' comic books to ascertain what happens in regard to the American superhero comics genre when it is produced in the Middle East, and what this might say about the genre's ability to reculturate.

Superhero Comics

Even though there were predecessors, most comics historians agree the superhero genre's urtext is Superman's first appearance in *Action Comics* #1, cover dated June 1938.[1] Early on in the academic study of the genre, superhero comics were often seen as a subset of larger, more extensive genres,

---

1. Reynolds 1992, 8.

such as the adventure story,[2] but it has since been recognized as a self-contained, even "self-aware" genre.[3]

Definitions

Several attempts have been made at defining the conventions of the superhero genre. An early endeavor was made by comics historian Richard Reynolds in 1992, who started with the original story of Superman and found seven "laws," including the orphan hero, the earthbound god, a personal rather than legal sense of justice, a contrast between the superhuman hero and the ordinary surroundings, a mundane alter-ego, a patriotic theme, and finally a blending of science and magic.[4]

A more comprehensive definition of "primary conventions" was later established by comics scholar Peter Coogan: a selfless, pro-social mission; superpowers based on extraordinary abilities, advanced technology, or highly developed physical and/or mental skills; and an identity comprised of a codename, a costume, and often a secret identity.[5]

A central theme of the superhero genre not addressed by the above-mentioned definitions is the conflict with the adversaries of the superheroes, the supervillains. Religion scholar Karline McLain included this in yet another attempt at establishing the conventions of the genre. She singles out six "essential features": extraordinary powers, enemies, a strong moral code, a secret identity, a costume, and an origin story.[6] The existence of enemies inevitably results in physical violence, so much so that in a content analysis of the genre, it was found that 97% of superhero stories contain violence.[7] The researchers analyzed animated TV shows from the U.S. featuring superheroes, but my experience after having read superhero comics for more than three decades is that their findings are valid also for superhero comics.

Another prevalent convention of the superhero genre left out of earlier definitions is the sexualization of the main characters. Most superheroes and superheroines have exaggerated (superhuman) physiques, which are amplified through skin-tight spandex costumes.[8] This is especially true for the superheroines, who are often clad in quite revealing costumes, and seen through the male gaze.[9] Finally, most superhero comics are set in a cohe-

2. Cawelti 2014, 40; Rollin 2013, 84.
3. Klock 2002, 26; Brooker 2013, 73.
4. Reynolds 1992, 16.
5. Coogan 2010, 607.
6. McLain 2009, 1.
7. Wilson et al. 2002, 32.
8. Duncan and Smith 2009, 235.
9. Avery-Natale 2013, 72.

sive storyworld, shared by other superheroes and based on the present-day world of the average reader, with varying degrees of deviation – the most obvious being that superheroes and supervillains exist.

My definition of the superhero genre would thus include the following conventions:

1. Superhuman abilities, for heroes and villains.
2. A strong personal moral code as driving force for the heroes.
3. An origin story that explains the abilities and the moral code.
4. A clear visual branding of each hero, mainly through costume design.
5. A mundane secret identity that contrasts with the superhuman identity.
6. Recurring violent clashes between heroes and villains.
7. A sexualization of the heroes, mostly seen through the male gaze.
8. A cohesive and contemporary, although alternative, version of the reader's world.

I view this as a prototype definition, meaning that not all conventions must be present to establish that something is a superhero comic, but that if they are, the comics in question can be said to be typical of the genre.[10]

Superhero Comics in the Middle East

Comics is not, nor has it ever been, a major popular medium in the Middle East.[11] The comics culture in the Middle East has its roots in imports from the U.S. and Europe during the first half of the twentieth century. In the 1930s, *Mickey Mouse* comics were translated and printed in Arabic magazines, as were American comic strips, and French-style albums like *Tintin* soon followed.[12] A new era was initiated in the 1970s, when money from the oil boom facilitated indigenous, original production. Comics from the Middle East have since mostly been published in children's magazines and are traditionally didactic and political in their content, with recurring themes of pan-Arab solidarity, anti-imperialism, and the glory of Arab history and heritage.[13] In the twenty-first century, an alternative comics scene has also emerged in many Middle Eastern countries, with notable anthologies such as *Samandal* in Lebanon and *Tok Tok* in Egypt.[14]

10. Swales 1990, 52.
11. Pilcher and Brooks 2005, 306; Otterbeck 2011, 137.
12. Douglas and Malti-Douglas 1994, 9.
13. Machin and van Leeuwen 2007, 36.
14. Bakhat 2013.

American superhero comics have been exported to the Middle East since the 1960s, particularly *Superman*. The Arab version has been adapted for a Middle Eastern audience: a high Arabic language has been used in the translation to increase its educational value, pages with didactic games and stories have been added, and older, less violent comics have been published, to suit the censors.[15] There had also been superheroes of Arab origin even before the advent of AK Comics and Teshkeel but mostly in the form of parody, as in the Algerian *Maachou, the Algerian Superman* (1983) by Menouar Merabtene or *Super Dabza* (1986) by Abd al-Karim Qadiri.[16]

AK Comics

In light of the above, AK Comics was an anomaly when it was founded in 2001/2002[17] by the Egyptian businessman Dr. Ayman Kandeel (whose initials gave the publishing house its name), with the aim of producing superhero comics that would promote peace and understanding in the Middle East.[18] AK Comics started publishing in 2003/2004, with four different titles collectively called *Middle East Heroes: Zein, Aya, Jalila*, and *Rakan*.[19] Even though – or maybe because – the comics were aimed at both Middle Eastern and Western audiences, there was an explicit desire to stay true to the Middle Eastern origin of the comics, as indicated by the following quote from a promotional pamphlet:

> Our mission is to fill the cultural and social gap that was created over the years between the West and East, by providing essentially needed role models – in our case, Middle Eastern superheroes. Ultimately, we are presenting to the entire world a strong and optimistic vision for a futuristic Middle East, void of war, violence and turmoil.[20]

15. Pilcher and Brooks 2005, 302; van Leeuwen and Suleiman 2010, 234.

16. Douglas and Malti-Douglas 1994, 180.

17. There are different datings for AK Comics's founding. The year 2001 comes from founder Ayman Kandeel's own webpage (*www.aymankandeel.com/about-ayman*). Van Leeuwen and Suleiman (2010, 237) instead propose 2002, which is also the year stated in the colophon in the English-language editions of AK Comics.

18. O'Loughlin 2005.

19. The first issues of the English editions are copyrighted for 2003, but seem to have been distributed in the early months of 2004. Brooks and Pilcher (2005) date the U.S. launch in 2004 and the release of the comic books in the Middle East in 2005. See also BBC World Service 2005. Throughout the chapter, references to *Zein* comic books below are to Nashar and Raapack 2006; *Aya* comic books to Vicino, Goldman, and Smith 2006; and *Jalila* comic books to Kandeel et al. 2006.

20. The promotional pamphlet was distributed at the 2005 San Diego Comic Con. See AK Comics 2005.

Kandeel, as founder, seems only to have been involved in the production of the initial comics, after which writing was left mostly to lesser-known U.S. scriptwriters and the art chores to studios based in South America. AK Comics were initially distributed in a number of Middle Eastern countries and the publisher twice attempted to enter the American comics market, first in 2003–2004 and again in 2005–2006. However, despite respectable, but not spectacular, sales figures during the second U.S. launch,[21] the fact that the whole enterprise comprised only about twenty issues in total, with all titles both ending in the middle of ongoing stories and including ads for further issues that were never published, indicates that it was not a resounding financial success. Ultimately, when all titles were cancelled in 2006, a statement was issued proclaiming that the publisher would focus on producing material directly for the graphic novel market.[22] Thus far, nothing has come of this.

Teshkeel

Teshkeel Media Group was founded in 2004/2005,[23] initially as a publisher of translated American superhero comics. But already by 2006, Teshkeel's endeavors had been refocused on the publication of its original superhero comic book, *The 99*. By 2008, *The 99* was outselling all but two of the translated comic books, and Teshkeel ceased distribution of other publishers' works the same year.[24] Teshkeel was founded by the psychologist Dr. Naif al-Mutawa, who has gained worldwide attention and acclaim for his efforts to create a cultural bridge between the Middle East and the Western world.[25] Al-Mutawa has had a didactic aim with his comics: "Islamic culture

21. Williams 2005.

22. See Economics 101 2006. This is a post on the blog *Friends of Jalila – AK Comics – Middle East Heroes*, dated November 20, 2006 and entitled *AK Comics – Graphics Novels!* Although published under the pseudonym "Economics 101," the intimate knowledge of the ins and outs of AK Comics indicates that the writer was in some way associated with the publisher.

23. As with the history of AK Comics, there are different years associated with the start of Teshkeel. Most sources claim that Teshkeel was founded in 2005, but some, like Deeb (2012), make 2004 the starting point. Al-Mutawa himself often recounts a story of how the idea for *The 99* came to him in a New York taxi in 2003 and that the need for better Muslim role models for his children became a concern for him after 9/11 in 2001 (al-Mutawa 2011).

24. Santo 2014, 682.

25. Clements and Gauvain 2014, 37; Deeb 2012, 392. Al-Mutawa has, among other things, been given the Eliot-Pearson Award for Excellence in Children's Media from Tufts University, the United Nations Alliance of Civilizations Market Place of Ideas Award, and the Schwab Foundation Social Entrepreneurship Award. He has also been named one of the 500 Most Influential Muslims by the Royal Islamic Strategic Studies Center four years in a row and, in 2013, *Gulf Business* included him among its "Top 100 Most Powerful Arabs."

and Islamic heritage have a lot to be proud and joyful about. *The 99* is about bringing those positive elements into global awareness."[26]

While al-Mutawa was officially involved as co-writer of almost all of *The 99*, he also enlisted high-profile U.S. scriptwriters like Fabian Nicieza and Stuart Moore, and he employed respected American artists such as John McCrea and Ron Wagner. Teshkeel's comic books seem to have been more successful than those of AK Comics, as the enterprise kept going from 2006 up until September 2013, when publication ceased after a run of over forty separate issues. However, in a 2010 TED Talk, al-Mutawa admitted that the comic books were losing money and that they were part of establishing an intellectual property, aimed at making money from other enterprises using *The 99* brand.[27]

Genre Analysis

For this chapter, I have studied all English-language issues published by the two publishers: twenty-three comic books from AK Comics[28] and forty-two from Teshkeel.[29] The comic books have been printed in the standard American format: they are about seventeen by twenty-six centimeters and contain between twenty-four and fifty pages in color. The majority of Teshkeel's comics have only been published digitally.[30]

Due to censorship issues in the Middle East, there are small differences

---

26. al-Mutawa 2008.

27. al-Mutawa 2010. For a thorough examination of Teshkeel Media Group from the perspective of brand marketing, see Santo 2014.

28. AK Comics published their comics twice in English, first in 2003–2004 and then restarting the enterprise in 2005–2006. I have tracked down all English language issues, as far as I can tell, and there do not seem to have been any issues only published in Arabic. Since there were fewer comics published in the first run, and since the comics were republished in the second run with different numbering and new covers, I have for the sake of clarity chosen to use the second-run numbering, from which I have located issues #1–6 of *Aya, Jalila,* and *Rakan,* and issues #1–5 of *Zein.*

29. Teshkeel published a total of 36 regular, numbered issues of *The 99,* but also 5 slightly longer (50 pages) "specials" and an "origin" issue, making for a total of 42 issues. All issues were published in both in an English and an Arabic version. The comics were initially printed as physical copies, but Teshkeel shifted to digital-only publication after seven issues. As this happened, it seems that the first printed issue was replaced by two new issues, making the old issue two the new issue three, and so on. For the sake of clarity, I have used the digital numbering, which represents the only complete run of *The 99.*

30. The four #1s of the English-language AK Comics re-launch were, for some reason, published in a slightly smaller format, with sturdier covers. This deviation from the American standard format was quickly abandoned, presumably to fit into existing shelving systems in the comic shops.

in the artwork of the Arab- and English-language editions of the AK Comics.[31] The written text, however, differs widely between the two, which have been adapted for their respective audiences. As a comparative study of the different versions of an issue of *Zein* indicates, the tone was different between the formal Arabic and the more informal English language, but the English adaptations also shifted focus somewhat towards a more Orientalist view. "Colonizers," for instance, became "imperialists," and "their largest colonies" became "their most cherished of imperial possessions."[32] Teshkeel's comics seem to be visually identical in the English and the Arabic editions. The translations seem to have been fairly direct as well, having been done from English to Arabic by a third-party translator as al-Mutawa and his main co-writer Fabian Nicieza originally worked in English.[33]

Figure 1: Part of the material studied. Photo: Fredrik Strömberg.

31. Williams 2005
32. van Leeuwen and Suleiman 2010, 237.
33. Clements and Gauvain 2014, 60.

The first question concerning this material was whether the comics actually belong in the superhero genre. Both publishers advertise them as such, but are they according to the conventions established earlier? To answer this, I analyzed four sample comics from each publisher: the first issue of each of AK Comics title and the first four regular issues of *The 99*.

The comics from AK Comics were clearly created to be close in form and content to their American counterparts. Three of the titles (*Aya, Jalila,* and *Zein*) contained all eight conventions, making it obvious that they belonged within the genre. *Rakan,* based on the archetype of the massive, sword-wielding barbarian made famous by *Conan the Barbarian,* did not feature a secret identity or a clear visual branding through a costume, nor was it set in the contemporary world. Even though this title has been presented as a superhero comic, presumably to fit in with the other three in marketing, it more correctly belongs within the sword-and-sorcery comics genre.[34] Thus, *Rakan* was excluded from further analysis here. *The 99* was also evidently modeled on the American superhero genre. In one sense, it can also be said to contain all eight conventions. Two of the conventions, however, were clearly adapted: violent clashes were often brief or avoided altogether and the sexualization of the heroes was almost non-existent, especially for the female heroes.

Based on these initial results, I decided to go forward with a complete analysis of all issues of *Aya, Jalila, Zein*, and *The 99*, analyzing more closely how the eight conventions have been treated, focusing especially on the two conventions that seems to separate the comics by AK Comics from those by Teshkeel, i.e. violence and sexualization.

Superhuman Abilities

The first and most basic convention of the superhero genre is that of superhuman abilities. These can be acquired through magic, science, or a combination of both, but they can also come from highly developed physical and/or mental skills, often attained through arduous training.[35] Supervillains almost always also have superhuman abilities, both allowing them to challenge the superheroes on a figurative "level playing field" and letting the scriptwriters keep suspension high issue after issue, as these are often continuous, serialized stories.

The three heroes from AK Comics all have archetypal superhero abilities, though. In fact, the basic ideas for the titles were more or less openly copied either from iconic American heroes or the archetypes from which they

34. Cf. Duncan and Smith 2009, 216.
35. Coogan, 2010, 607.

have risen: *Aya* was based on the lone vigilante/detective, most famously portrayed in Batman, and has trained herself to her seemingly superhuman proficiencies; *Jalila* was based on the strong, godlike, flying superheroine, most prominently embodied by *Wonder Woman*; and *Zein* is a mix of the god-like archetype of the supreme superhero (Superman) and the self-taught detective (Batman).

The heroes of *The 99* have more specific abilities, many of which seem less easy to connect to the traits of earlier superhero characters. There are heroes whose abilities are based on divine attributes and include the power to "turn chaos into order," to "track any object or pinpoint any location," to "chemically induce love and good feelings into a person's brain," to "instill mercy in other people," or to "turn discrimination back on the offending party."[36] These abilities, which might seem too specific or even too flimsy for a traditional U.S. superhero, have been chosen because one of the main ideas of *The 99* is teamwork.[37] A major narrative device is that the heroes are supposed to form "triads" where they link together, three at a time, enhancing each other's abilities. The powers of each hero thus becomes more or less a tool for their leader Dr. Ramzi, who composes each triad, based on the assignment that he wishes to send them on.

Personal Moral Codes

Why does the superhero keep fighting injustice instead of leading a normal life or even harnessing the extraordinary abilities for personal gain? There needs to be a believable motivation for heroic action within the narrative. This is where the personal moral code is introduced both as a driving force for the hero within the diegesis and as a key for the reader in understanding the hero's motivations. The moral codes of superheroes stem from the general perception of what it means to be a hero, i.e. to courageously help others both without any expectation of a reward and, at times, at great personal risk. Even though many variations on this theme do exist based on different cultures, these general traits still seem to be universal.[38]

The heroes of AK Comics all certainly have similar and, for the superhero genre, generic personal moral codes. Aya is determined to defend the innocent and fight crime in her hometown; Jalila wants to do the same in "The City of All Faiths"; and Zein sees himself as the last defender of the ancient land of Egypt. Their underlying reasons are not explained extensively

36. al-Mutawa, Moore, Brigman, and Richardson 2011.
37. al-Mutawa 2007b, 39.
38. Jayawickreme and Di Stefano 2012, 167.

in their respective origin stories, however, nor given any depth in the ongoing stories. The most engaging explanation for a hero's actions belongs to Aya, who wants to prevent more murders like that of her own father, which is copied more or less directly from *Batman*.

The creator of *The 99*, al-Mutawa, has explicitly stated that the stories and the characters should be based on universal values, and most of The 99 have moral codes that adhere to the generic principle of the hero, i.e. that they wish to help others both seemingly without any kind of reward and at personal risk. What sets *The 99* apart is that the heroes' prevailing moral compass is provided by their leader and mentor Dr. Ramzi, who is a psychologist (just like *The 99* creator al-Mutawa) and the founder of the 99 Steps foundation, a non-profit organization with the goal of "bringing hope and assistance to those people who need it the most."[39] He seeks out young adults who have been given powers by magical stones and then convinces them to use their newfound abilities to work for a world at peace.[40] It is not always explained how, or even if, the members of The 99 actually accept Dr. Ramzi's vision, aside from assertions that he is pure of heart.[41] The new heroes all simply leave their former lives, becoming more content with themselves and their situations, and unquestioningly throw themselves into the battles that Dr. Ramzi directs them towards. This goes against the conventions of the U.S. superhero genre, as the moral code that drives a superhero is usually personal and more specific.

A more communal sense of moral obligation is not a completely new idea in superhero comics. There is, for instance, a resemblance to Marvel's *X-Men* comics, which feature mostly young superheroes assembling around their self-appointed leader Professor Xavier, who acts as their moral compass. That the writers were aware of this comparison is made likely in the story "The Stinging Tree: Part One,"[42] where Rughal, the main villain of the series, is presented as reformed and starting an alternative school for young heroes. The resemblance is evident to the classic dichotomy in the pages of *X-Men* between the two leaders/mentors, the altruistic Professor Xavier and the more aggressive, sometimes villainous, sometimes heroic Magneto, who has been shown in several storylines to be reformed, even taking on the role of leader for other groups of young mutants.

---

39. al-Mutawa, Moore, Brigman, and Richardson 2011, 7.
40. *The 99* #7, 26. For this and future references to the ongoing series, see al-Mutawa et al. 2006–2013.
41. *The 99* #1, 30.
42. *The 99* #28.

Figure 2: The villain Rughal announces his intention to become a second mentor/leader of the young heroes. From *The 99* #28, p. 6. © Teshkeel Media Group 2011.

Origin Stories

Ever since Superman first appeared, most superhero comics somewhere contain an origin story that explains the hero's abilities and moral code. Communications scholars Randy Duncan and Matthew J. Smith even go so far as to claim that the origin story is the only recurring narrative pattern of the whole genre.[43]

In all the AK Comics titles, the origin stories are printed on the inside of the front covers to make sure that the reader never forgets the background story of the hero in question. These stories show clear inspiration from

43. Duncan and Smith 2009, 231.

American superheroes. Almost completely copying Batman's origin story, Aya is said to have been "traumatized when her father was shot in front of her" and has since devoted her life to "mastering all forms of martial arts, forensic techniques and other detective skills" in order to "defend the weak and innocent."[44] Zein is described as the last descendant of an ancient dynasty who was sent by his father in a specially designed vessel from a doomed civilization into the present to be the designated defender of their land in the future. The similarities to Superman's origin story are obvious, even though Superman was sent across space and Zein across time.[45] Jalila is a nuclear scientist who gains her powers in a nuclear blast, which mirrors the origin story of Marvel Comics's Hulk. But the fact that her parents, who died in the blast, were nuclear physicists who devoted their lives to protect their city through their work is an original variation and also the reason why Jalila decides to follow in their footsteps and to use her powers to protect the city and its inhabitants. None of these stories seem to resonate explicitly with the religious affiliations of the heroes, who, although this was never overtly revealed in the comics, were supposed to be adherents of different monotheistic religions.[46]

Conversely, the background story of *The 99* is different from that of most American superhero comics. The series has an overarching origin, which is retold several times. It is the story of ninety-nine stones that have been imbued with the collected wisdom of ancient Arab culture. When they come in contact with worthy persons, stated as "the right personality and inclination, plus an essentially pure heart"[47] – the latter a reference to the concept in Islam of the heart as the essence of an individual, where a sense of right and of faith resides – the so-called Noor Stones imbue them with special powers. These stones also epitomize the ninety-nine qualities of Allah, making the heroes embodiments of Allah's names. This is not unprecedented, as it can be said to be in line with the Sufi concept of *al-takhalluq bi-asma' Allah*, i.e. that by striving to embody the names of God, the Sufi manifests the traits of the names.[48] Still, it is not something that is unproblematic within Islam where it can be seen as idolatry. Al-Mutawa made sure to consult with religious scholars before creating *The 99,* but he has still been attacked and has even had a fatwa leveled against him from the Grand Mufti of Saudi Arabia, specifically based on the naming of the heroes.[49]

Still, al-Mutawa did give each of his heroes names that reflects the

44. Daniels 2004a, 34.
45. Daniels 2004b, 38.
46. O'Loughlin 2005.
47. al-Mutawa, Moore, Brigman, and Richardson 2011, 44.
48. Clements and Gauvain 2014, 63.
49. al-Mutawa 2014.

qualities of Allah. Some are taken directly from the Qur'an, such as the su-per-strong Jabbar, who gets his name from *al-jabbar* meaning "irresistible." The name Sami, from *al-samiʿ* meaning "listener," is given to a character with superhuman hearing. Other names are slightly adapted, such as Widad, a character who has the power to fill others with love, the name coming from *al-wadud*, meaning "full of love and kindness" – or Noora, a character who can see the light inside other people, based on *al-noor* meaning "light."[50]

In addition, all of The 99 have individual origin stories. Throughout almost the entire series, one new hero is introduced in every issue, mak-ing each issue an origin story. These stories are often based on trauma. The young people who are empowered by the Noor Stones have, for example, trodden on land mines, been kidnapped, or experienced traffic accidents. This, as observed by comics artist Paul Chadwick, is in line with many U.S. superheroes; as he has noted, the origin stories that resonate most with readers are those that "mine the vein of trauma."[51] But it is also a way for the writers of *The 99* to connect with the everyday lives of readers in the Middle East, where landmines, kidnapping, and traffic accidents can be common in the daily news.[52]

Visual Branding

The clear visual branding of each hero has been a mainstay since the early days of superhero comics, when the printing processes available to com-ic book publishers necessitated the use of simple designs that would both make the most of four-color printing and ensure that the images were leg-ible despite numerous misprints.[53] While printing techniques have vastly improved, most superheroes still have colorful, iconic costumes, designed to symbolize their identities and powers.

AK Comics's heroes have traditional, tight-fitting, brightly colored, spandex-like superhero costumes. Jalila, for instance, wears a skintight blue costume with gold details. This, combined with long, flowing black hair and the ability to fly, makes her resemble Wonder Woman (who is dressed in a blue and red costume with gold details), although Jalila's body is compara-tively more covered due to censorship issues in the Middle East.[54]

The 99 are also easily discernable through color schemes and symbolic attire, although their costumes are less skintight spandex and more like or-

---

50. Ali 2006, 135, 535, 876, 1450.
51. Duncan and Smith 2009, 232.
52. Deeb 2012, 400.
53. Clark 2014, 59.
54. Williams 2005.

dinary, though individualized, clothes. The first hero in *The 99*, Jabbar, is one of the few who actually has a body-hugging spandex costume, making him stand out among later additions to the team.

Secret Identity

The secret identity is a well-established convention of the superhero genre, again harking back to Superman and his alter ego, the timid, bespectacled Clark Kent. The reason given within the diegesis is often that the superheroes need to protect their friends and families from being attacked by supervillain enemies. The secret identity also gives writers and artists a chance to contrast superhuman abilities and personas with a more mundane existence and to provide readers a more plausible identification object.[55] Although this specific convention has somewhat fallen out of style recently (e.g. Captain America, Iron Man, Robin), it remains a useful generic marker.

The AK Comics superheroes have traditional secret identities. Jalila is a nuclear scientist, just as Bruce Banner is in *The Incredible Hulk*; Aya is a law student, seemingly combining backgrounds from *Spider-Man* and *Daredevil*; and Zein is a university professor. Little is made of these secret identities, however, with the exception of Jalila who is shown to have a brother who has been drawn into an organization run by the villains. Like Clark Kent, Jalila seems to be able to show up in her superhero costume without any mask and still not be recognized, not even by her own brother. She wears glasses at work, but not in private, making her look similar both in and out of costume. The only other difference is that she wears her hair in a ponytail when she is in her civilian identity as Ansam Dajani. The fact that no one recognizes her is consistent with how Superman can don a pair of glasses and not be recognized as Clark Kent within the DC Universe as that storyworld's most recognizable superhero.

In *The 99*, all heroes initially also have secret identities, but this is problematized and discussed within the story. Initially, the heroes use secret identities for protection, as they are often underage, and Dr. Ramzi's role as mentor includes him giving them superhero names and advising them to keep a secret identity. In the seventh issue, "Hiding in Plain Sight,"[56] the whole story is devoted to Dr. Ramzi discussing with the heroes' parents if and how to reveal their existence to the world. In the end, they are revealed at a press conference, but with masks on.

In the later story "Masks," after experiencing people's fear of them, the heroes rebel and demand to be allowed to work without secret identities and

55. Duncan and Smith 2009, 228.
56. *The 99 #7*.

masks.[57] This story can be read as an allegorical tale of the heroes growing up and breaking free from their surrogate parent Dr. Ramzi, but it is also indicative of the self-reflective, self-aware relationship that the writers of *The 99* have to the superhero genre. Having a secret identity is so integral to the idea of superheroes that when the characters in *The 99* discard their masks, the fact that it goes against the constraints of the genre adds emphasis to the story's message of openness and international solidarity.

Figure 3: From the story "Masks" (The 99 #17, p. 27). © Teshkeel Media Group 2009.

Violent Clashes

The superhero genre has a built-in narrative tension that pits hero against villain – all of whom possess extraordinary abilities – and they inevitably

57. *The 99* #17.

end up fighting each other physically. This violence has often inspired critique of superhero comics, a debate that has existed almost as long as the genre itself.[58] The AK Comics titles very much adhere to this convention. Almost all of the stories follow a fixed narrative system based on a classical three-act structure, where the first two-thirds of an issue are used as a set-up for a fight between hero and villain, which then goes on for between three and seven pages, out of a total of twenty-four. That is not to say that there is no violence in the first two thirds, but the final third is often one uninterrupted fight scene. Examples of this can be found in, for instance, *Aya* #5, where the climactic battle between Aya and a supervillain group covers pages 9 through 20; in *Jalila* #3, where Jalila fights a group of terrorists on pages 16 through 22; or in *Zein* #3, where Zein battles the villain Ammit on pages 15 through 21.

Teshkeel's balance of clashes is very different, and clearly based on al-Mutawa's thoughts that violence is to be avoided at almost all cost.[59] In *The 99*, much thought has been put into figuring out non-violent solutions to stages in the narrative where, traditionally, a fight between hero and villain would have erupted. Some such solutions include having the hero who is all about brawn, Jabbar, hit the ground, not the villain, thus making the opponent fall down and lose consciousness;[60] having Noora shine a light so bright that the villains are blinded and the heroes can run away;[61] and having Mumita destroy the villains' escape vehicle instead of fighting them.[62]

The theme of non-violence is built into *The 99* throughout the whole series, including the creation of the Noor Stones, said to have taken place during the Mongols' ransacking of Baghdad in 1258. In contrasting the senseless violence, including the destruction of the city's famous library, with the valiant efforts of the librarians who save all the knowledge through magic into the Noor Stones, al-Mutawa not only transmits the idea of the importance of knowledge but also that only the ignorant who do not know any better engage in violence. At the same time he connects this to a pivotal moment in Arab history, a story that is taught to most young Muslims in the Middle East.[63]

This non-violence theme equally includes the villains, who use things like knockout gas and sound to incapacitate the heroes.[64] But they also run

58. Cf. Beaty 2005, 114.
59. al-Mutawa 2007a, 39.
60. *The 99* #6, 25.
61. *The 99* #14, 11.
62. *The 99* #24, 15.
63. Deeb 2012, 394.
64. In *The 99* #14, 10; #23, 23.

Figure 4: A two-page spread from *Aya* #5 (p. 12–13), part of a longer fight scene between the heroine and a group of super villains. © AK Comics 2006.

away instead of fighting or simply remove the heroes' Noor Stones and thus their powers.[65] Much is done in order to win without ever throwing a punch. Several times there are generic build-ups to fights between a group of heroes and a group of villains, only to end up with both teams standing around glaring at each other.[66]

Figure 5: Image from *The 99* #33, p. 27. © Teshkeel Media Group 2013.

There is an awareness of this deviation from the convention of the genre in the diegesis. In the story "House Party: Part One," near the end of the series, a character whose superpower is fighting enemies and destroying things, Mumita – called "The Destroyer" – complains that during her last three missions she has been held back and therefore been "fighting against

65. *The 99* #24, 7; *The 99* #12, 3.
66. E.g. *The 99* #12, #15, and #24.

my nature." This is used as as the starting point of a story that introduces the hero Rahima the Merciful, who, when joined up with Mumita's power, can solve problems without the use of violence.[67]

Even in the cross-over series *JLA/The 99*, the Justice League of America is made to play along with The 99's rules of the genre. There is one evident exception to the non-violence rule, in *The 99 Special: Sacrifice*, where Jabbar solves a problem with violence for the first time, and Mumita actually hits the villains, Arab mercenaries, repeatedly and very graphically.[68] These scenes contain more violence than in all other issues put together, which could owe to this being the only issue not officially co-written by al-Mutawa.

Sexualization of the Heroes

Sexualization of the heroes, and in some cases the villains, is a long-standing convention of the superhero genre, harking back to the tight spandex costume of Superman and the revealing costume of Wonder Woman. Over decades, the bodies of superheroes, male and female, have become ever more exaggerated, and the costumes have revealed more and more. Or, as cultural theorist Scott Bukatman writes: "superhero bodies have always been naked bodies exhibited to a very public gaze."[69]

This convention is evident in the AK Comics titles, mostly the two featuring female heroes. Both Aya and Jalila have costumes that cover more of their bodies than is customary in U.S. superhero comics, where superheroines often sport costumes with bare arms and legs, as well as exposed cleavages. This was done to appease censors in the Middle East,[70] but both AK Comics superheroines nonetheless wear skin-tight, body-hugging costumes which reveal more than they hide. And they are frequently drawn in poses that focus the reader's attention to their breasts, buttocks, and crotches. Both superheroines are also often drawn with impossible combinations of thin waists and big, seemingly weightless breasts.

In *The 99*, all female characters have costumes that cover their bodies, they have more normal physiques, and there are no poses that draw particular attention to the bodies of the heroes. As in the titles from AK Comics, there are no overt references to the religious affiliation of the characters in *The 99*, but many female characters wear different variations of the veil, from the assistant to Dr. Ramzi, Miss Ibrahim, who wears a modern veil that

---

67. *The 99* #33.
68. al-Mutawa et al. 2007, 16, 34–38.
69. Bukatman 2013, 190.
70. Williams 2005.

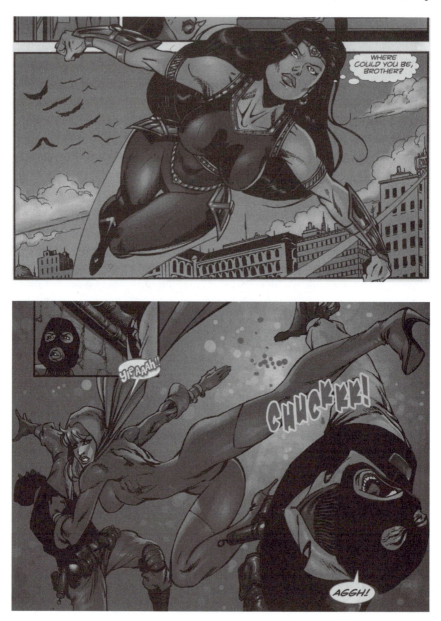

Figure 6: Two examples of the sexualization of heroes, from *Jalila* #1, p. 12 and *Aya* #2, p. 18. © AK Comics 2006.

Figure 7: Examples of the less sexualized heroes of The 99. From *The 99 Special: Beginnings*, p.1.
© Teshkeel Media Group 2007.

shows part of her hair and goes with a modern business suit,[71] to the super-hero Batina the Hidden, who wears a full *abaya* with *niqab*. Batina does reveal her face when among friends,[72] though, and many of the female characters do not wear any veil. The heroes' clothing and costumes adhere to the Islamic code of sobriety and modesty, while at the same time signaling their unique personal and superhero qualities.[73]

Again, there is a self-reflexivity about this issue within the diegesis. In the story "Problem Solving,"[74] two of the young heroes are seen looking into a shop window with quite revealing clothes:

Figure 8: From *The 99* #3, p. 14. © Teshkeel Media Group 2007.

Also worth noting in this connection is that, in comparison to equivalent American comics like *the X-Men*, there is a marked absence of love affairs between the young heroes gathered together.

An Alternative Version of the World

Most superhero stories are set in an alternative version of the reader's world. Locating these fantastical stories within a more mundane, easily recognizable setting makes the comics relevant, relatively accessible, and understandable to the readers, but it also provides a familiar setting against which to contrast the extraordinary personas and powers of the superheroes and supervillains.

AK Comics set all three of its titles in a version of the Middle East where the confrontations between Jewish, Christian, and Muslim forces have come to an end, and people live in peace. The text that can be found on the inside covers of all titles proclaims that their shared diegesis is a world "after the 55 year war," but the setting looks like it is supposed to be the contemporary Middle East. Thus, AK Comics are not set in a science fiction-like future but

71. *The 99* #1, 36.
72. al-Mutawa et al. 2011, 47.
73. Edwin 2012, 195.
74. *The 99* #3.

simply an alternative version of the reader's contemporary reality, which is consistent with the genre convention.

Two of the titles are set in Egypt, where the comics were produced. Zein is placed in a version of Cairo, as indicated by frequent visuals of the nearby Pyramids of Giza. Aya is situated in "Alexia" (Alexandria), Egypt's second-largest city, presumably so that the two heroes' stories can be kept separate. This mirrors the way two of the oldest superheroes, Superman and Batman, have been associated with two different cities, Metropolis and Gotham City, respectively, within the diegesis of the DC Universe. Then there is Jalila, who operates in and around Jerusalem, in the locale called "City of All Faiths." This is the most political of the three titles, with mentions of things like the opposing forces of the "United Liberation Force" (PLO) and the "Xenox Brigade" (the Israeli armed forces) and Dimondona, a thinly disguised reference to Israel's probable nuclear weapons facility at Dimona.

Despite setting the comics in geographical areas that are supposed to resonate with readers in the Middle East, it is evident that the artists were not from the Middle East themselves, as many characters look like traditional characters from U.S. superhero comics. In *Jalila* #4, for instance, there is a bank robbery scene, where the innocent bystanders are fair-haired, while the robbers all seem to be dark-haired,[75] something that in a comic made in the U.S. or Europe at the same time would probably have been deemed racist even though it was more common earlier on in comics history.[76]

Image 9: From *Jalila* #4, p. 16. © AK Comics 2006.

In *Zein*, references to ancient Egyptian culture such as the pyramids and the Sphinx are abundant, but in scenes from the diegetic Cairo, no veils are shown on the women, despite the fact that many in Egypt do cover their

75. *Jalila* #4, 16.
76. Lund 2013, 199.

heads.[77] The opening scene of *Zein* #3 looks like it was copied from an *Indiana Jones* film, complete with a Westerner in a fedora excavating an old gravesite in Egypt, a scene that in a U.S. comic book would most likely be considered Orientalist.

There is a greater diversity of locations in The 99's alternative version of our world. The heroes travel the world on missions, with the help of a team member who can teleport himself and others. Many of these missions are in the Middle East, but The 99 are headquartered in Paris for the main part of the series and, later, move to Spain for the last few issues. This geographic diversity and the idea that each of The 99 comes from a different country is, of course, good for a series that is set to have an international appeal,[78] but it is not new. Both Marvel and DC, the two big U.S. superhero publishers, have been doing this for years, albeit not as deftly as it is done in *The 99*. The American publishers' international heroes have often been stereotypes, made to represent their whole country, with costumes made out of the colors of their country's flag, such as the heroine Sabra, who wears a version of the flag of Israel. *The 99*'s writers and artists have, mostly, avoided these particular stereotypes.

Tyranny of Genre?

This chapter shows that AK Comics and Teshkeel have consistently applied intrinsically different methods in their efforts to use the American superhero genre in the Middle East. It is evident that the two genre conventions that gave these publishers the greatest problems were those of violence and sexualization.

Censorship is an ever-present force in many Middle Eastern countries, both in the shape of official, governmental censorship and in the risk of having a publication banned by various religious groups for not complying with their rules. This also applies to comics, which are mostly viewed as culture for children and young adults and can be censored for containing sexually implicit or explicit content, for being too violent, or for not being educational enough.[79]

Despite this, AK Comics decided to stay true to the conventions, with revealing costumes and recurring bouts between superheroes and supervillains aplenty. Particularly the sexualization seems to have clashed too much with Islamic principles in the Middle East and, even though AK Comics had the comics redrawn with more modest costumes after critique from the cen-

---

77. Slackman 2007.

78. Meier 2013, 187.

79. Clements and Gauvain 2014, 60; Douglas and Malti-Douglas 1994, 5; van Leeuwen and Suleiman 2010, 234; Zitawi 2008, 143.

sors, both titles featuring female heroes were banned from sale in several Middle Eastern countries.[80]

Teshkeel, perhaps with the benefit of hindsight from starting a few years later, chose a different approach, excluding violence and letting the superheroes, male and female, wear less tight-fitting costumes. The more modest, though still varied costumes conform to a modern-day feminist reading of the Qur'an, where the egalitarian message is stressed while Islamic traditions remain respected.[81] The restrictive view on the use of violence is in line with the interpretations of the Qur'an that can be found in what social scientist Mohammed Abu-Nimer calls "war and peace" studies within Islam, i.e. that violence should be heavily restricted and can only be justified in defense.[82]

These adjustments of the genre meant that the comics from Teshkeel were more sedate, making it possible for them to be more acceptable in the Middle East, but they were at the same time perceived as less exciting compared to American superhero comics. Looking at the way AK Comics and Teshkeel have treated *all* of the conventions of the superhero genre, it becomes evident that there is more to it than just how sexualization and violence can be treated in popular culture for young readers, due to cultural differences between the U.S. and the Middle East. Just as American superhero comics can be said to resonate with Jewish and Christian culture, so do the stories from AK Comics and Teshkeel Comics resonate with Islamic principles in the Arab culture.[83]

The term "tyranny of genre" was introduced by Richard M. Coe to describe the creative constraints that can be felt when working within a defined genre.[84] Staying close to the tradition of a certain genre – using most or all of its conventions – can generate strong genre identification. Using fewer conventions will, conversely, result in weak or ambiguous genre identification.[85] Simply using all the conventions of the superhero genre does not inevitably make for interesting comics, however, and tedious repetition often does not attract an audience. There needs to be a certain amount of adaptation of the genre, a manipulation of the conventions, in order to excite readers.[86] This leads to an extended definition of the "tyranny of genre," that the use of a certain genre demands a trade-off between conservative applications and innovative transformations of generic conventions. Again,

80. Pilcher and Brooks 2005, 307; Williams 2005.
81. Edwin 2011, 195.
82. Abu-Nimer 2000–2001, 223.
83. Otterbeck 2011, 138.
84. Coe 2005, 188.
85. Schauber and Spolsky 1981.
86. Fishelov 2010, 36; Neale 1980, 50.

the comics from AK Comics and Teshkeel show different ways of handling this balancing act.

AK Comics stayed true to all of the conventions of superhero comics, going so far as to copy most of the characteristics for their characters from well-known American counterparts, as well as imitating drawing styles and storytelling techniques. This meant that the only difference between their comics and the ones published in the U.S. was that the AK Comics's stories were set in the Middle East. The content only superficially mirrored the Middle Eastern origin, despite the openly stated intent of doing the exact opposite. This resulted in weak copies of American superhero comics, which did not excite readers in either the Middle East or in the U.S.

Teshkeel chose a largely different method and, to a greater or lesser degree, adapted almost all of the conventions. Elimination of violence and significantly downplaying the sexualization of the heroes were the major adaptations. But other changes were made, such as the use of superpowers that were designed to fit into a group rather than work independently, and the heroes' communal moral code also radically changed the way the stories in *The 99* were told, as compared to their American counterparts. The latter can be referred back to the fact that all of The 99 have been chosen to be the embodiment of Allah's named attributes, which unites them despite differences in age, nationality, and cultural backgrounds.[87] This can also be seen as a reference to the *umma*, the Islamic community all over the world, which fits in with the fact that all The 99 heroes are from different countries.

This meant that Teshkeel, through adaptation, really did create something new. By adapting almost all of the conventions, however, they changed so much that their comics moved closer to the genre of information comics, comics "designed to educate, inform, or teach the reader something."[88] This is consistent with the way comics made in the Middle East are often viewed, as didactic vessels intended to convey information for young readers. When moving towards the more educational information genre, *The 99* lost some of the appeal of the original genre, risking disappointment from readers expecting more traditional superhero comics.

So, do genres travel geographically and/or culturally? The material studied indicates that the conventions of the superhero genre are too immersed in U.S. culture to be directly appropriated into a Middle Eastern setting without adapting the conventions, and in doing so, risk straying too far from the genre's core. This could lead to the creation of a new genre, but does not seem to have done so yet.

87. Edwin 2012, 175.
88. Caldwell 2012.

Works Cited

Abu-Nimer, M. 2000–2001. "A Framework for Nonviolence and Peacebuilding in Islam." *Journal of Law and Religion* 1/2 (15): 217–265.

AK Comics. 2005. *AK Comics: Middle East Heroes.* Cairo.

Ali, A.Y. 2006. *The Meaning of the Holy Qur'an.* Beltsville.

al-Mutawa, N. 2007a. Naif's Notes. In *The 99* #6. Safat: Teshkeel.

——. 2007b. Naif's Notes. In *The 99* #8. Safat.

——. 2008. Naif's Notes. In *The 99* #12. Safat.

——. 2010. "Superheroes Inspired by Islam. *TED.* https://www.ted.com/talks/naif_al_mutawa_superheroes_inspired_by_islam.

——. 2011. Naif's Notes. In *The 99* #20. Safat: Teshkeel.

——. (2014). "The Latest Challenge of 'The 99' Superheroes Is Tackling a Fatwa." *The National,* April 26. http://www.thenational.ae/thenationalconversation/comment/the-latest-challenge-of-the-99-superheroes-is-tackling-a-fatwa.

al-Mutawa, N., S. Moore, J. Brigman, and R. Richardson. 2011. *The 99 Special: Beginnings.* Safat.

al-Mutawa, N., F. Nicieza, J. McCrea, S. Yeowell, J. Hodgkins, S. Moore, R. Wagner, S. Parsons, J. Rubinstein, J. Dennis, J. Brigman, K. Justice, J. Marzan Jr., J. Davies, L. Bradley, and R. Richardson. 2006–2013. *The 99* #1-33. New York.

al-Mutawa, N., F. Nicieza, S. Moore, P. Diaz, C. Schons, S. Yeowell, R. Wagner, J. Rubinstein, P. Diaz, C. Schons, S. Yeowell, K. Kobasic, D Hudson, M. Buckingham, and S. Buccellato. 2007. *The 99 Special: Sacrifice.* New York.

Avery-Natale, E. 2013. "An Analysis of Embodiment Amon Six Superheroes in DC Comics." *Social Thought and Research* 32: 71–106.

BBC World Service. 2005. "Middle East gets first superheroes." *BBC,* March 7. http://news.bbc.co.uk/2/hi/middle_east/4312547.stm.

Bakhat, I. 2013. "Arab Comic Strips Experiencing Their Own Spring." *swissinfo.ch,* March 28. http://www.swissinfo.ch/directdemocracy/picture-power_arab-comic-strips-experience-their-own-spring/35337848.

Beaty, B. 2005. *Fredric Wertham and the Critique of Mass Culture.* Jackson, MS.

Brook, W. 2013. "Fandom and Authorship." In *The Superhero Reader,* edited by C. Hatfield, J. Heer, and K. Worcester, 170–198. Jackson, MS.

Bukatman, S. 2013. "A Song of the Urban Superhero." In *The Superhero Reader,* edited by C. Hatfield, J. Heer, and K. Worcester, 170–198. Jackson, MS.

Caldwell, J. 2012. "Information Comics: An Overview (pp. 1–7)." Presented at the Professional Communication Conference (IPCC 2012).

Cawelti, J. 2014. *Adventure, Mystery, and Romance: Formula Stories as Art and Popular Culture*. Chicago.

Clark, M. J. 2014. "From Motion Line to Motion Blur: The Integration of Digital Coloring in the Superhero Comic Book." In *Superhero Synergies: Comic Book Characters Go Digital*, edited by J. N. Gilmore, and M. Stork, 57–76. Lanham, MD.

Clements, J. and R. Gauvain. 2014. "The Marvel of Islam: Reconciling Muslim Epistemologies Through a new Islamic Origin Saga in Naif al-Mutawa's *The 99.*" *Journal of Religion and Popular Culture* 26 (1): 36–71.

Coe, R. M. 2005. "An Arousing and Fulfilment of Desires: The Rhetoric of Genre in the Process Era-and Beyond." In *Genre in the New Rhetoric: Critical Perspectives on Literacy and Education*, edited by A. Freedman, and P. Medway, 181–190. London.

Coogan, P. 2010. Superheroes. In *Encyclopedia of Comic Books and Graphic Novels*, edited by M. K. Booker, vol. 2, 605–613. Santa Barbara.

Daniels, L. 2004a. *Batman: The Complete History*. San Francisco.

———. 2004b. *Superman: The Complete History*. San Francisco.

Deeb, M.-J. 2012. "*The 99*: Superhero Comic Books from the Arab World." *Comparative Studies of South Asia, Africa and the Middle East* 32 (2): 391–407.

Douglas, A. and F. Malti-Douglas. 1994. *Arab Comic Strips: Politics of an Emerging Mass Culture*. Bloomington, IN.

Duncan, R. and M. J. Smith. 2009. *The Power of Comics: History, Form and Culture*. New York.

Economics 101. 2006. "AK Comics – Graphic Novels!, November 20." http://ak-comics.blogspot.com/2006/11/ak-comics-graphic-novels.html.

Edwin, S. 2012. "Islam's Trojan Horse: Battling Perceptions of Muslim Women in *The 99.*" *Journal of Graphic Novels and Comics* 3 (2): 171–199.

Fishelov, D. 2010. *Metaphors of Genre: The Role of Analogies in Genre Theory*. University Park, PA.

Jayawickreme, E. and P. Di Stefano. 2012. "How Can We Study Heroism? Integrating Persons, Situations and Communities." *Political Psychology* 1 (33): 165–178.

Kandeel, A., A. Goldman, C. Lopes, F. Perzich, T. Moore, Z. Hennesey, R. Al-burquerque. 2006. *Jalila #1-6*. Giza.

Klock, Geoff. 2002. *How to Read Superhero Comics and Why*. New York.

Lavandier, Y. 2005. *Writing Drama; a Comprehensive Guide for Playwrights and Scriptwriters*. Paris.

Lewis, A. . 2014. "Whither the Muslim Superhero?" *ISLAMICommentary,*

June 3. http://islamicommentary.org/2014/06/whither-the-muslim-superhero.

Lund, M. 2013. *Rethinking the Jewish-Comics Connection*. Lund.

Machin, D. and T. van Leeuwen. 2007. *Global Media Discourse: A Critical Introduction*. London.

McLain, K. 2009. *India's Immortal Comic Books: Gods, Kings, and Other Heroes*. Bloomington, IN.

Meier, S. 2013. "Truth, Justice, and the Islamic Way: Conceiving the Cosmopolitan Muslim Superhero in *The 99*." In *Transnational Perspective on Graphic Narratives: Comics at the Crossroads*, edited by D. Stein, S. Denson, and C. Meyer, 181–193. London.

Nashar, M. el and J. Raapack. 2006. *Zein #1-5*. Giza.

Neale, S. 1980. *Genre*. London.

O'Loughlin, E. 2005. "Middle East's First Superheroes Out to Change Their World." *Sydney Morning Herald*, September 24. http://www.smh.com.au/news/world/middle-easts-first-superheroes-out-to-change-their-world/2005/09/23/1126982230864.html?from=moreStories.

Otterbeck, J. 2011. "Superhjältar med islamsk klangbotten." In *Perspektiv på islam: En vänbok till Christer Hedin*, edited by S. Olsson and S. Sorgenfrei, 137–143. Stockholm.

Pilcher, T., and B. Brooks. 2005. *The Essential Guide to World Comics*. London.

Reynolds, R. 1992. *Super Heroes: A Modern Mythology*. Jackson, MS.

Rollin, R. B. 2013. "The Epic Hero and Pop Culture. In *The Superhero Reader*, edited by C. H., J. Heer, and K. Worcester, 84–98. Jackson, MS.

Santo, A. 2014. "Is It a Camel? Is It a Turban? No, It's The 99: Branding Islamic Superheroes as Authentic Global Cultural Commodities." *Television & New Media* 15 (7): 679–695.

Schauber, E., and E. Spolsky. 1981. "Stalking a Generative Poetics." *New Literary History* 12 (3): 397–413.

Slackman, M. 2007. "In Egypt, a New Battle Begins Over the Veil." *The New York Times*, January 28. http://www.nytimes.com/2007/01/28/weekinreview/28slackman.html.

Swales, J. 1990. *Genre Analysis: English in Academic and Research Settings*. Cambridge: Cambridge.

van Leeuwen, T., and U. Suleiman. 2010. "Globalizing the Local: The Case of an Egyptian Superhero Comic." In *The Handbook of Language and Globalization*, edited by N. Coupland, 232–254. Chichester.

Vicino, T., A. Goldman, and C. Smith. 2006. *Aya #1-6*. Giza.

Williams, D. 2005. "Arab Superheroes Leap Pyramids in a Single Bound." *The Washington Post*, February 16, p. C01.

Wilson, B. J., S. L. Smith, W. J. Potter, D. Kunkel, D. Linz, C. M. Colvin, and E.
  Donnerstein. 2002. "Violence in Children's Television Programming:
  Assessing the Risks." *Journal of Communication* 52 (1): 5–35.
Zitawi, J. 2008. "Contextualizing Disney Comics within the Arab Culture."
  Meta: Journal Des Traducteurs / Meta: Translators' Journal 53 (1): 139–153.

Hero and/or Villain?
The 99 and the Hybrid Nature of Popular Culture's Production of Islam

Ken Chitwood

POPULAR CONCEPTIONS OF COMIC BOOKS present them as a means of mild escapism rather than vehicles for critique. However, it is made obvious in this volume and other monographs, articles, and popular works that popular culture materials are often replete with real-world relevance and shaped by political processes.[1] Nonetheless, when a comic book takes a contemporary issue as its starting point, vociferous debate and division over its politics and popular relevance often emerges.

Such is the case with entrepreneur and psychologist Naif al-Mutawa's *The 99* comic book series, which features a predominately Muslim cast of characters whose gifts and superhero powers embody the ninety-nine attributes of Allah from the Qur'an. Debuted in 2006, *The 99* captured imaginations and interest, especially with its protagonists in perpetual battle with Rughal, a character styled, in part, off the likes of dissident jihadi leaders such as Osama bin Laden. Al-Mutawa received praise from U.S. President Barack Obama and other national leaders in the Middle East and Europe, but also faced litigation at home in Kuwait and detractors in the U.S. who believed his characters personify terror and so-called "radical Islam."[2]

Indeed, in this chapter I will make the case that *The 99*'s contents and creator – situated in their historical and political context and analyzed according to subsequent critical receptions on multiple sides – can be read as hybrid entities that undermine simplistic readings of Islam along the lines of the "clash of civilizations" perspective.[3] *The 99* positions Islam as a multivalent religious repository that resists essentialization. The comic does the same with "the West" and instead posits both as intermeshed and

---

1. Cf. DiPaolo 2011; McKinney 2008; Pustz 2010; and various articles in journals such as the *Journal of Graphic Novels and Comics, Studies in Comics,* and *Journal of Popular Culture.*
2. Schonfeld 2014.
3. Huntington 1993.

entangled, wrapped up in a dialectic of tension and cooperation that reveals both as hero and villain. Yet, at the same time, *The 99* becomes a situational case-study allowing musings on how Islam is apperceived and appreciated in popular culture and public opinion, as both a real object of study and a socially constructed and politically imagined classification.

To understand *The 99* as such, it will be necessary to read reactions to it as contact zones and/or "borderlands," where religion and popular culture meet. It is this hybrid nature, this "third space,"[4] that is crafted in, and around, *The 99* and its attendant media that will be explored in this chapter. Engaging current discussions on culture and hybridity, I propose that *The 99* is a pertinent case study to understand not only how religion and popular culture are a two-in-one mélange, but also that this dual, hybrid nature is an inherent feature of global Islam.

This argument will not only prove beneficial for considerations of the study of Islam in popular culture, but also will hopefully lead to conclusions for non-Muslims who consider, study, and comment on Muslim communities and creations such as *The 99*. Specifically, it can help researchers and laity better come to terms with Islam's inherent complexity, chaos, and contradictions, in both content and conceptualizations.

Blurred Lines: *The 99* between Religion and Popular Culture

In their work *God in the Details: American Religion in Popular Culture*, editors Eric Michael Mazur and Kate McCarthy propose that "[b]oth the field of popular culture studies and the material it examines [...] seem to be growing at a pace that outstrips the analytical categories and methods available."[5] They make the point that the conventional distinction between religion and popular culture is perhaps worth calling into question. At the very least, it is necessary to pay attention and to listen to, learn from, and discern the meanings of the "intersection of religion and culture in the ordinary experiences" of individuals across the globe.[6] This is paramount in terms of understanding and interpreting not only materials and productions, but also of cultures and people. Mazur and McCarthy write, "the borderland where religion and culture meet in popular expression is also a borderland of another sort. [... T]hese quasireligious popular culture sites serve as points of intersection – sometimes harmonious, often conflictual – for people of very diverse and disparate identities."[7] This mash-up of religion

4. Bhabha 1991.
5. Mazur and McCarthy 2010, 2.
6. Mazur and McCarthy 2010, 3.
7. Mazur and McCarthy 2010, 3.

and popular culture, which *The 99* represents, challenges essentialized real-world dualisms by its intrinsic hybrid nature.

This discussion draws from the deep well of borderland research that emerged from the pioneering work of Chicana, feminist, and queer theorist Gloria Anzaldúa in her seminal text *Borderlands/La Frontera: The New Mestiza*.[8] The borderland, in Anzaldúa's conceptualization, is a place of ambiguity and contact, a discursive space imbued with issues of political hegemony, contested cultural arrangements, and marginal agency. It is, at its base, a place where two or more cultures, classes, races, or ideologies make contact and collide. In this contact zone marginalized individuals and communities are given, and make, multiple and juxtaposed identities and discourses from which to draw and mark out their own concepts of selfhood and self-representation. Anzaldúa first wrote of borderlands in direct connection to her experiences along the U.S./Mexico border. Since then, the concept has been dispersed and spread across disciplines.[9] Across multiple fields, there is a notion that borderlands proliferate in a globalized world, wherein the modernist conception of the nation-state is beginning to crumble and populations are ever-more connected through worldwide flows of people, technology, finances, ideas, religions, and media.

This concept of borderlands and its related terminology (e.g. *hybridity*) have come to mean all sorts of things concerning the mixing and combinative forces acting in the moment of cultural exchange.[10] Hybridity is that "in-between" that refers to the "third space" as a space of cultural separation and merging.[11] It is the place where "transculturation" takes place, which involves the acquiring of limited aspects of one culture, the loss of some elements of another one, and the creation of a new, hybrid-but-coherent body of both amalgamated together.[12] In this instance, the "third space" is the content, concepts, and critical reception in conversation with *The 99* and its creator. In this space structures and practices, thought to be discrete and separate, combine to produce, and to be produced by, new structures, conversations, objects, practices, and ideas.[13]

In fact, it is in these contact zones, this "third space," that this chapter accesses popular culture and Islamic studies and from which multiple levels of interpretation are drawn. These borderlands are vital to the interpretation of religion and culture because they often display the conflictual,

8. Anzaldúa 2012.
9. Cf. Anzaldúa 2012, "Preface to the 25th Anniversary Edition."
10. Bhabha 1991, 112.
11. Bhabha 1991, 55.
12. Bhabha 1991, 131.
13. Drawing on the work of Canclini 2005, xxv.

powerful, and institution-laden processes that are part and parcel of the contact and entangled content of religion and popular culture. As scholar of religion David Chidester writes of popular culture, it is "[n]ot a stable system of production and consumption, [but] a battlefield of contending strategies, tactics, and maneuvers in struggles over the legitimate ownership of highly charged symbols of meaning and power."[14] To appreciate the ways in which ideas about Islam are created, contested, and cross various social, political, economic, psychological, and cultural borders throughout the globe, it is thus necessary to study it at these frontiers.

Of course, notions of hybridity and borderlands inherently call into question whether or not there are identifiable and definable categories to be amalgamated in contact zones in the first place. Is religion a sui generis phenomenon to be differentiated from pop culture (or, for that matter, politics, psychology, economics, etc.)? As others scholars illustrate, religion is bound up in socio-historical, psychological, and other beliefs and practices such as popular culture.[15] Thus, in some sense it is meaningless to postulate comic books such as *The 99* as a means of contact between religion and popular culture, as if they were singular spheres. It is not helpful to position religion as a unique institution in order to understand how it is laced in with other processes of politics and culture, economics, and social realities. That is, in point of fact, a contention of this chapter – that religion and popular culture, Islam and the West, are intermeshed in one another and cannot be so easily distinguished *from* one another. Thus, it is the task of the researcher to enter into these borderlands of power, perception, and production to tease out what we can about the objects/subjects of study.

This chapter engages in a limited discourse analysis of *The 99* and its critical reception. This methodology assumes that the language of *The 99* is tantamount to a form of social interaction and is also aware of, and concerned with, the socio-political and cultural context in which this discourse is situated. Hence the need to investigate various installments of *The 99* to discuss those themes, characters, and narrative arcs that provide evidence of hybridity. Not only that, but there is also the necessity of analyzing the popular receptive discourse surrounding the series and how it serves as confirmation of a wider context of cross-bred entities and imagined communities.[16] Those sources I will look to include not only the comic books themselves but also other forms of media including videos, news articles related to al-Mutawa's work, opinion pieces written about the comic book

---

14. Chidester 2005, 21.
15. Cf. Asad 1993; McCutcheon 1997.
16. Anderson 2006.

series, and scholarly articles discussing the themes in *The 99*. This method will be grounded both in theories concerning discourse analysis and in discussions about global Islam. These theoretical interludes will help ground the analysis further and provide a backbone for the core concepts to form around and take shape. Thus, the methodology herein identifies both the "local" structure of discourse within *The 99* and the "global" structures of reception and critical reaction as significant to the overall thesis of the chapter.

The Cross-Bred Content and Conceptualizations of *The 99*

The 99 represents a "third space" or "borderland" where not only religion and popular culture contact and collide, but also where ideations of Islam and Muslims converge. The following section details the creators, content, and characters of *The 99*, before moving on to the mixed reception it received across the globe.

Born and raised in Kuwait, but with postgraduate qualifications in clinical psychology from the U.S., al-Mutawa has stated aim with *The 99* was to spawn a narrative to counteract "the hijacking" of Islam by so-called "extremists."[17] In his own words, al-Mutawa wants *The 99*'s audience to celebrate "Islamic culture and Islamic heritage [of which Muslims] have a lot to be proud and joyful about," and he describes the goal of *The 99* as "bringing these positive elements into global awareness."[18] Surely, al-Mutawa wanted to produce a consumable and entertaining comic book product, but through its narrative, representations, and characters he simultaneously looked to offer a vision of the proper place and purpose of Islam in the contemporary world.

To do so, al-Mutawa created *The 99* as a series that features superheroes whose powers are based on the ninety-nine Virtues of Allah (*asma' Allah al-husna*) and who pursue values that appeal to modern, Western contexts, simultaneously serving as universal exemplars. Al-Mutawa said the hope was that "[i]t doesn't matter what culture you're from, it can still resonate. What *The 99* does is saying, 'Hey, our values, they're the same as yours; they're the same as the rest of the world.'"[19] Thus, from the beginning, al-Mutawa's creation was intended to be a bridge between worlds, popular culture artifacts of action that spanned the imaginaries of Islam. And yet, as will be illustrated, even as al-Mutawa framed his work as being about the positives of these connections and interstices between two worlds, the comic book series si-

17. Solotaroff 2011.
18. al-Mutawa et al. 2011, "Naif's Notes," #12.
19. Curry and Soffel 2013.

multaneously showcased the inherent frictions and contradictions between and within each culture. Although al-Mutawa wanted to bequeath the Muslim world its own superheroes while also encouraging a more generous and magnanimous apperception of Islam across the globe,[20] he concurrently offered a conglomerate vision of Islam and the world – creating characters that were both hero and villain, hidden and manifest, historically grounded and yet strikingly modern and young. In turn, these characters, concepts, and storylines were received both positively and negatively, among Muslim and non-Muslim critics and popular readers.

Al-Mutawa was not the sole progenitor of *The 99*. He brought together multiple streams of collaborators and teamed up with famed comic book writer Fabian Nicieza of *X-Men* and *Captain America* fame. Moreover, the graphic teams that illustrated the comic book series and online videos were made up of commissioned illustrators and writers who came from the powerhouse companies of Marvel and DC Comics in the U.S.[21] Not only did al-Mutawa enlist Western assistance in bringing his idea to life, but also he consulted Islamic scholars of *fiqh* (Islamic law).[22] Together, this mixed team created a comic book brand that sought to translate supposedly universal values through original, Islam-inspired superhero characters and content.

At the same time, the Islam-inspired creations conformed to broader superhero conventions.[23] Even so, these media choices contributed to the hybrid meaning and impact of *The 99*. The use of a medium such as comic books (and YouTube videos, even) can be considered culturally "lowbrow."[24] By extension, it can suggest affiliation with marginalized communities and identities (in this case Islam and Muslims), even as it is distributed among multiple markets, both high- and low-end.[25] Moreover, "the hybrid nature of comic's verbal and visual components"[26] – the framed panels and blank gutters, and the interstitial spaces created by these multimodal effects[27] – create thresholds in which greater reader participation and interaction is possible.[28] These permeable spaces create more room for meaning-making and the potential transgression of proposed meanings put forth by the comics' creators and illustrators. Thus, the very structure of a comic book invites

20. Cartoonist's Rights Network International 2014.
21. Deeb 2012.
22. Clements and Gauvain 2014.
23. Deeb 2012. For more on this, see also Fredrik Strömberg's chapter in this volume.
24. Cawley 2011.
25. Santo 2014.
26. Taylor 2004.
27. Kuechenmeister 2009.
28. Cawley 2011.

hybrid readings where the blank spaces between frames and the gutters as well as between images and words serve also as liminal interpretive space.

These mixed readings, made possible by the hybrid nature of the media themselves, are discussed by communications scholar Avi Santo, who has argued that in attempting to re-brand Islam through media and market conventions, al-Mutawa underestimated "brand culture's ambivalence" and the asymmetry of global initiatives, particularly of the comic book kind.[29] Thus, al-Mutawa's hopes were not fully realized given the unsure nature of media and the inability of media to guarantee cultural change and shifts in popular perceptions.

Beyond the media's hybrid natures, al-Mutawa crafted hybrid characters that illustrate the universal duality of humanity regardless of creed, culture, or class. Three examples will suffice. First, al-Mutawa sought to reposition and re-conceptualize Islam's history through the narrative of the Noor Stones. Also known as *ahjar al-nur* or Stones of Light (*nur* being "light" in Arabic), these ninety-nine mystical gemstones, each of which represents one of the ninety-nine names attributed to Allah in the Qur'an, give the characters their unique powers. In doing so, al-Mutawa posits Baghdad and Spain as harbingers of Islam's true heritage. Perhaps seeking to resolve some of Islam's historical political and epistemological differences, al-Mutawa "streamlined, homogenized, and essentialised" the "true light" of Muslim history into a condensed version that neglected the Prophet Muhammad, the Qur'an, and scores of other historico-cultural timelines, scholars, and notables, to focus on a connected chain of thought from from the eight-century reign of the Moors in al-Andalus, Spain to eleventh-century Baghdad, and to the rest of the world through the passage of the Noor Stones to *The 99*.[30]

These choices are not neutral ones. There are those who would argue that the essence of Islam passes from the time of the Prophet and the Pious Predecessors (*al-salaf al-salihin*) through al-Ma'mun's Bayt al-Hikma (House of Wisdom) to the philosophical intermingling of scholars in Spain.[31] It is their hope that today's Muslim world would model itself on these periods, evincing the golden era of scientific progress, discovery, and innovation in Baghdad and the splendor, religious diversity, and tolerance of al-Andalus. Of course, there is nary a mention – in either this popular discourse or in al-Mutawa's comic – of political, theological, or cultural disputes during these "golden ages," or the fact that there is a strong current of argument that posits that the respective Abbasid and Umayyad caliphates were dicta-

29. Santo 2014.
30. Clements and Gauvain 2014, 39.
31. Cf. Hoodbhoy 1991; Bakar 2009; Menocal 2002.

torial, elitist, and intolerant.[32] Effectively, vast swathes of debated Muslim history are "smoothed over, then re-spun" to appeal to Muslim youth and offer in *The 99* a new understanding of Islam's role in society, culture, and even politics.[33]

Indeed, as al-Mutawa would have it, the historical memory of these places and people positions Islam as a bridge between worlds, in his estimation between popular conceptions of Islam and the West. In the very first issue – *The 99*'s "origin story" – Andalusia (Seville, Spain) becomes the central node of *nur* (light) that The 99 represent. Later, The 99 Steps Foundation – the NGO The 99 operates out of – relocates to Spain for their headquarters. As his team travels throughout the globe on its missions, Dr. Ramzi explains to his team from Spain that the Noor Stones came from Baghdad, the "land of wisdom" (*dar al-hikma*) under the Mu'tazilite scholars and caliphs, who become nouveau "Pious Predecessors."[34] The scholars used alchemy to preserve within the Noor Stones the knowledge contained in Dar al-Hikma and smuggled them out of the city when it fell to the Mongol armies in the thirteenth century. In this story, librarians-cum-alchemists become the heroes, engaging in the mixing and amalgamation of physics and faith, chemistry and concepts, secrecy and scholarship. These gemstones eventually make their way to Spain to be protected inside a "Fortress of Knowledge" by guardians who are the descendants of the librarians.[35] Theirs is a *jihad* (struggle) of defense, to preserve the knowledge of Dar al-Hikma. To do so, their mission spans centuries, contexts, and cultures. As Dr. Ramzi explains, the effort to bring the Noor Stones' light into the world flows through processes of globalization, migration, and modernization.

English scholar James Clements and Middle Eastern studies scholar Richard Gauvain make the point that, in this narrative, al-Mutawa re-imagines classical Islamic culture and heritage as made up of both rationalism and what they call Islamic "Gnosticism" or mysticism. Left out of The 99's chronicle of Islamic light are more traditional scholars. This omission is telling, as the traditional strain of scholarship is arguably the most influential in the history of Islam, for its supposedly more strict adherence to the Qur'an and the *hadith* – those defined as authoritative by the traditionalists themselves – and the methods and conclusions of approved legal procedures and apparatus. Rationalism, typified in the Mu'tazilite school, places more emphasis on reason in the appropriation and apperception of knowledge

---

32. Cf. Denny 2011; Griffel 2009.
33. Clements and Gauvain 2014, 36.
34. al-Mutawa, #1.
35. al-Mutawa, #1.

(*'ilm*). Islamic "Gnosticism" or "mysticism" is typified in the hiddenness of the knowledge that is passed on through the gemstones. The authors argue that, while rationalism and mysticism struggled to gain ascendency, or even to exist, throughout Muslim history, al-Mutawa gives them pride of place. In channeling the re-telling of Muslim history and knowledge through "the rationalism of Baghdad's (Abbasid/Mu'tazilite) polymaths and the esotericism of (the Andalusian) guardians"[36] and finally embodied in the perfect and pure polymath (Dr. Ramzi), al-Mutawa privileges one brand of Islam over others in his re-telling of Islamic history. Thus, even as al-Mutawa imagines and crafts in comic book form a relevant and orthodox Islam that is hybrid, his vision of Islam also lacks certain streams and elements of Islamic history he deems unnecessary to the bridge-building project of *The 99*.

Not only is Islam a composite creation of al-Mutawa's in *The 99*, but characters themselves are two-in-one. This theme is embodied in the story of Noora. Noora is one of the principal characters of the comic, who "uses the power of her gem to see the light of truth in others," according to the official *The 99* website. Further, "[t]he light of truth shows her how truthful and good each person is. She can also use her power to produce illusions of light and uses this power to hide THE 99 when the team needs secrecy."[37] Although the theme of juxtaposing light and dark, good and evil, is a common trope throughout the comics, the motif is epitomized in Noora's narrative.

It seems that al-Mutawa's themes of light/dark, particularly in the story of Noora, reveal two points: that there is light and dark in everyone and that light can hide as much as it can reveal. Throughout these comics, characters seem to be fighting the darkness within themselves, using the Noor Stones to keep the darkness at bay. In one particular scene, Noora, having recently discovered her powers to see light/dark in everyone and everything around her, runs through the streets of a city center in the United Arab Emirates, her home country. As she runs past people and places, different objects shine with light that is blotted with dark splotches representing evil. As she sees the evil within them, she remarks how "afraid" she is. She sees darkness in street thugs, in her own father, and notably in the minaret of a mosque.[38] This narrative serves to remind the reader of what popular author Anne LaMott expressed, "the villain has a heart, and the hero has great flaws."[39] Al-Mutawa, it seems, agrees. Through these vignettes, and through Noora's frequent use of her powers to reveal the light/dark in others, al-Mutawa

36. Clements and Gauvin 2014, 45.
37. Teshkeel Media 2014b.
38. al-Mutawa, #1.
39. LaMott 1995, 78.

appears to be making the point that there is darkness and light within each of us. Indeed, he even appears to suggest that there is light and dark within Islam, its structures, and its adherents. At the same time, the whole world is light *and* dark. As al-Mutawa would have it, there is both good and evil within everything and everyone. Thus, the representations of heroes *and* villains are always blurred amalgamations of light and dark, good and evil in *The 99*. In this comic narrative, there is almost no pure *nur* in the world.

There is one exception: the Noor Stones are pure light, juxtaposed against the evil of the world. In addition, when Noora first meets Dr. Ramzi, he appears in pure light.[40] Is this evidence that al-Mutawa is suggesting that Ramzi is the perfect man (*al-insan al-kamil*)? Is he a pure bearer of light in the world? Could he be a stand-in for the Prophet? Rather than saying that Dr. Ramzi in and of himself is pure, it could be said, reading along the lines above, that Dr. Ramzi is pure light because of the two-in-one aspects of Islam that he represents. As al-Mutawa brings together two diverse streams of Islamic thought and practice in the content of *The 99*, the two streams of Islamic consciousness come together in the character of Dr. Ramzi. This is why he is pure light. He represents the simultaneously amalgamated, but pure, channels that flow together into himself and his project – The 99 Steps Foundation. Thus, in al-Mutawa's "*The 99* universe," pure light is only possible in mixing and matching, in bringing together the tensions in Islamic discourse and ritual, the so-called Muslim and Western worlds (as they are represented by al-Mutawa), and diverse characters from across the world, who bear the pure light of such traditions and tributaries.

Even Rughal, the principal villain of the series, is a hybrid entity, not purely backwards or evil but redeemable and resplendent with a certain light. Rughal, described as "an Osama bin Laden-inspired villain who could just as well be the face of ISIS or 'any other self-styled messiah' in our post-al-Qaeda world,"[41] is the principal villain The 99 face in the series. The central contest between Rughal and Ramzi/The 99 is that the former seeks to find and use the Noor Stones to "gain unlimited power and dominate the world."[42] Essentially, he wants to co-opt Islam's wisdom – as it is refracted in the Noor Stones – for his own nefarious and selfish purposes. This would seem to be al-Mutawa's swipe at the aforementioned self-styled messiahs. And yet, Rughal was formerly a fifteenth-century Guardian of the Fortress of Knowledge in Andalusia. He is a brilliant scientist who had an alchemy experiment with the Noor Stones go awry that made him become vapor for centuries.

40. al-Mutawa, #1.
41. Akbar 2015.
42. Teshkeel Media 2014c.

He is depicted in modern, Western dress in the contemporary scenes and in robes and traditional dress in the past. While each mode of dress is suitable for its times, Rughal is drawn as a representative of a tributary of Islamic thought that stands in contradistinction to that represented by the Noor Stones. Thus, as Rughal is depicted as both medieval and modern, specter and embodied adversary, scientist and spiritual alchemist, he parallels the time-travel of the Noor Stones, even as he juxtaposes their traverse across geographies. As such, al-Mutawa represents Rughal as the characterization of the school of thought that seeks to situate traditionalist, and so-called extremist, strains of Islam as both ancient and modern, emergent and historical.[43]

Furthermore, there is a story arc regarding the hidden and manifest nature and posture of *The 99* heroes that is also telling in regard to the hybrid nature of the comic's content and characters. Issue #17 is titled "Unmasked." Up until this issue, the main characters had worn masks to obscure their identity in public, à la traditional superheroes, who keep their true identities hidden through obfuscating wardrobes (masks, glasses, etc.). To "unmask" is to reveal, uncover, expose, bring to light, and lay bare. Masked in their previous adventures, The 99 are in this issue represented in the popular media as "convicted felons," who subsequently hide their identities from the public. The line of reasoning goes, "if they have nothing to hide," why do they not show themselves to the public?[44] The masks, The 99 find, produce fear among those they seek to serve. In the following issue, divisions arise within The 99, as they debate whether or not to reveal themselves and go unmasked in public.

While the unmasking of a superhero is perhaps a common trope in comic books, the issue takes on particular relevancy regarding Islam when the "Mysterious Batina" – a character depicted in full *burqa* – is revealed as a member of The 99. As al-Mutawa wrote, "little is known about Batina the Hidden, whose mastery of her gemstone gives her the ability to blend into any background and become invisible. Batina uses her powers to hide THE 99 when there is a need for secrecy. She can sometimes define and understand things that have been hidden by others."[45] She joins a group that includes Muslim women in *hijab*, *niqab*, and without any hair covering – a diverse group from across the globe. As the public gathers outside, they demand the revelation of The 99's true identities with signs, such as one that reads: "Superheroes or menaces?" Meanwhile, Batina feels confused by the

43. Cf. Kane 2003.
44. al-Mutawa, #17.
45. Teshkeel Media 2014a.

overwhelming darkness being pressed upon her by the anger of the crowd outside. When Batina is revealed to The 99 in full *burqa*, they assume she is the cause of the crisis blamed on them and responsible for the negative public reaction. She responds, "You don't understand. Any of you. You assume that anyone different from you is an enemy," and claims they are not ready for a gem-bearer that is different.[46] Not only is this a commentary on the need to include even the most traditional Muslims in the *umma*, it highlights the need to reveal and unmask, but also to respect, hiddenness and secrecy. Again, these characters cannot be cast in any one mold. They are transnational individuals, living between locations and transmigrating across the globe (e.g. Aleem, from Qatar, is discovered in New York but lives in L.A.; Musawwira, from Ghana, moved to New York with her family; Samda, from Libya, flees to Paris), bequeathed unique powers and reflecting the stunning diversity of the *umma*.

Moreover, it has been pointed out that al-Mutawa presents a hybrid vision of Islamic feminisms in his comics. As anthropologist Saba Mahmood argues in *Politics of Piety: The Islamic Revival and the Feminist Subject,* there are multiple ways and means that feminism can be expressed as a set of norms, practices, and political projects that do not necessarily conform to liberal notions.[47] Picking up on this theme and interpreting al-Mutawa's formulation of female characters in *The 99,* English scholar Shirin Edwin argues that these superheroes embody the "complex dimensions of feminisms in Islam that also include women's weaknesses, struggles, and problems."[48] Thus, as visualized in *The 99,* Muslim women do not necessarily conform to either/or formulations of femininity but transcend boundaries between various discursive concepts and realized practices.

In point of fact, anthropologist Talal Asad has written that Islam is "a discursive tradition" – a set of religious symbols that take on meaning, value, and expression in various social and political situations, where multiple processes, discussions, and negotiations are involved.[49] From this perspective, it can be deduced that there is no "Islam," per se, but a "discursive tradition" that "addresses itself to conceptions of the Islamic past and future, with reference to a particular Islamic practice in the present."[50] There are, in other words, a myriad of Islams. In *What is Islam? The Importance of Being Islamic,* Islamic studies scholar Shahab Ahmed attempts nothing short of offering a

46. al-Mutawa, #18.
47. Mahmood 2005.
48. Edwin 2011.
49. Asad 1986, 14.
50. Asad 1986, 14.

brand-new, bold, and reconceived notion of *what Islam is,* standing in stark contrast to essentialist notions, whether they be popular, traditionalist, or radical. Taking a cosmopolitan and far-reaching approach to more than a millennium of Muslim history, poetry, music, science, philosophy, theology, and practice, Ahmed re-conceptualizes Islam as a *hermeneutical engagement* comfortable with the contradiction of its own stunning diversity and immense variety.[51] Thus, Ahmed posits that the main challenge in interpreting Islam is coming to terms with the considerable diversity of beliefs, practices, and postures of global Islam, while simultaneously appreciating that there are shared principles which act as a cri de coeur for Muslims across the world.

It is intimated in the above that al-Mutawa's approach perhaps aligns with Asad's line of thought and Ahmed's postulations. The conceptualizations of *The 99*'s characters and contents presented above suggest that essentialized abstractions that say that "Islam = violence" or "Islam = peace" are insensitive to the alterations and negotiations that characterize lived Islam in interaction with myriad Muslim constituencies and non-Muslim actors across the globe (e.g. Saudi Arabia, Southeast Asia, the Balkans, and even Latin America and the Caribbean). *The 99*'s characters evince Islam's contradictions and make people on all sides uncomfortable. They also undermine notions of a clearly codified West. As will be discussed further, this presentation undercuts "clash of civilizations" and "orientalist" discourses as it merges cultures, light and dark, good and evil, and, again, hero and villain. This becomes even more evident when investigating the mixed reception *The 99* has received since its first publication.

Mixed Receptions, Hybrid Readings

Not only is *The 99* a hybrid creation, but it also was received and critiqued in multivalent fashion by communities of discourse that are themselves diverse. Some aspects of this reception were due to identity politics and channels of power. Even so, *The 99* has been used, critiqued, and praised by both the hegemonic *and* the subaltern, the so-called mainstream *and* the marginalized. In the end, neither can fully understand or agree about the essence of al-Mutawa's hybrid characters. Whether it be progressives hailing the comic book series for its bold interfaith enterprise or conservatives damning it for either its perceived heretical notions or its supposed support of "creeping Sharia,"[52] all are examples of individuals and structures trying

51. Ahmed 2014.
52. Pipes 2012.

to simplify a hybrid work to either/or notions of religion, politics, and social expression.

On the one hand, The 99 and its various sites and artifacts of cultural production have been commercially successful and well-received by the media, government representatives, and popular readership. With comic books, a subsequent TV spinoff, online content, and a theme park, it could be said that The 99 "is one of the most significant media sensations for young Muslims around the world."[53] The television series is shown in over seventy countries and the series' Facebook page had nearly 1.4 million likes at the time of writing. The 99's creator was given the opportunity to share his story and his concept through a 2010 TED Talk entitled, "Superheroes Inspired by Islam," which has enjoyed over 700,000 views online.[54] On the other hand, regardless of region or religion, reception was mixed. In the U.S. and Europe, the reception of al-Mutawa's work was, on the whole, positive. Forbes magazine hailed The 99 as "One of the Top 20 Trends Sweeping the Globe,"[55] and U.S. President Barack Obama highlighted al-Mutawa's work as the "most innovative response to the need to 'deepen ties between [...] the United States and Muslim communities around the world' and offered it as an example of 'the teachings of tolerance in Islam.'"[56] And yet, though The 99 was envisioned as popular culture to promote peace between Islam and the imagined West, it has also been lampooned. Andrea Peyser, a controversial New York Post columnist who comments on everything from politics to popular culture, wrote that the syndicated television program version of The 99 should be cancelled "before it starts."[57] She wrote in warning: "Hide your face and grab the kids. Coming soon to a TV in your child's bedroom is a posse of righteous, Sharia-compliant Muslim superheroes – including one who fights crime hidden head-to-toe by a burqa. These Islamic butt-kickers are ready to bring truth, justice and indoctrination to impressionable Western minds."[58] Others joined in by warning that U.S. parents should keep their children from the subversive series and its participation in the supposed process of "creeping Sharia" – whereby Muslims slowly assert their vision for personal and political governance in multiple arenas of Western culture, and in turn come to power through ultimately seditious means.[59] Still others warned of

---

53. Clements and Gauvain 2014, 37.
54. al-Mutawa 2010.
55. Eaves 2008.
56. Clements and Guavain 2014, 36.
57. Khouri 2009.
58. Khouri 2009.
59. Khouri 2009; Pipes 2012.

a "cultural jihad,"[60] "Islamic missionizing," and the "indoctrination of Western children."[61] As Avi Santo writes, while al-Mutawa tried to design *The 99* as "a transnational cross-media brand"[62] in order to ameliorate Islam's global reputation, the opposition that the comic book and its TV spinoff faced in the U.S. "demonstrates some of the limitations of applying market logic to efforts to rehabilitate Islam's image."[63]

Reaction to *The 99* in "the Muslim world"[64] was also mixed. The Royal Islamic Strategic Studies Center based in Amman, Jordan, named al-Mutawa one of its 500 Most Influential Muslims in the world for four consecutive years.[65] The Dubai-based magazine *Gulf Business* featured al-Mutawa as one of its "Top 100 Most Powerful Arabs," and described him as an "inspired thinker" for the Middle East and the globe.[66] Simultaneously, criticism from Arab Muslim countries and Islamic constituencies has been vociferous. Some Salafi critiques "focus on the risks of representing the Divine Names in human form (an act of idolatry, or *shirk*) and, secondarily, on the un-Islamic nature of this representation (there are complaints that so few of the female characters wear the *hijab,* that the characters use 'magic' and so on)."[67] And although the Kuwaiti government initially endorsed his work, a fellow Kuwaiti has now brought a legal suit against al-Mutawa for blasphemy, and a fatwa was issued against him by a grand mufti in Saudi Arabia. A Twitter campaign has also singled out al-Mutawa for heresy, calling for him to be brought to trial or even to be killed (the hashtag "#whowillkillalmutawa" made the rounds). As *The Independent* reported:

> Al-Mutawa received a hail of abuse and death threats culminating in an ironic sequence of events: "Shortly before New Year 2014, I received an email informing me that The 99 had won in the media category of the Islamic Economy Awards [in Dubai]. A few days later, I received an email from my lawyer updating me on the case lodged against me in Kuwait for heresy and insulting religion through The 99. This is the same book President Obama, Sheikh Mohammed, even His Highness the Emir of Kuwait, publicly endorsed as being a bastion of tolerance."[68]

60. Geller 2011.
61. Pipes 2012.
62. Santo 2014, 679.
63. Santo 2014, 691.
64. See discussion about "the Muslim world" at the beginning of the chapter.
65. PR Newswire 2012.
66. Buller 2012.
67. Clements and Gauvain 2014, 38. Cf. Leslie 2011; Sabra 2011.
68. Akbar 2015.

Not to be left out, ISIS (a.k.a. IS, ISIL, Daesh) has pronounced a fatwa of con-
demnation against *The 99*'s real-life progenitor and called for his death.[69]
Thus, although al-Mutawa consciously avoided direct references to the
Qur'an or depictions of the Prophet Muhammad and created *The 99* in con-
sultation with Islamic scholars and a team of Western illustrators, he has
come up against stiff criticism from all sides.

The above illustrates the variegated nature of *The 99*'s reception and how
cultural interpreters on both sides attempt to place Islam in their own pre-
conceived boxes. Notably, Islamic traditionalists joined a chorus of cultural
conservatives in the West to condemn *The 99* in a confluence of criticism.
For the former, it was upsetting that women were not wearing *burqas*; for
the latter, it was disturbing that a woman in the series *was* wearing a *burqa*.
As CNN reported, "for some he [al-Mutawa] is a defender not of peace but
of profanity: ironically, he has hardline detractors in both America and the
Arab world, though they hate him for opposing reasons. To U.S. conservatives, he is a terrorist and a pawn of hardline Islam; to Islamist Arabs, he is
a heretic and a pawn of the liberal West."[70] It may be that the detractions'
seemingly opposing viewpoints concerning al-Mutawa are due less to the
interlocutors' opposing perspectives and more to the hybrid nature of *The
99*'s content and characters. The complex and two-in-one nature of the comic book and its subjects – both Islam and the West as al-Mutawa constructs
them – significantly shaped not only (mis)perceptions of the comic book,
but of Islam as well. The interlocutors' own identity politics and preconceptions only exacerbated the issues surrounding the reading of a hybrid text
distributed across varying contexts.

Conclusion

A theme running throughout this chapter has been that Islam – in reality, in
popular culture representations such as *The 99*, or in discursive construction
and conception – should never be essentialized into any one entity, even
though it often is. While there is some notion of Islam as a unified religion
based on certain texts and traditions, its myriad manifestations across the
globe make it so that *what Islam is* can never be fully defined. It evades our
grasp. Yet, it also exists in the world and, as a concept, is on the loose.

There are an estimated 1.6–1.7 billion Muslims worldwide, comprising
twenty-three percent of the global population.[71] While particularly concen-
trated in the Asia-Pacific, Middle East, and North African regions, there are

69. Cf. Schonfeld 2014; Pecquet 2014.
70. Curry and Soffel 2013.
71. Pew Research Religion and Public Life Project 2014.

significant populations in sub-Saharan Africa and increasing numbers in Europe, North America, and Latin America and the Caribbean. With such intercontinental distribution, is there any unifying aspect of Islam that makes it a singular entity? Various scholars have proposed different fusing factors for Muslims across the globe. Anthropologist Ralph Grillo proposes three, specifically: transnational networks; bi-national/plurinational frameworks; and the concept of the *umma*.[72] He also references the forces of migration, multicultural diasporas, and the "Islamic teaching elite" that impact global Muslim discourse. Scholar of law Abdullahi Ahmed An-Na'im takes up migration as a particularly unifying Muslim global occurrence, relating it all the way back to the experience of the Prophet Muhammad, saying that "for Muslims migration is an honor, in line with the movements of the Prophet between Mecca and Medina."[73] And what of these physical locales? Can Mecca, in particular, serve as a centrifugal "node" for the global Muslim population – its creator, capital, crucible, and centering cogency, as Middle Eastern studies scholar miriam cooke and scholar of religion Bruce B. Lawrence suggest?[74]

Because of the decentralizing character of Islam and its global distribution, there is an ongoing debate, what scholar of religion and popular commentator Reza Aslan calls "a civil war,"[75] raging over what is authentic ("orthodox") Islam and where the boundary lines of Islam can be drawn. Islam, as a world system, is not static, but is always changing according to the various lines of its own "discursive traditions." The tone of these various streams of thought about Islam are not solely determined by interconnected Islamic networks and global forces (though these do play a role), but local realities. There is also, as Shahab Ahmed has claimed, outright *contradiction* in Islam.[76] Therefore, any explanation of *what Islam is* must in some way encompass both striking complexity and some underlying unity. Or, as Ahmed later puts it, conceptualizations of Islam must recognize "how Islam makes Muslims as Muslims make Islam."[77] He goes on to also say how even non-Muslims are part of the "discursive and praxial diffusion"[78] of Islam in the world, and that understanding Islam in this way will lead to further questions and answers as to what Islam is.

As anthropologist Anthony Cohen has argued, culture is not something

---

72. Grillo 2004.
73. An-Na'im 2014.
74. Cooke and Lawrence 2005, location 55.
75. Aslan 2005.
76. Ahmed 2015, 6.
77. Ahmed 2015, 543.
78. Ahmed 2015, 544.

sui generis and is less a matter for documentation than interpretation. Instead, he posits that communities are best understood as "communities of meaning." The reality of community, Cohen argues, lies more in symbol and perception than in any unique essence. "People construct community symbolically, making it a resource and repository of meaning, and a referent of their identity."[79] Correspondingly, Islam is fascinating because of its versatility, not in spite of it. Because of its multivalent expressions, it can serve as a strong identity marker. Furthermore, it is perhaps better portrayed in hybrid metaphor and media than it is in textual depictions or strict typologies.

Investigating a "third space," such as the contact point between religion and popular culture, is a field wherein these questions can be explored. Thus, the above is meant to serve as a means to examine the ways in which Islam as a concept is perceived as diffuse, both by self-identified Muslims and those who who do not identify. Thus, al-Mutawa's vision of Islam comes up against an amalgam of political perceptions of what Islam *is* and *is not*. In some ways it points to the dialectic between Muslim and non-Muslim hybrid subjects and subjectivities that continue to create a mixed opinion of Islam. Moreover, given its hybrid nature, *The 99* adds to this amalgamation of conceptions. Although al-Mutawa sought to position Islam as a bridge between "Islam" and "the West," his mission faltered in mixed readings and complex conceptions of Islam. This underlines the fact that hybridity is constantly channeled, and hemmed in, by contours of power, identity politics, and the specificity of prejudices manifest in hierarchies of exclusion. While there may be promise in a vision of religious subjects and objects as both hero and villain, there is no escaping the fact that hybridity cannot yet transcend dichotomies of difference concerning what is considered good and/or evil.

This chapter has sought to show that *The 99*'s content and characters are hybrid creations and that, as such, they provide an opportunity to consider the variegated nature of Islam. This analysis offers a lens through which to view the complexities and potential contradictions found within Islam, in contradistinction to Western concepts and norms. While not necessarily a novel conclusion, it is ever more pertinent, given misperceptions and misconceptions of Islam in mass media and popular understanding. Poignantly, it posits comic books as particular areas where such misperceptions might either be played out or challenged, given their hybrid nature and complex content. In the end, such an analysis seeks to provoke more investigation concerning Islam's relationship with the West and the many ways it is charted.

79. Cohen 1985, 118.

Works Cited

Ahmed, S. 2015. *What is Islam? The Importance of Being Islamic.* Princeton.

Akbar, A. 2015. "The all-Islamic super-heroes: Muslim children love 'The 99' comics, but hardliners loathe their creator – whose trial for heresy is looming." http://www.independent.co.uk/arts-entertainment/books/features/the-all-islamic-super-heroes-muslim-children-love-the-99-comics-but-hardliners-loathe-their-creator-10101891.html.

al-Mutawa, N. 2010. "Superheroes Inspired by Islam." *TED.* https://www.ted.com/talks/naif_al_mutawa_superheroes_inspired_by_islam?language=en.

al-Mutawa et al. 2011. *The 99,* issue #1. New York

———. 2008 *The 99,* issue #12. New York.

———. 2012a *The 99,* issue #17. New York.

———. 2012b *The 99,* issue #18.

Anderson. 2006. *Imagined Communities: Reflections on the Origin and Spread of Nationalism, Revised Edition.* New York.

An-Na'im, A. A. 2014. "Immigration and Integration." Panel, Religion Newswriters Association Conference, Emory University, Atlanta, GA, September 18, 2014.

Anzaldúa, G. 2012. *Borderlands/La Frontera: The New Mestiza.* 4th edition. San Francisco.

Arjana, S. R. 2015. *Muslims in the Western Imagination.* London.

Asad, T. 1993. *Genealogies of Religion: Discipline and Reasons of Power in Christianity and Islam.* Baltimore.

———.1986. "The Idea of an Anthropology of Islam," *Occasional Paper Series, Center for Contemporary Arab Studies, Georgetown University*: 14. Washington, D.C.

Aslan, R. 2005. *No god but God: The Origins, Evolution, and Future of Islam.* New York.

Bakar, O. 2009. "Commentary: The Importance of al-Ghazali and Ibn Rushd in the History of Islamic Discourse on Religion and Science." In *Science and Religion: Christian Muslim Perspectives,* edited by David Marshall, 102–110. Istanbul.

Beal, T. 2008. *Religion in America: A Very Short Introduction.* New York.

Bhabha, H. K. 1991. *The Location of Culture.* London.

Buller, A. 2012. "The 99: Inspired Thinking." *Gulf Business,* May 3. http://www.gulfbusiness.com/articles/insights/interviews/the-99-inspired-thinking/.

Canclini, N. G. 2005. *Hybrid Cultures: Strategies for Entering and Leaving Modernity.* Minneapolis.

Cartoonist's Rights Network International. 2014. "Naif Al-Mutawa Sentenced to Death by Isis." *Cartoonists Rights Network International.* http://cartoonistsrights.org/naif-al-mutawa-sentenced-to-death-by-isis/.

Cawley, S. 2012. "Hybridity and Comics." https://blogs.stockton.edu/postcolonialstudies/hybridity-and-comics/.

Chidester, D. 2005. *Authentic Fakes: Religion and American Popular Culture.* Berkeley.

Chitwood, K. 2015. "Human Consciousness and Religious Reality." *Religious Studies Project.* http://www.religiousstudiesproject.com/2015/09/24/human-consciousness-religious-reality/.

Clements, J., and R. Gauvin. 2014. "The Marvel of Islam: Reconciling Muslim Epistemologies through a New Islamic Origin Saga in Naif al-Mutawa's *The 99*," *The Journal of Religion and Popular Culture* 26 (1): 36–71.

Cohen, A. 1985. *The Symbolic Construction of Community.* Hempstead.

Cooke, M. and B. B. Lawrence, eds. 2005. *Muslim Networks: From Hajj to Hip Hop.* Durham.

Curry, N., and J. Soffel. 2013. "The 99: Islamic Superheroes Going Global." *CNN,* June 20. http://www.cnn.com/2013/06/11/showbiz/comic-book-heroes-the-99-write/.

Deeb, M.-J. 2012. "The 99: Superhero Comic Books from the Arab World." *Comparative Studies of South Asia, Africa and the Middle East* 32 (2), 391–407.

Denny, F. M. 2011. "Muslim Creeds and Theologies: Their Purposes and Varieties." In *An Introduction to Islam.* 4th edition. Boston.

DiPaolo, M. 2011. *War, Politics, and Superheroes: Ethics and Propaganda in Comics and Film.* Jefferson, NC.

Ekman, M. 2015. "Islamophobia and the Politics of Fear: Manufacturing the Green Scare." *Ethnic and Racial Studies* 38 (11): 1986–2002.

Edwin, S. 2011. "Islam's Trojan Horse: battling perceptions of Muslim women in *The 99*." *Journal of Graphic Novels and Comics* 3 (2): 171–199.

Geller, P. 2011. "86 'The 99'." *World Net Daily,* October 11. http://www.wnd.com/2011/10/354477/.

Green, T. 2015. *The Fear of Islam: An Introduction to Islamophobia in the West.* Minneapolis.

Griffel, F. 2009. "The Project of Enlightenment in Islamic-Arabic Culture." In *The Cultures of Maimonideanism: New Approaches to the History of Jewish Thought,* edited by James T. Robinson. Leiden.

Grillo, R. 2004. "Islam and Transnationalism." *Journal of of Ethnic and Migration Studies* 30, no. 5: 864–868.

Hjärpe, J. 1997. "What Will Be Chosen from the Islamic Basket?" *European Review* 5 (3): 267–274.

Hoodbhoy, P. 1991. *Islam and Science: Religious Orthodoxy and the Battle For Rationality.* New York.

Huntington, S. P. 1993. "The Clash of Civilizations?" *Foreign Affairs.*

Kane, O. 2003. *Muslim Modernity in Postcolonial Nigeria: A Study of the Society for the Removal of Innovation and Reinstatement of Tradition.* Leiden.

Khouri, A. 2009. "99 Problems But a Cape Ain't One: Conservatives Attack Islamic Superheroes." *Comics Alliance*, October 19. http://comicsalliance.com/the-99-muslim-islamic-superhero-comic/?trackback=tsmclip.

Kuechenmeister, B. 2009. "Reading Comics Rhetorically: Orality, Literacy, and Hybridity in Comic Book Narratives." *SCAN: Journal of Media Arts Culture* 5 (3).

LaMott, A. 1995. *Bird by Bird: Some Instructions on Writing and Life.* New York.

Leslie, L. 2011. "Sharing faith through comics, animation." *Muslim Voices*, October 14: http://muslimvoices.org/sharing-faith-comics-animation/.

Mahmood, S. 2005. *Politics of Piety: The Islamic Revival and the Feminist Subject.* Princeton.

Manger, L. 1999. "Muslim Diversity: Local Islam in Global Contexts." In *Muslim Diversity: Local Islam in Global Contexts*, edited by Leif Manger, 1–36. Copenhagen.

Mazur, E. M., and K. McCarthy. 2010. *God in the Details: American Religion in Popular Culture.* New York.

McCutcheon, R. T. 1997. *Manufacturing Religion: The Discourse on Sui Generis Religion and the Politics of Nostalgia.* New York.

McKinney, M. 2008. *History and Politics in French Language Comics and Graphic Novels.* Jackson, MS.

Menocal, M R. 2002. *Ornament of the World: How Muslims, Jews, and Christians Created a Culture of Tolerance in Medieval Spain.* Boston.

O'Leary, S. D. 1996. "Cyberspace as Sacred Space: Communicating Religion on Computer Networks." *Journal of the American Academy of Religion* 64 (4): 781–808.

Pecquet, J. 2014. "Kuwaiti cartoonist battles IS death threats, US bigots." *Al-Monitor*, November 12. http://www.al-monitor.com/pulse/originals/2014/11/99-netflix-comic-cartoon-kuwait-death-threats-isis.html.

Pew Research Religion and Public Life Project. 2014. "Global Religious Landscape: Muslims." *Pew Research Religion and Public Life Project*, December 18. http://www.pewforum.org/2012/12/18/global-religious-landscape-muslim/.

PR Newswire. 2012. "The World's 500 Most Influential Muslims." *PR Newswire*, November 27. http://www.prnewswire.com/news-releases/the-muslim-500-the-worlds-most-influential-500-muslims-180970281.html.

Pustz, M., ed. 2012. *Comic Books and American Cultural History: An Anthology.* New York.

Roy, O. 2004. *Globalized Islam: The Search for a New Ummah.* New York.

Sabra, P. 2011. "Superheroes Inspired by Islam." *American Muslim Mom,* February 13. http://americanmuslimmom.com/99-superheroes-inspired-islam.

Said, E. W. 2001. "The Clash of Ignorance: Labels like 'Islam' and 'the West' Serve Only to Confuse Us about a Disorderly Reality." *The Nation,* October 4. https://www.thenation.com/article/clash-ignorance/.

Santo, A. 2014. "'Is it a Camel? Is it a Turban? No, Its *The 99*': Branding Islamic Superheroes as Authentic Global Cultural Commodities." *Television and New Media* 15 (7): 679–695.

Schonfeld, R. 2014. "ISIL vs. Naif Al-Mutawa and The 99." *Huffington Post,* November 25. http://www.huffingtonpost.com/reese-schonfeld/isil-vs-naif-almutawa-and_b_5883926.html.

Solotaroff, I., dir. 2011. *Wham! Bam! Islam!* Arlington, VA.

Taylor, L. N. 2004. "Compromised Divisions: Thresholds in Comic Books and Video Games." *ImageTexT: Interdisciplinary Comics Studies* 1 (1). http://www.english.ufl.edu/imagetext/archives/v1_1/taylor/.

Teshkeel Media. 2014a "Batina." *The 99.* http://www.the99kids.com/about/the99/batina/

———. 2014b "Noora." *The 99.* http://www.the99kids.com/about/the99/noora/.

———. 2014c. "Rughal." *The 99.* http://www.the99kids.com/about/villains/rughal/.

Qahera Here and There:
Navigating Contexts in the Translation of a Muslim Egyptian Superheroine

Aymon Kreil

Q AHERA IS A SUPERHEROINE, the protagonist of a webcomic written and drawn by the Egyptian writer and artist Deena Mohamed. One of Qahera's most striking features to unfamiliar audiences is her *hijab*, which sometimes hides her face, resembling nothing so much as a ninja outfit. She is accompanied by a non-veiled friend named Layla Magdy. Qahera's own name comes from the Arabic spelling of Cairo, al-Qahira, meaning the "victorious" or the "subduing." It is a very uncommon name, and in one of the stories, she is gently teased by Layla for this: "Is you sister's name Alexandria?" she asks.[1] Qahera answers by diverting the conversation. Even though the name remains unexplained in Mohamed's stories, it carries connotations both of a powerful woman, in reference to the original meaning of the word *qahira*, and of local ties, due to its homonymy with Egypt's capital.

Published as a webcomic on Tumblr,[2] there are at the time of writing eight *Qahera* stories, published between June 30, 2013, and August 26, 2015. Mohamed also posted a single image on April 4, 2016, which shows the superheroine holding up a bridge.[3] The comic is meant by its author to be a tool of social commentary, mainly addressing issues related to feminism and to Islamophobia. Initially, Mohamed was writing primarily for English-educated Egyptians and for foreigners, and her first two *Qahera* stories were published only in English. They were intended as responses to Western stereotypes about Muslim women. Mohamed eventually decided to translate her stories to Arabic for a local readership. From that point on, she has become much more specific in her stories, leaving Islamophobia aside, concentrating instead on women's rights and political accountability in Egypt.

1. In the Arabic version, Alexandria is replaced by Madina Nasr, a neighborhood of Cairo.
2. http://qaherathesuperhero.com/
3. Eds. note: This image is featured on this volume's cover.

While the existing academic writing about Qahera focuses on how the fictional character questions Western stereotypes about Muslim women,[4] I will in this chapter put the stress on translation issues. For this, I can partly rely on a text written by Mohamed herself, on the use of English and Arabic in her stories.[5] What makes the topic compelling from my perspective is how Mohamed uses different writing strategies when addressing an English-speaking and Arabic-speaking readership, respectively. As can be seen through some translation gaps in her stories, she has different expectations for each audience, about its prejudices, norms, and knowledge.[6]

As I see it, the author's specific positionality between two cultural contexts adds both force and weakness to her social agenda. It allows her to act as a mediator for feminist messages, providing her with better tools for outreach thanks to her own inscription in the Egyptian context. On the other hand, as is suggested in the last story published to date, she seems to share a sense of estrangement over the authoritarian turn that many Egyptians who were inspired by the 2011 uprising felt. In 2013, the Egyptian army seized power and took over the country. In this, as I observed firsthand, they had the support of a significant part of the population.[7] This left many activists feeling orphaned by "the people" (*al-sha'b*) they had thought of themselves as fighting for.

In this chapter, I first briefly sketch the history of comics in Egypt, to provide some background to Mohamed's work. Then, I discuss the effects of the 2011 uprising on how cultural production in Egypt has been reported abroad, to better understand what, besides the quality of Mohamed's stories, led to Qahera's immediate success among journalists and researchers. After that, I discuss the role Islam plays in Qahera's adventures, which also provides an opportunity to discuss the existing research literature on this superheroine. Next, I compare the English and Arabic versions of Qahera to see how Mohamed adapts her discourse to fit the intended readership. Finally, in the last section, I return to Mohamed's position at the fringe of both English-speaking and Arabic-speaking sets of references, and how this can both increase her work's outreach potential and foster feelings of alienation.

---

4. Bailey Jones 2015, 144–148; Duncan 2015; Hunter 2015; Ivey 2015.

5. Mohamed 2016.

6. For a similar method of comparison between English and Arabic for an Egypto-Qatari website, see Abdel-Fadil 2013, and for another superhero comic set in the Egyptian context, see van Leeuwen and Suleiman 2010.

7. For a discussion about the reasons for this support, see Schielke 2014.

Comics in Egypt: A Short History

Writing on the history of comics in Egypt is complicated by the lack of a recent comprehensive study on the topic. Arabist Bertrand Millet's *Samir, Mickey, Sindbad et les autres: Histoire de la presse enfantine en Egypte*, published in 1987, and historian Allen Douglas and Arabist Fedwa Malti-Douglas's *Arab Comic Strips: Politics of an Emerging Mass Culture*, published in 1994, are key sources on this history, but both are more than two decades old.[8] Documentarian Muhammad Isma'il Amin's 2013 film *Kumiks bi'l-Misr* provides important information about the recent history of comics in the country. However, due to the narrative constraints of the film, it also takes many shortcuts, leaving it incomplete. Further, scattered information can also be found in the scholarship on Egyptian publisher AK Comics's superhero Zayn, by semiotician Theo van Leeuwen and communications scholar Usama Suleiman, and on the graphic novel *Metro*, by Middle East scholar and literary critic Brian T. Edwards.[9] Nevertheless, some topics remain completely undocumented, as for instance the circulation of manga in the country, and the sources sometimes contradict each other on dates and places of publication. Still, some of the axes of this history seem sufficiently established to be recounted here. This literature is a good starting point to clarify two cross-historical problems for comics in Egypt: first, it highlights the difficulty of adapting imported comics; and, second, it reveals the dilemma faced by publishers, who are torn between publishing comics with the aim of writing entertaining stories or educational tales. These problems are echoed in Qahera's adventures.

In Egypt, political cartoons were circulated to a wide audience already in the nineteenth century, with the satirical journal *Abu nazzara zarqa*, founded already in 1877 by the famous writer Ya'qub Sannu'.[10] Sequential art appeared only later in the country, however, first in the form of illustrated stories that had a narrative and paraphrased dialogues as a text block under the panels. The magazine *Al-Awlad*, which started publication in 1923 (and was cancelled in 1933), featured many such early comics. Its example was emulated by numerous followers, among them *Al-Atfal* (1936), a short-lived magazine which introduced Disney's Mickey Mouse in Egypt; *Baba Sadiq* (1934–1946); *Al-Bulbul* (1946–1951); *Al-Katkut* (1946–1949), a children's supplement to the feminist journal *Bint al-Nil*, which introduced the charac-

8. Millet 1987; Douglas and Malti-Douglas 1994.

9. van Leeuwen and Suleiman 2010; Edwards 2014. [Editors' note: See the article by Fredrik Strömberg in this volume.]

10. Zack 2014.

ters Tintin and Tarzan to Egyptian audiences;[11] *Baba Sharu* (1948–1950); and *'Ali Baba* (1951–1953), to name a few.

The overthrow of King Faruq in 1952 by the Free Officers, and the nationalization of the press that followed, did not stop the publication of comics in Egypt. Founded shortly after, *Samir* (1956–2002) remained the most famous comic magazine in Egypt for a long time. Its main competitors were *Sindibad* (1952–1961) and *Miki* (*Mickey*) (1959–). It was also during this period, at the end of the 1950s, that speech balloons finally made their way into Egyptian publications.[12] As these formal developments were taking place, official efforts at the highest level sought to Egyptianize and moralize comics. The magazine *Karawan* (1964), for example, was an attempt promoted by the state to create Egyptian comics that had an educational message for the nation's youth, aimed at mobilizing the children for national endeavors. The magazine quickly failed, probably due to management problems, but according to Millet, the setback was attributed at the time to the pressure of one of its competitors, *Subirman* (*Superman*), launched the same year.[13]

Later, beginning in the 1970s, with the liberal turn undertaken by President Anwar al-Sadat and prolonged by Husni Mubarak, the work conditions for authors in publication houses owned by the state deteriorated, with a subsequent loss in the quality of their magazines. This paved the way for new publications, some of them edited outside of Egypt, even as they employed many Egyptian authors. *Majid* (1979–), published in the United Arab Emirates,[14] and *Basim* (1987–), published in Saudi Arabia, were both widely distributed in Egypt. *Tan Tan* (*Tintin*) (1971–1980), *Flash* (1990–), and *'Ala' al-Din* (1993–), which first appeared in these years, are probably the most famous magazines published in Egypt.

Among the locally produced comics, some were created by foreigners, as for instance the Italian Morelli, who had first introduced speech balloons in Egypt, or the French Berny, who created the comics character Samir, who gave his name to the eponymous magazine. Berny's compatriot Ruffieux drew an official comics biography of Nasser published in 1973.[15] There were, however, many Egyptian comics creators active at this time, among whom

11. Millet 1987, 51–52.
12. Millet 1987, 108.
13. According to Millet, Nasser himself was behind the lauch of *Karawan*. Concerning *Subirman*, after the interruption of its publication in Egypt in 1964 partly due to the scandal around the failure of *Karawan*, it started again in Lebanon from 1971 to 1995 (Millet 1987, 69–73; Hisham 2015; van Leeuwen and Suleiman 2010, 234).
14. Douglas and Malti-Douglas 1994, 150–173.
15. Millet 1987, 121–122; Douglas and Malti-Douglas 1994, 27–45.

Muhyi al-Din al-Labbad and Hijazi stand out. Nevertheless, many of the stories in these magazines were translated material from the U.S., France, and Belgium, as it was cheaper than paying Egyptian authors for the work.

Hence, the issue of adaptation and translation of comics can be found at all periods of their production in Egypt. Importation of comics material created tensions with Egyptian authors. Al-Labbad, for instance, wrote many articles and drew cartoons critical of the influence of foreign comics, which is somewhat unsurprising, considering that he had a leading role in the launch of the magazine *Karawan*.[16] Different strategies have been used to counter the problem. Arabizations (*ta'rib*) occurred, for example by changing the names and the aspect of characters, or sometimes even the narrative style of the stories. For instance, the first Mickey adventures in Arabic in 1936 were all translated in the classical style of *zaghal* poetry, in order to further Arabize the material. For his first appearances in the magazine *Katkut*, Tintin was renamed Human, his hair became brown, he lost his famous quiff hairstyle, and he sometimes wore a tasseled *tarbush* cap.[17] Likewise, Clark Kent, the alias of Superman, was called Nabil Fawzi in some Lebanese translation in the seventies, and an Iraqi version of the character from the end of the 1980s, who was called *al-Rajul al-Khariq* (Miraculous Man), was redrawn with a moustache.[18] Much later, in 2004–2006, there was an attempt to further Arabize superheroes by the publisher AK Comics, who produced four superhero titles called the "Middle East Heroes," but the experiment did not last long.[19]

Beside the debates that could arise concerning the national anchoring of comic characters, the debates surrounding the cancellation of *Karawan* hint at another major rift in Egyptian comics production, which runs throughout its history: this is the question of whether comics should primarily be a tool for educational or for commercial purposes, the latter implying a focus on entertainment without strong considerations for moral aims. Thus, another purpose of *Karawan* was to moralize the production of comics and to make them a tool for mobilizing the nation's youth. However, rather than a blank opposition, there is a continuum between comics that put the stress on the message or on the narrative. As American comics pioneer Will Eisner has noted about instructional comics in the U.S., authors most often mix entertaining and explanatory sections in their stories, to make them attractive

16. al-Labbad 2012, 30–35, 67, 94–95.

17. Millet 1987, 107–108. Millet suspects that it was also a way to avoid paying rights on the stories.

18. Hisham 2015.

19. van Leeuwen and Suleiman 2010.

for readers.[20] The same strategies were used in Egypt. Serious topics and educational content was always present, even in commercial magazines.

Since the beginning of Egyptian comics history, magazines devoted to comics for children and adolescents were the main publication venue for comics. Therefore, the publication in 2008 of the graphic novel *Metro* by Majdi al-Shafi'i was seen as the birth of a new genre.[21] A new wave of projects followed, including independent magazines targeting an adult audience, as for instance *Tok Tok* (2011–)[22] and *Garage* (2015–). Further, the Internet has offered an additional platform for comic artists. *Qahera* is just one example of such webcomics. There is, for instance, the Facebook page *Waraqa* by Islam Gawish, which has more than a million "likes." Gawish's work went relatively unnoticed on the international level until he was interrogated by the police for his mild satire of President Abd al-Fattah al-Sisi in 2016.[23]

Journalists, Researchers, and the Egyptian Art Scene after 2011

The Egyptian uprising in 2011 has been the subject of much writing by journalists and researchers. Many factors contributed to this new focus on Egypt: the surprise effect of an event that nobody had really foreseen; the enthusiasm elicited by the promise of a revolution; and, on a more practical level, the increased demand of expertise on the region, as well as the cor-related willingness of scholarly funding agencies to allot money to projects related to the upheaval in the Arab world. For instance, a survey of academic bibliographies I conducted revealed that 455 publications in English were dedicated to the Egyptian uprising in 2011–2012.[24] In a critique of the phenomenon, sociologist Mona Abaza even talked of "academic tourists sight-seeing the Arab Spring."[25]

This period also witnessed a shift in academic attention that reflects the proximity of current research to journalism and policy-making. Until 2011, the bulk of research in the Middle East was on Islamization. The Egyptian uprising, by contrast, has hastily been labelled as a revolution of the liberal educated youth.[26] This was congruent with the image of a new "wave of democratization," where democratic ideas are seen as suddenly flooding the Middle East, after having done so in southern Europe, South America,

---

20. Eisner 2008, 147–148.
21. Edwards 2014.
22. Carle 2016.
23. Qualey 2016.
24. Kreil and Sabaseviciute forthcoming.
25. Abaza 2011.
26. El-Mahdi 2011.

and eastern Europe between the 1970s and the 1990s.[27] This bias of seeing events in the Middle East as a revolution of the liberal educated youth was amplified by a narrative of technological progress that figured them as a "Revolution 2.0" led by social media activists.[28]

The social components of the 2011 uprising were far more diverse than the media and scholarly narrative suggests, and included, for instance, syndicates, militants from older political organizations, and Islamists. Likewise, without denying the importance of the organizational tools provided by social media, independent information and exchange platforms provided by the Internet, they alone cannot explain why the uprising started or the forms it took.[29]

Nevertheless, the figure of young Egyptian activists became an object of unprecedented interest in the period following 2011. This interest extended to cultural productions. Graffiti, hip-hop, and electro artists were courted by journalists and academics. It seems that the forms of art that were privileged in the moment were those immediately considered as subversive according to Western standards. Comics, with its historical links to the underground in North America and Europe, was one of the art forms that many could spontaneously associate with youth at that time.[30]

Mohamed, the author of *Qahera*, was herself surprised by the amount of attention that her work attracted from journalists and scholars from the very start.[31] A newcomer, less than twenty years old, still a student, and with no networks in the Cairene comics scene, she started drawing these stories mostly for herself and her close network of friends, more as a "joke," as she notes in an interview.[32] The success encountered by the first publications encouraged her to continue, and she began to realize how much weight her social commentaries could potentially have.

Indeed, Mohamed's positioning allowed her to fit perfectly into the expectations of the new observers of cultural life in Egypt. As an English-trained student, she has a very good grasp of U.S. cultural references. The way she writes about gender issues was also greatly informed by her education, to the point that she had difficulties using the Arabic terminology, if they even existed.[33] Further, her first comics were noticeably influenced

27. Stepan and Linz 2013.
28. Ghonim 2012.
29. Bennani-Chraïbi and Fillieule 2012; Gonzalez-Quijano 2012.
30. Taher 2011.
31. For an overview of articles published about Qahera, see http://qaherathesuperhero.com/elsewhere.
32. Lewis 2014.
33. Mohamed 2016, 140.

by her readings on the Internet. Islamophobia is not a common problem in Egypt, where more than ninety percent of the inhabitants are Muslim.[34] Hence, she was very aware of how Qahera's appearance would likely be interpreted by Western audiences, and rather uncertain about its relevance for the Egyptian audience.

A Muslim Hero against Islamophobia

The three academic publications to date that discuss Qahera are dedicated to the issues of the veil and Islamophobia. English scholar Jackie Duncan compares *Qahera* with Marjane Satrapi's *Persepolis* – the story of Satrapi's childhood in Iran – in order to underline the diversity of practices and purposes associated with the veil.[35] Education scholar Rachel Bailey Jones presents Qahera as an example of an insider discourse that can be usefully mobilized by teachers in the U.S. to deconstruct stereotypes about Muslim women wearing the *hijab*.[36] Finally, communications scholar Christina Ivey focuses on the second Qahera story, wherein the superheroine encounters the feminist activist group Femen, founded in the Ukraine and based in Paris, as a symbol of empowerment for Muslim women.[37]

I find some aspects of these papers problematic. They reflect the biases that a reading centered on debates on Islam in the U.S. can elicit. For example, Ivey interprets the Qahera-meets-Femen story as a response to the "epistemic violence"[38] that Western feminists commit against Muslim women and their culture, due to a lack of awareness of differences and of their own privileged status. From Ivey's point of view, "Qahera wears the hijab not to *conceal* her identity (as many superheroes do) but to *project* her identity. Indeed, her power seems to come from her traditional dress, as she is empowered by her choice to wear the hijab despite critiques of the possibilities of Islamic feminisms."[39] Although this statement is well phrased, a problem with some of Ivey's assumption comes from her homogenizing approach concerning "Egyptian/Muslim culture," which erases tensions within the culture described. Furthermore, to label the *hijab* as "traditional" does not give an accurate account of its history in Egypt, which, as we will see below, is far more complex. Likewise, I would not claim, as Bailey Jones

---

34. Elsässer 2014, 5.
35. Duncan 2015.
36. Bailey Jones 2015.
37. Ivey 2015.
38. The concept is originally from Gayatri Spivak 1999, 127.
39. Ivey 2015, 384. Emphasis in original.

does, that Qahera is "using her identity and clothing as a source of power."[40] Mohamed never explains the origins of Qahera's superpowers. As such, she is a superhero who happens to be veiled, who defends her freedom of choice as a woman, but who does not necessarily feel any sense of superiority because of it.

Thus, it seems necessary to clarify the way Islam is mobilized as a reference in the Qahera strips. As noted above, the fact that she is a Muslim woman wearing the veil may be one of Qahera's most striking attributes. However, the *hijab* has lost most of its distinctive power in Egypt nowadays. It was reintroduced in the cities in the 1970s, in the wake of a process of Islamization of public space that was started under the Sadat presidency. It reappeared in a form clearly distinct from the veil worn by peasant women or the *burqa* worn until the 1920s, which made it suitable for educated young Egyptian women, who were among the main proponents of the reintroduction of the veil. The resurgent veil's success and progressive hegemony also meant a weakening of its meaning. As the vast majority of Muslim women ended up wearing the veil, with plenty of different styles and colors to choose from, and accessorized it with all kind of outfits, ranging from the prudish to the sexy, it could no longer be associated with a special sense of piety.[41] It is difficult to assess at this time, but the short presidency of Muhammad Morsi (June 2012–July 2013) might have contributed to further losses of semantic power for the *hijab*.[42]

Further, it should be made clear from the outset that Mohamed is not drawing religious comics. Religious comics in an Islamicate context were studied by Douglas and Malti-Douglas. They mostly illustrate stories from the Qur'an, from the hadith, and from the biography of the Prophet Muhammad, or they are educational tales about the rewards of being a good Muslim, sometimes mixed with nationalist content.[43] Mohamed does not address such religious issues directly in her stories. She does invoke a religious discourse about women's rights from time to time, but never from a theological point of view.

This is the case with the first story of the serial, for instance, where a bearded sheikh lectures a group of smiling men, telling them that: "A good wife is an obedient wife! It is your Islamic duty to keep your women at home and in check!" In reaction to hearing this, what Qahera calls "the sound ...

40. Bailey Jones 2015, 55.
41. Hoffmann-Ladd 1985; Füger and Haenni 1996; Abaza 2007.
42. This remark is based on my own observation, and determining whether it is truly a trend would require further inquiry and longer observations.
43. Douglas and Malti-Douglas 1994, 82–83.

of misogynistic trash!" she says that "[her] super-hearing can't handle this nonsense," before springing into action. She swoops down on the sheikh, telling him that he is right, that "[h]ousework is women's work, absolutely." "I especially enjoy doing *laundry*," she says in the segment's final panel, in the background of which the reader can see the sheikh, now hanging from a clothesline and kept in place with clothespins. That this strip was published on June 30, 2013, is probably not a coincidence. The sheikh and his audience represent Islamists. This was the day of the huge demonstrations which led to the overthrow of Morsi, who belonged to the Muslim Brotherhood. Morsi's overthrow was first enthusiastically backed by many supporters of the 2011 uprising.

To be sure, the didactic means of a superhero like Qahera – fists, swords, and sticks – are rather basic and would probably not allow for an elaborate discussion about the religious validity of the relegation of women to the domestic sphere by some Muslim scholars. However, her indignation seems less propelled by the religious inadequacy of the teachings of the sheikhs whom she attacks than by their misogyny. She claims an autonomous position for Muslim women, where they are free to make their own choices and are aware of their rights. At the end of this same story, she turns against a teacher explaining to a group of women clad in Western clothes that Muslim women are oppressed and need saving. "Oh no! My super hearing is detecting more rubbish," Qahera says in response. "Here we go again," she adds in the final panel, and unsheathes her sword. This should also be understood as a way to avoid being seen as aligning with Islamophobic discourses. Along the same lines, in the second Qahera story, the superheroine fights the Western feminist activist group Femen, who likewise set out to "save" her. While they, like their real-world counterparts, might think they are doing something good, it is clear from the strip that they are regarded as actually doing harm, because of racism conscious or unconscious. They end up being left by Qahera to dangle off the branches of a tree.

To put it in Mohamed's own words:

> The simple fact that it was being published in English meant that
> key aspects of Qahera/*Qahera* as a character and a comic were
> established from the very beginning – especially that she had no time
> for exclusionary Western feminism that dismissed her, and that she
> did not exist as a vehicle for viewers to project their own narrative of
> oppressed Middle Eastern Muslim women on her. The language choice
> also influenced the projection and reception of other important,
> visible aspects of her identity, the most obvious of which is the hijab,
> which is viewed far more negatively in the West where visibly Muslim

women tend to bear the brunt of Islamophobia. Had the comic been created with a predominantly Egyptian or Arabic-speaking audience in mind, it is doubtful these qualities would have been developed as central to the character.[44]

This is why she later did not find it relevant to translate her two first stories into Arabic. For her, they made little sense in the Egyptian context.[45]

Qahera's religious options seem influenced by the trend of *wasatiyya*, a word which is difficult to translate but conveys the meaning of "moderation" and "middle way" at the same time, as it comes from *wasat*, the middle. As such, it is claimed by many different actors in the Egyptian religious field. The difficulty resides in the problem of defining the poles between which this interpretation could figure as a middle way. The term can perhaps best be described as a mode of Islamic universalism, whose claims of being adapted to our times relies on an eclectic and varying mix of references to religion, to science, to rights, and to the everyday habits of the Egyptian middle and upper classes. Supporters of *wasatiyya*, hence, often distinguish themselves strongly from the Salafi approach, deemed as too rigid and narrow-minded,[46] as Mohamed does in some of her stories.

Further, Mohamed refuses to be considered as a spokesperson for anyone.[47] However, is she not somehow trapped in this role by her initial creation of Qahera with the *hijab* as her main attribute, unintentionally inviting interpretations of the comics in generalizing culturalist terms? Is the paradigm of identity in which Mohamed inscribed her work at the beginning now an inescapable straightjacket? In the quotation above, Mohamed explains that she probably would not have put such an emphasis on the religious identity of her character if she had written the stories for an Egyptian or Arab-speaking audience. Thus, the stories which she wrote after starting to translate Qahera into Arabic tend to embed her work more within the Egyptian context.

An Egyptian Hero for Women's Rights

The first Qahera story Mohamed translated into Arabic is about sexual harassment. According to her, it was created in response to insistent demands from some of her followers, and, as she told me, she did not take the translation quite seriously at the time. She did not even care enough to reverse the reading direction of the panels from left to right to right to left, which would

44. Mohamed 2016, 140.
45. Interview with Deena Mohamed, 04/05/2016.
46. Kreil 2015b.
47. Lewis 2014; with Deena Mohamed, 04/05/2016.

have been standard in Arab comics. Hence, Arabic readers had to refer to the numbering of the panels to understand their order. Later, from the fourth story on, she has reversed the order.

In this story, Mohamed's third strip, Qahera's non-veiled friend Layla Magdy makes her first appearance. A man grabs Layla's rear in the street, and when she tries to file a complaint at the police station, the policeman patronizingly says that he "understand[s] you say that man harassed you, and to be honest I believe you, I really do," but adds that the way she is dressed is "immodest ... inappropriate."[48] Once she is out, she rebuffs the comments and advances of another group of men, and they try to attack her with a knife. At that moment, Qahera suddenly appears, takes the men down with her fighting stick, and leaves them hanging outside the police station, with a message written on the wall both in English – "These men are per-verts" – and in Arabic: "*mutaharrishin,*" which means harassers. In the Arabic translation, published later, the English sentence disappears.

That the issue of sexual harassment allowed Mohamed to build a bridge between her English- and the Arabic-speaking readerships is linked with the internationalized context in which the struggle against harassment has taken place since the mid-2000s. Since the opposition to and prevention of sexual harassment was made part of the United Nations agenda in the 1990s, this has opened the way for initiatives by NGOs to fight against the phenom-enon. Funding and logistical support have been made available to them for this purpose. Establishing a standard translation for the concept of sexual harassment was part of the strategy. The Conference on Women in Beijing in 1995 institutionalized *taharrush jinsi* as the standard Arabic translation. The word has permitted situations which otherwise would have been either deemed as issues of women's modesty or as a way of flirting – as in the Qa-hera example above – to be redefined as crimes. Thus, the responsibility of men in cases of harassment and the severity of the act can more easily be put forward.

The issue gained further visibility on the international level after large-scale sexual aggressions against women during the mass demonstrations on Tahrir Square in 2011–2013.[49] Hence, sexual harassment is a topic that is easy to grasp for both an English-speaking and an Arabic-speaking readership. (There was even another Egyptian superhero helping harassed women at that time, but with no Islamic reference in his aspect: *Subir-Makh*, drawn by Makhluf for the magazine *Tok Tok*.) Mohamed dedicated the fourth Qahera strip to the topic of sexual harassment during mass demonstrations. In the

48. Ellipsis in original.
49. Kreil 2016.

story, Qahera is observing a demonstration. On the ground, some men stare lustfully at demonstrating women. Their faces are framed in subpanels, giving prominence to their glances and setting them apart from the women and from the rest of the demonstration. A panel shows money passing from an arm in a suit to a bare arm with a bracelet. In the following panel, the arm with the bracelet grasps the arm of a woman. Then, the woman is carried away by the group of harassers previously shown.

For this sequence, the comments to the pictures, which reflect Qahera's thoughts, are scattered between three panels and read: "I do my best to protect women. From harassment, as they like to call it. A light word, all things considered. It's not harassment. It is a *crime*."[50] Hence, Mohamed describes the word, which has already been introduced strategically to criminalize the harassers' behaviors, as a light word compared to the indescribable horror of the crimes against women that were perpetrated during the demonstrations. The Arabic version is similar to the English one. Qahera later intervenes and saves the women. Her comment goes on:

> They threaten women in every way. Because women are half of
> society. Remove their voice, and society is vulnerable. Sometimes,
> I don't make it in time ... and sometimes, I am not needed. But no
> matter what they keep on going. I am a superhero because I have
> superpowers. They are superheroes because they do not.

"I remember at one point during the revolution, people would use statistics of attacks on women to discredit political movements – and Egyptians – at large," Mohamed adds in a short text below the English version. Hence, she seems to subscribe to the narrative that political agents hostile to the demonstrations financed these attacks.

As mentioned in the introduction, Mohamed considers her work a tool, not as social commentary. As such, it has educational tones and is structured around social causes. What is obvious from the moment she starts translating her stories into Arabic, and later begins to conceive them in this language, is that the issue of Islamophobia vanishes completely. The focus instead lands on issues of social responsibility and women's rights. Likewise, as I have already noted above, she allots much more space to specific details that only readers with sufficient knowledge of Egypt can understand.

The fifth story, for instance, in its Arabic version, is about the music video for Egyptian pop-singer Tamir Husni and the U.S. rapper Snoop Dogg's song "Si al-Sayed" (*Si al-Sayyid*), which is a reference to the ambiguous patriarch in a trilogy of novels from the mid-1950s by writer Naguib Mahfuz. The

---

50. Emphasis in original.

expression "Si al-Sayed" has since become a colloquialism in Egypt, used to designate a man dominating his wife and family. To my knowledge, the song had little success outside of the Middle East. Thus, in the English version, the title is only evoked in small letters blasting out of a computer, surrounded by parodied "misogynistic lyrics" in big letters (the words "misogynistic lyrics" themselves are the largest in this panel).[51] Later in the English-language version, Mohamed adds a note to explain that "Si al-Sayed" is "a term denoting a lot of manliness, the context being that said manliness is superior to all else." In the Arabic version, the main text blasting out of the computer simply reads "I am Si al-Sayed" with other lyrics in small type. Mohamed seems to assume that the reader is familiar both with the song and the figure. The Arabic version contains a pun Mohamed confessed that she had problems translating. Daydreaming in response to the song's lyrics, Qahera fantasizes about holding the singer in the air, and seeing how, out of fear, his "I am Si al-Sayyid" becomes "I am *sis*." *Sis* designates a flimsy man in Egyptian colloquial Arabic. In English, instead, "I am Si al-Sayed" simply becomes "I am sorry." It is obvious that the story was originally conceived in Arabic, which Mohamed corroborates.[52]

The sixth story, on the reactions to the Israeli bombings in Gaza in July 2014, evokes arguments against Palestinians which could typically be heard in Egyptian coffee shops at that time. Hamas is an offshoot of the Muslim Brotherhood, and as such, it was suspected of helping its Egyptian brother-party in the fight against the overthrow of Morsi. Qahera is outraged by the lack of compassion of her compatriots for the victims. The only person apart from her who speaks on behalf of the Palestinians is a bearded man, clearly an Islamist, who deplores that Muslims were killed there, to which Qahera answers that there are also Christians in Gaza. The whole scene is set in a coffee shop. After Qahera is asked to leave, because she is "causing a fuss," a fire erupts and the customers are trapped inside, in analogy with the situations of the people of Gaza, which Qahera makes clear, by echoing the words of one of the men in the coffee shop: "So here is a situation ... If I stand aside [as the men had advocated about Gaza], you will almost certainly die ... But it's not like I started this fire ... And saving you may come at a cost to myself ... Why should I help?" Qahera saves them, of course, "because [she does not] want to have [their] blood on [her] hands." In the next panel, a sheet covered with the names of the victims of the bombings written on

51. One of the lines reads "almost as bad as blurred lines." This is a reference to U.S. singer Robin Thicke's 2013 song "Blurred Lines," which sparked controversy because of lyrics that many thought were suggestive of rape.
52. Mohamed 2016, 144; interview with Deena Mohamed, 04/05/2016.

it in Arabic, is shown unfurled. The identity of the last victims is stated as "unknown" (*majhul*). Mohamed dedicates three panels with no dialogue in balloons for the sheet, which enhances the dramatic effect of its appearance and creates the sensation of an unlimited time span.[53] In a fourth panel, a wide shot shows that the sheet hangs from the presidential palace at Qasr al-Qubba. The sheet has the words "Martyrs of Gaza" at its top. Written on the ground where the sheet ends, in front of the palace, are the words: "We have their blood on our hands." Noticeably, Mohamed does not translate the list of names on the sheet into English, which also suggests that the story was first drawn in Arabic. The titles also differ: in Arabic, it reads "On Nationalism and Humanity," and in English "On Accountability." Apparently, Mohamed did not consider the issue of nationalism as equally relevant for the English-speaking readership.

The seventh story, the second one in which a religious argument occurs, is another good example of the way Mohamed's stories became more and more embedded in the Egyptian context. The setting is a coffee shop again. Two Egyptian men debate about the *hijab*. The first one argues against it. He interprets it as a sign of backwardness, praises countries where the *hijab* is forbidden, and adds, in the Arabic version, that it seeing non-veiled women is "a thing that opens the feelings and uplifts the heart." The panel projects the men outside of Egypt, to an imagined place where women are all dressed in Western fashion, with a waitress taking their orders. A man who speaks in a mix of classical Arabic and colloquial Egyptian argues against him, in favor of the veil. He uses well-known metaphors about the issue: for instance, that a woman without veil is like an unwrapped candy attracting insects or like money without a wallet: "We cover our women for the same reason you carry money in a wallet! Because it's valuable and we don't want it exposed to everyone!" Qahera and her friend Layla listen to these men talk until Qahera has enough and interrupts them, telling them that women's choices are none of their business: "Women's lives are not for you to prove a point! Our choices are not your political punchlines. And they are worthy of respect." In this story, there are references to places outside of Egypt, but the topic is not Islamophobia. It is part of an intra-Egyptian and intra-Muslim debate.

Thus, by switching languages, Mohamed also switched from an argument against Islamophobia to what she herself describes as an outreach tactic to convey messages to the people of her country.[54] This way, her discourses on women's rights could get rid of suspicions of being a foreign import alien to Egypt, as it is a visibly Muslim woman who is defending them in the stories.

53. McCloud 2006, 164–165.
54. Interview with Deena Mohamed, 04/05/2016.

This tactic of Islamizing messages about women's rights or sexual health issues, in order to make people accept them more easily, is rather common in Egypt. It is one of the reasons for the collaboration between the United Nations Fund for Population (UNFPA) and Islamic University of al-Azhar, for instance. Likewise, sex-education classes given by Egyptian counselling associations always started with citations of the Qur'an and the hadith evoking sexual matters, as a way to explain to the audience that it was licit to speak about this topic openly.[55] Yet, to resort to such outreach tactics can also hint at the difficulties encountered by proponents of women's rights in legitimizing their discourses.

Outreach and Alienation

Despite the history of adaptation to Arabic of foreign comics heroes, super-heroes, in Mohamed's eyes, cannot rid themselves of their sense of being imported goods. This is an issue that she is struggling with.[56] This is part of her more general concern about the accuracy of the stories she writes for the different readerships she tries to reach. Her attempts to make Qahera's adventures relevant for both the English-speaking and the Arabic-speaking public provide important hints about the ways she envisions cultural contexts. She expects different reactions and sets of knowledge from each of these publics, and this has a deep impact on the way she conceives her stories and dialogues. As already noted, she does not consider it useful to translate her two first stories about Islamophobia into Arabic, because she did not consider the topic relevant for her Egyptian readership. Likewise, her stories in Arabic are full of references and details that she omits for the English-speaking readership. Sometimes, she even feels compelled to add an exploratory note in the English versions of the story, as in the example of Si al-Sayed described above. Thus, her strategy for translating the strip into English seems to oscillate between simplifying the story and adding explanations that are not there in the Arabic version.[57]

To understand the purpose of these choices, it is necessary to briefly come back again to the aim Mohamed assigns to her work, namely as a tool for social commentary. This explains the didactic undertone of some of Qahera's stories. Thus, the balance between the didactic (*khatibi*) dimension and the development of story is a concern for her.[58] In this regard, Qahera's

55. Kreil 2015a.

56. Mohamed 2016, 140–141.

57. For an example of translation strategy relying on the specification of context and the erasure of conflicts, see van Leeuwen and Suleiman 2010.

58. Interview with Deena Mohamed, 04/05/2016.

stories could be seen as a project to present purposeful art molded into the entertaining frame of comics, a use of this medium, which, as noted, has precedents in Egypt.[59] However, as Mohamed's stories are addressed to an adult audience, they have no patronizing or lecturing tone.

Hence, entertainment is part of the outreach potential of the *Qahera* stories. The romping character of the superheroine's beatings is almost reminiscent of Punch and Judy or their Egyptian counterpart, Aragoz, except that Mohamed loads them with moral content. Further, she has deliberately decided to write the Arabic dialogues in colloquial Egyptian, which invites a more direct emotional involvement from the readers. Is this choice the result of a lack of confidence with classical Arabic from a student with an Anglophone education, a way to more directly address the readership, or can it be attributed to the rise of a generation that is comfortable with transnational references and which does not fear mixing the repertories of high art and of pop culture?[60] The answer probably comprises a bit of all three elements.

Hence, Mohamed is straddling American and Egyptian referential universes. This places her and her work in an ambivalent position, on the margins of the Egyptian cultural field. On one hand, the strength of this position resides in the potential for outreach it provides, allowing mediation of women's rights issues to a broad local readership. On the other hand, belonging to the liberal educated youth can foster feelings of alienation toward Egyptian society and doubts about the legitimacy of one's discourse. In this regard, *Qahera* follows the same trajectory as many participants to the 2011 uprising, who grew increasingly disaffected, first as the military seized power in 2013, and then as this return to authoritarian politics was supported by significant parts of the population. The 2011 uprising started with the slogan "The people want the downfall of the regime." Suddenly, it looked like the people instead wanted a strengthening of the regime and its repressive forces in the name of order and stability.

Mohamed's eighth, and, at the time of writing, last Qahera story has a sad undertone. In it, Qahera expresses a sense of alienation, which results in a certain helplessness. In this episode, the superhero saves a woman from robbers. However, instead of being grateful, the victim rebukes Qahera because of her privilege – her ability to fly – while the woman's own brother has to go through a difficult journey to emigrate. It is difficult not to read in this story the estrangement of the supporters of the 2011 uprising evoked above, seen especially in the fourth strip, where Qahera crowns the women

59. Millet 1987; Douglas and Malti-Douglas 1994.
60. Edwards 2014, 72; Jacquemond 2016.

demonstrators as the real superheroes. Hence, it was probably a shock for the revolutionaries to see a large and vocal part of the nation's population turn their wrath against them so soon after the regime change. At the end of the story, to solve her dilemma, Qahera offers a plane ticket to the woman. The last panel shows a plane bringing this woman out of the country. When I interviewed Mohamed, she asked me what it means for a superhero to solve problems by offering a plane ticket to a woman, to help her leave. If everybody could fly, Egypt would be emptied of its people, she said, adding that everybody wants to leave.[61] After the eighth strip, Mohamed published no new Qahera stories for approximately nine months. Only recently, on April 4, 2016, did she publish a new image of Qahera: in the picture, the superhero can be seen holding up a collapsing bridge. Apparently, Mohamed seems to think that the country still needs its superheroes to keep it from falling apart.

Conclusion

Qahera's stories illustrate problems that have persisted throughout the history of comics in Egypt. Issues of translation and of anchoring the comics art form in the nation are reflected in Mohamed's initial doubts about the relevance of making Arabic versions of Qahera's stories, and in the interest the character has proven to hold for an Egyptian audience. However, the more Mohamed develops the Arabic part of the serial, the more specific she gets about the country's difficulties. Hence, the problem seems to solve itself. *Qahera* has evolved from a story written for an international readership to a tale full of winks that are understandable only for the Egyptian reader. Even in the strip's sense of alienation, it expresses doubts that are shared by a significant part of the county's population.

Historian Beth Baron, in her book *Egypt as Woman*, describes the many ways the country has been personified by feminine figures in nationalist discourse.[62] What would it be, then, to think of Egypt as Qahera? It would hint at the circulation and reshaping of American figures of pop culture through an active reappropriation, and to a possible generational shift in art practice that started a few years before the 2011 uprising.[63] Further, she serves as a useful reminder of the hardships inherent in social and political commitments, in outreach and alienation, and of the sometimes unsolvable dilemmas that can result from activism. As such, Qahera testifies to an experience firmly anchored in the struggles of Egypt after 2013, but what she has to say about it reaches far beyond that time and place.

61. Interview with Deena Mohamed, 04/05/2016.
62. Baron 2007.
63. Edwards 2016; Jacquemond 2016.

Works Cited

Abaza, M. 2011. "Academic Tourists Sight-Seeing the Arab Spring." *Jadaliyya*, September 27. http://www.jadaliyya.com/pages/index/2767/academic-tourists-sight-seeing-the-arab-spring.

——. 2007. "Shifting Landscapes of Fashion in Contemporary Egypt." *Fashion Theory: The Journal of Dress, Body & Culture* 11 (2): 281–297.

Abdel-Fadil, M. 2013. "Islam Online Guides Spouses Towards Marital Bliss: Arabic vs. English Counselling Perspectives on Marital Communication." In *Muslims and the New Information and Communication Technologies: Notes from an Emerging and Infinite Field*, edited by T. Hoffmann, and G. Larsson, 49–71. Dordrecht.

al-Labbad, M. a.-D. 2012. *Naẓar!* Cairo.

Bailey Jones, R. 2015. *(Re)Thinking Orientalism: Using Graphic Narratives to Teach Critical Visual Literacy*. New York.

Baron, B. 2007. *Egypt as a Woman: Nationalism, Gender, and Politics*. Berkeley.

Bennani-Chraïbi, M., and O. Fillieule. 2012. "Pour une sociologie des situations révolutionnaires: Retour sur les révoltes arabes." *Revue française de Science politique* 62 5: 767–796.

Carle, Z. 2016. "Les phylactères du Caire: Entretien avec Mohammed Shennawy." *Vacarme* 74 (1): 66–71.

Douglas, A., and F. Malti-Douglas. 1994. *Arab Comic Strips: Politics of an Emerging Mass Culture*. Bloomington.

Duncan, J. 2015. "Beyond the Veil: Graphic Representation of Islamic Women." *The Compass* 1 (2). http://scholarworks.arcadia.edu/thecompass/vol1/iss2/4.

Edwards, B. T. 2014. "Jumping Publics: Magdy El Shafee's Cairo Comics." *NOVEL A Forum on Fiction* 47 (1): 67–89.

——. 2016. *After the American Century: The Ends of U.S. Culture in the Middle East*. New York.

Eisner, W. 2008. *Comics and Sequential Art: Principles and Practices from the Legendary Cartoonist*. New York.

El-Mahdi, R. 2011. "Orientalizing the Egyptian Uprising." *Jadaliyya*, April 11. http://www.jadaliyya.com/pages/index/1214/orientalising-the-egyptian-uprising.

Elsässer, S. 2014. *The Coptic Question in the Mubarak Era*. Oxford.

Füger, H., and P. Haenni. 1996. "Métamorphoses du voile "islamique" et distinction sociale." *Egypte/Monde arabe* 20: 43–66.

Ghonim, W. 2012. *Revolution 2.0: The Power of the People Is Greater Than the People in Power: A Memoir*. Boston.

Gonzalez-Quijano, Y. 2012. *Arabités numériques: Le printemps du web arabe.* Arles.

Hisham, M. 2015. "Kumiks Bi-L-'arabi Al-Fasih": "Subirman" Yatahawwal Ila "Nabil" Fi Al-Nuskha Al-Lubnaniyya ... Wa Batman "Khashshaf" Fi Al-'iraqiyya." *Al-Misri al-Yawm*, April 10. http://lite.almasryalyoum.com/extra/50001.

Hoffmann-Ladd, V. 1985. "Polemics on the Modesty and the Segregation of Women in Egypt." *International Journal of Middle East Studies* 19 (1): 23–50.

Hunter, L. 2015. "(Re)Producing Difference: The Pedagogy of Graphic Narratives for Critical Visual Literacy." *Pedagogy, Culture & Society* 24 (2): 301–305.

Ivey, C. L. 2015. "Combating Epistemic Violence with Islamic Feminism: Qahera vs. Femen." *Women's Studies in Communication* 38 (4): 384–387.

Jacquemond, R. 2016. "Une révolution culturelle?" *Vacarme* 74 (1): 57–65.

Kreil, A. 2015a. "Pudeurs des corps, impudeurs des mots en Egypte: Formes et usages de la 'rhetorique du bris de silence' sur la sexualité." In *Voile, corps et pudeur: Approches historiques et anthropologiques*, edited by Y. Foehr-Janssens, S. Naef, and A. Schlaepfer, 155–168. Geneva.

———. 2015b. "Science de la psyché et autorité de l'islam : Quelles conciliations?" *Archives de sciences sociales des religions* 170: 267–282.

———. 2016. "Dire le harcèlement sexuel en Egypte: Les aléas de traduction d'une catégorie juridique." *Critique internationale* 70: 101–114.

Kreil, A., and G. Sabaseviciute. Forthcoming. "Révolution." In *Dictionnaire des concepts nomades en sciences humaines 3*, edited by O. Christin. Paris.

Lewis, D. 2014. "'Qahera' Webcomic Creator Deena Mohamed Talks Superheroes, Gaza, and Women." *IslamiCommentary*, July 29. http://islamicommentary.org/2014/07/qahera-webcomic-creator-deena-mohamed-talks-superheroes-gaza-and-women/.

McCloud, S. 2006. *Making Comics: Storytelling Secrets of Comics, Manga and Graphic Novels*. New York.

Millet, B. 1987. *Samir, Mickey, Sindbad et les autres: Histoire de la presse enfantine en Egypte*. Cairo.

Mohamed, D. 2016. "On Translating a Superhero: Language and Webcomics." In *Translating Dissent: Voices from and with the Egyptian Revolution*, edited by M. Baker, 137–147. New York, London.

Qualey, L. 2016. "Popular Egyptian Cartoonist Islam Gawish Arrested and Released." *Arabic Literature (in English)*, January 31. https://arablit.org/2016/01/31/popular-egyptian-cartoonist-islam-gawish-arrested/.

Schielke, S. 2014. "There Will Be Blood: Expecting Violence in Egypt, 2011–2014." *ZMO Working Papers* 11.

Spivak, G. 1999. *A Critique of Postcolonial Reason: Toward a History of the Vanishing Present.* Cambridge.

Stepan, A., and J. Linz. 2013. "Democratization Theory and the 'Arab Spring'." *Journal of Democracy* 24 (2): 15–30.

van Leeuwen, T., and U. Suleiman. 2010. "Globalizing the Local: The Case of an Egyptian Superhero Comic." In *The Handbook of Language and Globalization*, edited by N. Coupland, 232–254. Malden.

Zack, L. 2014. "The Use of the Egyptian Dialect in the Satirical Newspaper *Abu Naddara Zar'a.*" In *Alf Lahja Wa Lahja: Proceedings of the 9th Aida Conference*, edited by O. Durand, A. D. Langone, and G. Mion, 465–478. Vienna.

Truth, Justice, and the Spiritual Way:
Imam Ali as Muslim Super-hero

Hussein Rashid

la fata illa 'Ali la sayf illa Dhu'l-Fiqar
There is no hero besides Ali, there is no sword besides Dhulfiqar.[1]

Introduction

THERE ARE NUMEROUS MUSLIM SUPERHEROES in American comic books. Characters such as Kamala Khan (Ms. Marvel), Sooraya Qadir (Dust), Monet St. Croix (M), and Faiza Hussain (Excalibur) are some of the more recent additions to the Marvel Universe. DC Comics introduced Bilal Alsselah (Nightrunner) as the Batman of Paris and Simon Baz as a Green Lantern to much fanfare. Each of these characters fits a Muslim into an established mold of comics superhero. Yet, there is also a long tradition of illustrated heroic tales in Islamicate cultures – cultures that are influenced by Muslims – that predates American comics. Islamicate traditions of heroic stories partnered with pictures continue into the present day. These heroic tales and archetypes are distinct from those present in the American comics medium. The rise of Muslim characters in the comics superhero genre should not obscure Muslim traditions of heroic stories.

One of the most important heroic figures in Islam is Ali, a close relation of the Prophet Muhammad. Ali's biographical details indicate that he was a figure of great moral vision. This moral core is a signature element of what becomes his heroic narrative. In Islamicate literatures, we find that heroes are individuals who serve as exemplars.[2] The Islamicate hero is extraordinary, but can and should be emulated. In some traditions, more fantastic elements are introduced to the heroic story, so that the hero now becomes a super-hero, as opposed to a superhero.

The distinction between "superhero" and "super-hero" looks small, but

1. Traditional Muslim expression.
2. Renard 1993, 1, 9.

it is crucial. A hero is someone who acts at the limits of human capability, or in a selfless manner. Everyday heroes may include firefighters or teachers. A superhero often exceeds the normal bounds of human capability, and achieves heroic feats as a result of these abilities. An Islamicate super-hero is a hero who may be given special abilities because of her heroic qualities. The superhero is heroic because of her super powers, while the super-hero is super powered because of her heroism.[3]

The stories of the hero and the super-hero are parallel collections referencing the same person. The distinction between a Superman and Clark Kent does not exist in Islamicate narratives, as the Islamicate hero does not have an alter ego. A possible parallel would be Jennifer Walters, aka She-Hulk. She is recognizable as the same person in both her roles as lawyer and superhero, but does different heroic actions in each capacity.

The Islamicate super-hero is also often granted her amazing abilities by divine favor, so this person is now uncanny and cannot be successfully emulated. The moral inspiration of the hero remains in super-hero stories, but the dominant didactic approach is gone. However, because the tales of the super-hero remind the consumer[4] of the hero, the consumer still seeks to emulate the hero.

To look for the super-heroic qualities in Islamicate tales, as a parallel of superheroism, is to misread the tradition. These stories do not have superheroes. The super-heroic qualities are incidental to the purpose of these traditions. It is the hero, and her heroic qualities, that consumers want to emulate. We can speak of Muslim superheroes to mean Muslim characters in a specific genre of comics. However, when we look at Islamicate traditions, the focus is on the hero. To focus only on what is happening in the American media at the expense of what is an organic part of Muslim cultures is a type of Orientalism. These two conversations of Muslim superheroes and Islamicate hero tales must happen simultaneously.

It is in this vein of having concurrent conversations that we use Sufi Comics, an Indian-based comic series that tells well-known stories of Ali in a graphic format. They work with more heroic tales of Ali, eschewing imaginative (*khayal*) elements, to create morally edifying stories. Their material is visually resonant with American comic styles, while incorporating elements from Islamicate illustrative forms. These variances from the ex-

---

3. Compare the distinction between "superhero" and "super hero" in Coogan 2006, 49.

4. The "consumer" is a broad category for the individual who approaches these stories. They are not always read, in the sense of an individual with a book, but may be read aloud, or part of a larger oral performances. The result is that we are not always considering a "reader," when discussing people who engage with these stories.

pected visuals are important elements in the storytelling for the authors of Sufi Comics.

This chapter explains how Ali fills the emic role of a hero in many Islamicate literatures. It begins by looking at him as a moral exemplar and the cultural expectations amongst many Muslims of what a hero is. His extraordinary qualities hint at more miraculous feats that will eventually develop around his person, turning him into a Muslim super-hero. This incorporation of super-heroic stories into Ali's narrative allows us to further define how "hero" and "super-hero" function in Islamicate literatures, including in comparison to notions of comics "superheroes." This context allows us to read Sufi Comics's interpretations of Ali with nuance.

Ali the Hero

For Muslims, Muhammad is considered the perfect man. By virtue of being a prophet of God and the first Muslim, his behavior is emulated through reports (*hadith*) of his custom (*sunnah*). There is a rich tradition of miracle stories (*mu'jiza*) attributed to Muhammad as well. However, while he is considered a role model – the Qur'an even refers to him as such *uswa hasana*, a "beautiful role model," Q. 33:21) – and has many heroic deeds to his credit, he is not the first person many Muslims think of when they think of a Muslim hero. That aspect of Muhammad's charisma is manifest through his family, specifically his daughter Fatima, his grandsons Hasan and Husayn, and especially through his cousin and son-in-law Ali.[5]

For Shi'i Muslims, Ali is the successor to Muhammad's religious and spiritual authority. It is through Ali's children with Fatima that his descendants continue to manifest this heroic quality. Many Sufi Muslims, who recognize a different authority structure than Shi'i Muslims, still assert that their line of masters begins with Ali. He is, for them, the inheritor of Muhammad's special wisdom. The lines of masters of the various Sufi orders all trace their teachings back to Ali.[6] Even for many Sunni Muslims, Ali represents heroic ideals and actions.[7] He is a universal hero amongst Muslims.[8]

Ali becomes the embodiment of *futuwwa/jawanmardi*,[9] terms, in Arabic and Persian respectively, that both translate roughly as "young-manliness."

5. Renard 1993, 1, 3, 9.
6. Ridgeon 2011 4.
7. Ridgeon 2011, 6, 17; Lewisohn 2006, 118. Cf. Shah-Kazemi 2015, 35.
8. Shah-Kazemi 2015, 33.
9. Renard 2008, 69. There is another related term, *muruwwah*, which means manly virtue. According to one Arabic aphorism, "there is no religion without *muruwwah*" (quoted in Renard 1993, 14). However, *futwuwwah/jawanmardi* take on a much more spiritual connotation that is relevant for the discussion of this article.

However, the connotative range of these terms is much larger. The Arabic *fu-tuwwa* comes from the same root as *fata*, or hero, found in the phrase which begins this chapter: *la fata illa 'Ali*, there is no hero besides Ali. *Jawanmardi* is the Persian equivalent of the Arabic word. Both terms speak to more than notions of battlefield heroics; they are about correct behavior (*adab*) and an ethical worldview (*akhlaq*) to be inculcated amongst the truly heroic. It is in being responsible to these ideals, inspired by the divine, that one draws oneself closer to God. Despite the literal translation, which implies a gendered ideal, the practices of *jawanmardi* are open to women, and women participate in them.[10] In several stories of Ali, we see him paired with his wife Fatima. She too represents the ideals of spiritual beings in the world. It is because she is also an exemplar that it is specifically Ali's children with Fatima who inherit the charisma associated with Ali's *futuwwa*.

Ali is the perfect *fata*, a status which is coupled with super-human events and actions (*karamat*), making him a super-hero. The *karamat* are not technically miracles, a status reserved for prophets, but are amazing, incredible, and even uncanny.[11] While these fantastic events are attention-grabbing parts of Ali's narrative, it is his quotidian actions that are the core of his heroic status.

We can discuss Ali's heroic charisma in three parts: his teachings on being a Muslim; the *karamat*; and his actions as a *fata*. Many of his teachings are compiled in a work called *Nahj al-Balagha*, *The Peak of Eloquence*. The title itself is a hint at the esteem in which many Muslims hold Ali's rhetorical skill. The *karamat* clearly establish Ali as a super-hero and demonstrate the ways in which Muslims in different cultures construct their (super-)heroes. While some of these stories are memorialized in painting, it is the actions of Ali as *fata* that persist across Muslim cultures, even in the contemporary period.

The creators of Sufi Comics represent Ali as the *fata*. The two brothers behind the comics, Mohammed Arif Vakil and Mohammed Ali Vakil, illustrate a variety of stories from Sufi and Shi'i sources, but which are firmly within the genre of *jawanmardi* literature. The two comic stories about Ali that we analyze in this chapter demonstrate his heroism. However, to get to the quality of his actions, we need to understand his thought.

Ali's writings span a breadth of genres, from ideas on governance to advice for his children. There is a consistent interest in equity and justice (*adala*). For example, he says that justice is one of the four foundations of faith. He continues:

10. Ridgeon 2011, 8.
11. Renard 1993, 119.

Justice also has four aspects: keen understanding, deep knowledge, a good power of decision, and firm forbearance. Therefore, whoever understands comes to acquire depth of knowledge; whoever acquires depth of knowledge drinks from the spring of judgement; and whoever exercises forbearance never commits evil actions in his affairs and leads a praiseworthy life among the people.[12]

One of Ali's most systematic engagements with how he sees justice manifest in the world appears in his letter to his governor in Egypt, Malik al-Ashtar. Reza Shah Kazemi, an expert in the Anglophone world on the teachings of Ali, has written extensively about this letter, so we need only focus on a few exemplary passages.[13] In these selections, Ali bridges Qur'anic injunctions with action in the world, without always being explicit in his references. He manifests an ethical worldview that is deeply informed by his faith, without being didactic.

Ali begins the letter by urging al-Ashtar to hold virtuous acts as his dearest treasure. Concurrent with these virtuous acts, the governor is advised to exercise self-restraint. He then offers guidance on specific virtuous actions:

1. Forgive, because God is forgiving. (See fig. 1 for an illustration from *40 Sufi Comics* of Malik al-Ashtar embodying this guidance.[14])
2. Do not act rashly, and always seek multiple courses of action.
3. Let your affairs be focused on justice.
4. Remember the common people over the elite people, because they are the basis of a society.
5. Appoint as the head of the army someone who is slow to anger; quick to pardon; kind to the weak; severe with the strong; and is not inclined to violence.
6. Pay attention to the lowest classes, especially those who have no access to you.
7. Set apart the most of your time to explicitly think of God and nurture your soul.[15]

This list ends with a reference to remembering God, but in many ways this admonishment frames the entire letter. It is in the recollection of God that one tempers the self. The actions that Ali recommends should flow from the mindfulness of God. Al-Ashtar must be forgiving, because God is

12. Ali b Abi Talib 1984, 576–77.
13. Shah-Kazemi 2006b.
14. Vakil and Vakil 2011, 17.
15. Shah-Kazemi 2006b, 219–36.

Figure 1: An illustration from *40 Sufi Comics* of Malik al-Ashtar embodying the guidance he received from Ali to be forgiving.

forgiving (#1), and the commander of his army will also be forgiving (#5). Forgiveness and pardon become a particular manifestation of justice,[16] which is ultimately the worldly focus of this advice (#3). For Ali, constructing the just society is dependent on remembering those who would not otherwise be remembered: the least amongst us. Leonard Lewisohn, a scholar of Islamicate literatures, makes an explicit connection between the ethics of Ali and the Sermon on the Mount from the Christian tradition.[17]

However, for Lewisohn, Ali's letter is more explicit in a call to action than Jesus' sermon. For Ali, justice is not an abstract concept, but one that is tied to action. As a result, his letter is a manifestation of a deeply spiritual worldview informed by the Qur'an, which does not need to be explicit in its reference to scripture. In the letter, Ali argues that justice is not just the central organizing principle of society: it is a personal virtue.[18] There is an inherent relationship between the struggle an individual has with herself to do what is right and the struggle an individual has with society to do what is right.[19] The internal and the external struggle are reinforcing positives: to do what is best for oneself spiritually is to create a better world, and a better world allows that individual to work towards spiritual advancement.

The Heroic Ideal

In Ali's teaching, we see the need to integrate individual achievement with moral impetus. This connection between action and intent is a staple of Muslim thought; to offer formal prayer without a statement of intent is considered an incomplete prayer.[20] The question of morality is a fundamental one to the understanding of an Islamicate hero, who is ideally both moral and competent.[21] In an Islamicate context, these requirements are further emphasized, because a hero has religious overtones. According to John Renard, an expert on themes of heroism in Islamicate contexts, a hero must "function as a model, an ideal of exemplary behavior as worked out in the context of adversity."[22]

However, this adversity does not suggest that the hero is "self-achieved,"[23] because in an Islamicate context the idea of a self-made hero is untenable.

---

16. Lewisohn 2006, 145.
17. Lewisohn 2006, 117.
18. Paya 2013, 24,
19. Renard 1993, 27.
20. See, for example, al-Qadi al-Nu'man 2002; Nasir-i Khusraw 2012.
21. Allison and Goethals 2011, 44; Morris and Loeb 2005, 12; cf. Klock 2013a, 74.
22. Renard 1993, 9; 2008, 53–54; cf. Allison and Goethals 2011, 29.
23. Campbell 2004, 15.

The hero is called by God, and has God-given abilities.[24] These abilities are used by each hero in unique ways and through free will, but the story is never a bildungsroman. By virtue of the hero's special relationship with God, the inner transformation of the hero – the realization of spiritual potential – happens before the hero begins engaging with the world.[25] It is only the spiritually perfected individual who can be a super-heroic force in the world.

Using Ali as a case study, we can create a working definition of an Islamicate hero. The hero has a special relationship with God, and as a result has a God-given ability. Many heroes have special weapons.[26] The hero is human and can die.[27] The special relationship with the divine is not a mark of invincibility or immortality. The hero is not supernatural but the "extreme realization" of human abilities, which means the hero has physical human weaknesses. Most importantly, the hero acts from a moral conviction, which is consistent with divine guidance and revelation. The hero can never be a vigilante who operates outside of the law, although she does fight against tyrannical and oppressive powers. Nor can the justice that the hero fights for simply be about personal strength and ability; it is not about the hero imposing her will.[28]

From a Muslim perspective, the relationship between faith and justice is one of dependency. Justice becomes a manifestation of faith for Ali, and faith is cultivated in justice. Julie Meisami, a scholar of Islamicate literatures, discusses the ways in which notions of heroism in Muslim cultures are criticized as being flat and uninspiring.[29] The argument rests on the belief that to valorize the individual would risk a type of idolatry. Yet, such a critique rests on two misconceptions. The first misconception is based on aesthetics and a reliance on Eurocentric notions of literature and heroism.[30] The second misconception is premised on the universality of moral education. The form of many Islamicate heroic narratives emerges from "a conviction that the individual example validates the general principle, and, further, a belief in the human potential for both creativity and perfectability."[31]

24. Hagen 2009, 55; cf. Allison and Goethals 2011, 44; Stuller 2010, 5; 2013, 19.
25. Renard 1993, 26–27.
26. Renard 1993, 142.
27. Renard 1993, 63.
28. Many of these characteristics of the Islamicate hero are similar to characteristics outlined by authors who attempt to create more expansive definitions of what a superhero can be. See for example, Eco 2004, 146; Kaveney 2008, 6; McLuhan 2004, 105.
29. Meisami 1987, 132–34.
30. Renard 1993, 24.
31. Meisami 1987, 135; cf. Renard 1993, 28.

Ali becomes the embodiment of moral action, who demonstrates virtues accessible to all people.[32] His heroism is grounded in his humanness.
Following the poet-philosopher Muhammad Iqbal (1877–1938), who inverts
Nietzschean thinking, Ali is an *Übermensch* because of his devotion to God.[33]
Therefore, while Ali is more than the average human, his status is theoretically achievable by anyone who is willing to learn from him and follow his
example. This accessible, perfecting quality of Ali's heroism, what John Renard describes as the "challenging, uplifting, and affirming [of] the potential
of real people," is the basis of my analysis of Sufi Comics.[34]

There is another, parallel set of traditions that see Ali as a super-hero.
The move from hero to super-hero is easy to make, because Ali is a religious
hero. He has a special connection to the divine that allows him to move from
the role of a perfected human to a person with abilities beyond the normal
human sphere.[35] His humanity makes him aware of death but he is also cog-
nizant of the promise of a life after death, and a role in a divine plan. As a
result, he is not afraid of conflict, as his confidence is not in himself, but in
God.[36] Therefore, he is almost always assured of victory, regardless of the
situation. With a premise of guaranteed success, it is easy for hero stories to
be linked to hagiography and, in turn, hagiography to become inflated into
super-hero stories.[37]

Peter Coogan, a researcher of American comics, creates a distinction between a hero, a hero that is super, and a superhero.[38] His particular schema
does not work well as a universal model. It has failings in American comics,
as it is too narrow in the distinctions it makes.[39] It is also too culturally specific to be applicable in an Islamicate milieu. The hero has a cultural context
that determines how his heroism is constructed.[40] Coogan is most interested
in the American idea of a superhero, who has a "universal, prosocial mission"; has superpowers, including technological or mystical abilities; and
has an identity tied to costume and codename.[41] His "hero that is super" is
missing at least one of these defining characteristics, but has superpowers.
For Coogan, the regular hero is specifically missing superpowers.

32. Lewisohn 2006, 131.
33. Rahim 1989, 485–487. Renard 1993, 63.
34. Renard 1993, 63.
35. Renard 1993, 19.
36. Renard 1993, 222.
37. Hagen 2009, 353; Soenarto, 78.
38. Coogan 2006, 49; 2013, 7–8.
39. Klock 2013b; Stuller 2013.
40. Renard 1993, 1.
41. Coogan 2013, 3.

Ali, as an Islamicate hero, has a universal, prosocial mission. However, that mission is defined by a religiously informed moral perspective. As a result, to live that moral life as an exemplar is a fundamental part of the mission, so there is no space for secret identities or costumes. The closest Ali comes to having a signature costume is his sword Dhulfiqar and his steed Duldul. Nor can Ali have superpowers that define his mission as *fata*; to do so would make him impossible to emulate and thus defeat his mission. Coogan's definition cannot meaningfully contribute to an Islamicate notion of the super-hero.

Without superpowers or a secret identity, Ali cannot function as a superhero in the sense of the U.S. comic book genre. However, he is a superhero. The heroic quality of Ali is elevated by the consumers of his stories, embellished with miraculous elements and retold as new tales. Ali's human qualities persist, as does his primary heroic function to serve as a moral exemplar. The ways in which he achieves that mission is fantastic, making him super in a sense of being awe-inspiring, without discouraging the belief that one can emulate his moral conviction.[42] The unrealistic elements of these stories index Ali's special relationship with the divine, as they can only emerge from Ali's perfected spiritual character.

The Islamicate super-hero is one whose humanity and heroic qualities are centered in a narrative of divine purpose. That centering does not have to be explicit, but can be implicit through references to the hero's relationship to the divine or the hero's moral character. Because of his special relationship to God, the hero is always assured victory. As a result, the hero can be put in fantastic situations that allow him to act in super-heroic ways. Primarily, the super-hero will have miraculous feats credited to him, but these miracles are favors from God, and not inherent in the hero.

In Ali's super-heroic narratives, miraculous events surround him from his birth, when his mother receives a premonitory dream that involves Muhammad and the holy site of the Ka'ba expands to bring Ali's mother inside, so that she can give birth to Ali inside of it. There are other signs of Ali's favored status, such as Muhammad tying his turban around Ali's head, a sign of blessing.

In a folk tale from the Pamir mountain range in Central Asia, a hero by the name of al-Walid is unable to defeat a despotic figure named Qahqahah. It is Ali who is ultimately able to defeat this villain. The basis for this victory is tied to Ali's unsurpassed piety, and "it is argued in the legend that the long reign of tyranny and injustice manifested in Qahqahah had to be replaced

42. Similar claims regarding the religious values of superheroes can be found in several works, most notably Weinstein 2006.

by freedom and justice brought by Ali, and that true salvation was due to Ali and his progeny."[43] In this story the human strengths of al-Walid are not sufficient to defeat the enemy; Ali's special connection to God is necessary.

Certain tropes emerge around Ali as hero and super-hero.[44] One trope is that he hears calls for help from people in need when they have no other recourse. This tradition actually dates back to Prophet Muhammad, who called on Ali for help on various occasions,[45] for help in battle; there is even a belief amongst Shi'a that a special prayer was revealed to Muhammad to call for the help of Ali.[46] The prayer has a line which says "call Ali, the manifestation of marvels." The reference to "marvels" contributes to the inflation of Ali's stories to the level of the super-hero. Another element of Ali's super-heroism is his strength, which allows him to slay dragons or lift doors that normally require eight men to carry.[47] Ali also has strong interpersonal skills, so that he is represented as a loyal man, a good father, and a good husband. To the latter point, his wife Fatima, who is arguably an under-appreciated hero in her own right,[48] often appears in stories with him. Finally, since Ali is a Muslim hero, he will often end up converting other characters in his stories to Islam, and this becomes a sign of heroic success.

Ali's tales of heroism cross cultural borders. Some stories are unique to particular communities; many tales are variations of a core narrative, with Ali defeating hordes of enemies. One of the most commonly retold stories seems to be a story wherein Muhammad, in a time of need, calls Ali. These are not embellishments of the events of Khaybar or Uhud but distinct battles that are clearly mythic, while referencing historical antecedents. For example, in one Swahili version, Muhammad is losing a battle, and the angel Gabriel appears to tell him to call Ali. After Muhammad calls for him, Ali miraculously appears from a great distance to slay three giants, take down 2000 men, and defeat the enemy's champion, at which point the remainder of the opposition converts to Islam.[49]

In another story, a Muslim is captured by the demon Rasi Li Ghuli, the Swahili version of the Arabic *ra's al-ghul* (or "Head of the Demon").[50] Ali

43. Iloliev 2015, 310.
44. Renard 1993, 112.
45. Shah-Kazemi 2006b, 15.
46. Amir-Moezzi 2011, 352–353.
47. Shah-Kazemi 2006b, 16.
48. Madelung 2014.
49. Knappert 1999, 77–88. According to Knappert, there seems to be an Arabic version of this tale as well; cf. 1967, 193–197.
50. This *ra's al-ghul* is not the same as Batman's nemesis, Ra's al Ghul. It is not inconceivable that the comic character is an Orientalist pastiche of Islamicate antecedents, but there is no direct evidence for such a linkage.

defeats the demon, rescues the Muslim and other captives, and in the process is able to show his cunning and prowess in defeating numerous foes.[51] This demon is not the most powerful supernatural foe that Ali fights. In an increasing escalation of Ali's prowess, there is a mythic retelling of the Battle of Badr, where Satan battles the angel Gabriel in the air and Ali on the ground. Ali is about to slay Satan but Gabriel prevents him from delivering the killing blow, because, according to a Muslim belief, "Satan cannot be killed before Judgement Day."[52]

Ali's fantastic qualities do not just center around battle prowess. His moral character is also an important part of his heroism that is manifest in super-heroic action. In one instance, a young man wants to win the heart of a woman by killing Ali. When Ali hears this tale, he tells the young man that if he becomes Muslim, Ali will offer his head to the boy, so he can win the heart of his beloved. The boy refuses to convert, and the two fight. Ali bests him, at which point the youth converts to Islam, and Ali says he will help the young man get his girl.[53] The tale illustrates Ali's dedication to his religion, as he is willing to die to have someone convert to the faith. He also represents a commitment to help those who ask for it, even though the boy fought with him.

Another story describes Ali's religious learning. A man feels an urge to travel and speak to Muhammad. After traveling, he arrives to find out Muhammad has passed away, but is advised to go speak to Ali. He asks Ali twenty difficult questions about faith, which Ali easily answers, and the man converts to Islam.[54] Ali's fluency with esoteric material of the faith demonstrates a special relationship to the divine, which allows him to access this knowledge.

Ali's relationship to Fatima, his wife, is emblematic of his conception of family. Their union is blessed by God, who tells Muhammad that they should be married, and who promises that Gabriel will be Ali's *vakil* (representative) and God will be Fatima's.[55] Fatima refuses the worldly gifts from God that are given as a wedding present, asking instead to be an intercessor for Muslim women in the afterlife.[56]

Fatima's rejection of material wealth from God is embedded in a larger discourse of one rejecting worldly attachment, including wealth, as one

51. Knappert 1999, 139–144.

52. Knappert 1985, 249.

53. Knappert 1985, 258–259.

54. Knappert 1999.

55. Knappert 1999, 45. In Islamic law, a bride and a groom do not marry each other directly, but through affirmations of their *vakils*, or representatives.

56. Knappert 1985, 240–241.

becomes more spiritually adept. Ali, as a person deeply invested in being God-conscious, is not rich. On a journey, he gives away the last of his money in charity. As he nears home, a man offers to sell him a camel on credit. Ali takes the camel, and a rich man offers to buy the camel. This transaction allows Ali to pay the initial cost of the camel and have money left over. The man he gives the money to and the man involved in the camel transaction are God's representatives. The tale demonstrates Ali's generosity to the consumer of the story.[57] An important subtext here is that trusting in God is the best guarantee of sustenance.

A story with a similar moral involves Fatima being ill. She asks for a pomegranate to make juice, so that her symptoms may be relieved. Ali finds the last pomegranate in the city. He then meets a sick beggar, and Ali gives him the fruit so that the beggar may reap its benefit. The angel Gabriel then visits Ali and Fatima to provide a collection of pomegranates for Ali to give to Fatima.[58] In both stories, Ali's generosity and reliance on God are expressions of his moral qualities. That moral expression of charity is what marks him as a hero. His heroism is then merged with mythic engagement with God and an angel to mark him as a super-hero.

Food and sustenance, in the context of family and God's power, continue to be important elements of Ali's super-heroism in cross-cultural contexts. In one story, Ali and Fatima are fasting for three days. Their sons Hasan and Husayn are ill, and the fast is a prayer for healing. At sunset, as Fatima finishes making five portions of food – for herself, Muhammad, Ali, Hasan, and Husayn – beggars come knocking on the door. Ali gives the beggars the food and the family's fast remains unbroken. On the second night, blind men come by and Muhammad gives them food, and the fast continues. On the third day, orphans come by and Fatima gives them food. After fasting for three days without interruption, God sends a message to the five of them that they will be granted Paradise, and thus will receive blessed sustenance, for their generosity.[59]

Amongst the Hui, an ethnic group in China, there is a similar story of fasting. An army led by Ali has been without food for three days. Ali promises food and asks Hasan and Husayn to go scouting for something to eat. Fatima begins cooking for the army, as though the food will appear. Hasan and Husayn find only sacks of sawdust. Fatima takes the sawdust and mixes it with rocks from a nearby river. The combination miraculously turns into a rich porridge that feeds the army. Ali's trust in God is shared by his family, which allows God to become an actor in the world.[60]

The miraculous nature of these stories emphasizes the manifestation of God's power in response to those who rely utterly on God. They feed into the super-heroic powers granted to Ali by being a *mard-e khuda*, a man of God. However, it is his role as *fata* that provides a more practical model of emulation. In his more human tales, the reader/listener/viewer is reminded of a core principle of Ali's teachings: knowledge must be turned into action.[61] As we saw in his letter to Malik al-Ashtar, knowing the ethical precepts of the Qur'an should result in specific actions that one can take to improve the lives of people.

The Stranger

Sufi Comics illustrate the stories of Ali as a hero. Two brothers, Mohammed Ali Vakil and Mohammed Arif Vakil, started the company in 2009. According to their website, they believe "that religion is not just about following a set of rules & regulations, but actually meant to reform us from inside so that we become better human beings," and they are "influenced by the spiritual and moral stories of the Prophet Muhammad (s) and his Holy Progeny (the Ahlul Bayt)."[62] In their explanatory statement of the comics, the brothers clearly articulate that they see these stories as a means of personal edification, to make them better Muslims.

"The Stranger" is a story that deals with obligations of family, loyalty, and commitments to those in need. The story begins with an image of a woman carrying water back to her family. She meets a man who asks why her husband is not doing the heavy work of the house. She responds that her husband was a soldier in Ali's army, and that he died in battle. The stranger offers to help her carry the load, and when they arrive at her home, he sees that she has children. He offers to help that day and he returns over the following days, bringing her food and taking care of the children. One day, a neighbor comes over and recognizes the stranger as Ali, and the woman begs his forgiveness for making him do house work.

One reading of this text is that Ali is committed to all the people in his

---

60. Li and Luckert 1994, 94–96.

61. Lakhani 2006, 36–37.

62. Unknown 2012. The "(s)" after the mention of Muhammad's name is a symbol for prayers to be offered by Muslims for Muhammad. It is often translated as "peace be upon him" in English. The "Ahlul Bayt" (i.e. *Ahl al-Bayt*) are are Muhammad's close family, including Ali, Fatima, Hasan, and Husayn.

care, as witnessed in his letter to al-Ashtar. No one will take care of the widow and the orphan if he does not do so himself. The familial argument can be extended based on what we saw as part of his miraculous stories about food. Here, the needy person and her family are also part of Ali's family, as the soldier was part of Ali's army. The man entrusted Ali with his life, and so Ali fulfills that trust by taking care of the man's family.

A variation of the story adds a detail of Ali standing in front of a cooking fire and saying that he was trying to feel the fire of hell. This imagery is consistent with Ali as *fata*, recognizing that his actions in this world are determined by God. It can also be that he reminds himself of what happens when he fails in his duties in faith. Another reading is that it is an earthly penance, a form of mea culpa, where he seeks forgiveness from the family, as the father died for Ali, and now the children are orphans.

Because stories of Ali are well known amongst Muslims, the one-page comic also serves as a rich archive of intertextual references. For example, a famous prayer of Ali states:

> There is a group who worship God out of desire [for something not yet attained], and this is the worship of the merchants. And there is a group who worship God out of fear, and this is the worship of the slaves. And there is a group who worship God out of gratitude, and this is the worship of the free.[63]

It seems consistent with the logic of this prayer to not worship God out of fear of hell, that Ali standing in front of the fire is most likely a connection between the worldly and otherworldly conceptions of justice in his actions. He is called to help the woman and her family by divine guidance, not from fear of punishment. However, that does not mean that he is not aware that there is a punishment for those who fail in their religious obligations. From a Muslim worldview, justice without consciousness of the divine leads to relativism, while a commitment to the letter of religious law that strips it of its intent is reductionism.[64] Ali is in equilibrium, navigating a balance between *din* (religion) and *dunya* (the world). Reza Shah-Kazemi argues that justice is fully realized when it is linked to "the spiritual precepts of the Islamic faith," and that "contemplation and action are seen in this perspective as complementary, not contradictory."[65]

This story of Ali as "The Stranger" seems to be well known in the oral tradition, but does not have any obvious visual depiction in the archives of

---

63. Shah-Kazemi 2011, 32. This prayer is illustrated in Vakil and Vakil 2011, 39.
64. Lakhani 2006, 56.
65. Shah-Kazemi 2006a, 61.

Figure 2: The story of "The Stranger" by Sufi Comics.

Ali's iconography.[66] The Sufi Comics version of the story appears to be a rare depiction of the story. While depictions of human beings are common in Muslim traditions, particularly in traditions of spiritual discipline, the artists of the comic chose not to depict Ali's face. The aura of a visual depiction carries with it *baraka* or blessing.[67] The image also collapses mythic time, so that the religious figure is present, rather than represented, and the viewer engages in "visual hagiography," conflating the life of the figure with her own life.[68] These images are further used for talismanic purposes, such as protection, or good fortune, and reminders to do good.[69]

The lack of details in Ali's face – and of Muhammad's family more broadly in Sufi Comics – signifies that his visage is too holy to behold. The blank space is a type of halo to indicate Ali's special status. It is also an acknowledgement of his position in certain Shi'i thought as a peerless hero, both because of his commitment to the faith, and because God has chosen him to be a hero. He is between hero and super-hero. This liminality of being both hero and super-hero is an important part of the Islamicate tradition.[70] The consumer of the tale is put in an aspirational position: to emulate the perfect human, whilst knowing they will fail. It is the struggle to better oneself that defines the religious life of many of these consumers. The fantastical elements of Ali's battle prowess are not as important in this story. In this story, the elements of Ali's super-hero identity are tied to his relationship with the divine. The average believer can only achieve part of his ability; the remainder can only be granted by God, and it has only been promised to Muhammad and his family. The visualization allows the reader to receive the blessings of the image, to be morally edified, and to know that Ali is to be followed because of divine command.

Despite the special lineage and characteristics of Ali, the first panel finds him walking by himself on the streets of a town (fig. 2). He sees a woman struggling with a heavy load and offers her his assistance. In the next panel, she tells him of her difficulties, so Ali becomes an emotional support as well. It is the humanity of Ali that is magnified and represented in this sequence.

---

66. Flaskerud 2010, 58.

67. Here, the work of Walter Benjamin, and to a lesser extent John Berger, are instrumental to understanding "aura." They speak to the tradition and history that is evoked by the image and how viewers integrate that longer narrative into understandings of the image. The viewer may then potentially integrate those understandings into their own lives. See Benjamin 1986; Berger 1973.

68. Roberts et al., 2003, 45.

69. Roberts et al. 2003, 48; Flaskerud 2010, 60.

70. For similar arguments about the liminality of superheroes, cf. Kaveney 2008, 5; Coogan 2006, 52.

The next panel captures three events: the joyfulness of the children at the return of the mother, Ali's restless night, and Ali's return the next day. The fact that there are two children represented is highly significant to a Muslim reader. Ali has two sons, Hasan and Husayn. The evocation of an empty house with two young children resonates with Ali and with the reader, who is familiar with Ali's life. The reader is not sure what is troubling Ali during his sleepless night: it could be guilt or it could be the suffering he witnessed in the family. The next day, Ali eases the family's material need by bringing them food. This construction of the visual flow invests the reader in the story because it alludes to Ali's own personal story. It also emphasizes the notion that religious knowledge must result in action. Here, Ali seeks to aid the widow and the orphans. These are Qur'anic commandments that Ali reiterates in his letter to Malik al-Ashtar. His unease at night, then, most likely relates to the difficulties of the family.

This idea of turning faith into action continues in the next panel, where Ali agrees to watch the children. It is an opportunity for Ali to seek forgiveness for not coming sooner to care for the orphans. He says, "forgive Ali if he has failed his duty towards you." The duty can only be the religious obligation that remains unrealized. This possibility is emphasized at the end of the panel, when Ali places his face near the fire and reminds himself that "the heat of the fire [...] is for those who fail in their duty to widows and orphans." The panel sees Ali the man, who seeks forgiveness, and also Ali the *mard-e khuda*, who knows his obligations to the divine. He is, once more, balancing the commitment to justice in this world and the next.

A neighbor announcing Ali's identity to the woman is the sole focus of the fifth panel. It is the shock of recognition and a lifting of the veil of secrets. This revelation is the equivalent of an epiphany in this telling of the story. It is the Freudian *unheimlich*, "everything that ought to have remained [...] secret and hidden but has come to light."[71] What was a relationship of equals is now turned into a relationship between the Commander of the Faithful, Ali, and the widow of one of his soldiers. He attempts to revert to the old order in the next panel, telling the woman that she does not need his forgiveness, but he needs hers.

The subtle shift in body language reinforces this idea of changed power relationships. In the first panel, Ali is upright. After that, he is always bowed, either carrying a load, or sitting on the floor. He only returns to his full height once his identity is revealed. It is only as Ali, and in seeking forgiveness as Ali, that his true self is reintegrated. He must take responsibility for his own actions. He cannot ask forgiveness for himself, as though he were

71. Bhabha 1994, 10.

a disinterested party. The action of making reparations is a part of what makes Ali a *fata*, a hero.

The story of "The Stranger" makes clear that Ali's heroism is not tied to battle prowess. Instead, it is manifest through his caring actions. He provides emotional and physical support to a woman and her children who lost the most important man in their lives. The man was a soldier for Ali, so Ali has an obligation to the family. More importantly, Ali is under divine command to help those who cannot help themselves. In Ali's quest for forgiveness, he must act in a way that benefits the family, but he must also directly ask for forgiveness. It is that challenge that makes the task difficult, but also worth doing.

Sheathing the Sword

Ali's emphasis on doing tasks correctly and well applies to his martial experience as well. Jalaluddin Rumi, a well-known thirteenth-century Persian poet, writes a story of Ali in battle.[72] The core of the story is that Ali is in a duel and defeats his enemy. As Ali is getting ready to slay his opponent, the man spits in Ali's face. At this point, Ali sheathes his sword. When asked why, Ali responds that when he was fighting before, he was fighting for God, but when he got angry, he was fighting for himself, and that is not the appropriate way to fight. His enemy, amazed at what he heard, converts to Islam.

This particular story is illustrated in numerous collections of Rumi's work. The Sufi Comics version seems to collapse several different stories, including Rumi's. There are hints of the story of the young man who tried to kill Ali to win the hand of a woman. The moral core of the story, "Follow Principles" (fig. 3),[73] is fairly consistent with Rumi's version, and it speaks to a different model of heroism than simple combat.

As Ali readies himself to deliver the killing blow to his opponent, he is stopped by a plea to give to a beggar. We have consistently seen that one of Ali's primary concerns is caring for the needy. By casting himself as being in need, Ali's enemy is able to save his own life. From panel one, we move to panel four, where Ali's explicit declaration of reliance on God indexes his actions as being those of a hero in an Islamicate vein. It is because of the surety of his faith and God's plan for him that Ali is able to willingly surrender his sword.

In this telling of the story, and in Rumi's version, it is when Ali stops himself from delivering the fatal blow that he exhibits self-control born of

72. Rumi 1989.
73. Vakil and Vakil 2011, 21.

Figure 3: "Follow Principles" by Sufi Comics.

piety, which is a precondition for leading others.[74] Ali's faith supersedes any other concern. Since charitable giving is commanded in the Qur'an above almost any other act, Ali must give his sword to his enemy. Reza Shah-Ka-zemi says that Ali's writings frequently reference a Qur'anic verse that the soul incites one to evil. The conception of evil includes the arrogation of the rights of God for oneself. One of the ways this arrogation manifests is to commit acts in a manner that is consistent with God's command, but which is opposed to the intent of the acts.[75] Had Ali killed his opponent, he would have been right in killing someone threatening to kill him. However, the point of conflict in Ali's view is not victory through destruction, but the ability to create peace.

In the Rumi version, Ali's refusal to slay his enemy epitomizes Ali's relationship to the divine, which causes him to be humble and conquer his own anger. Ali says that he is fighting to "quell anger, not because [he is] stirred by anger." Ali demonstrates that a physical struggle is meaningless without a concurrent spiritual struggle.[76] He must better himself in all ways, and thus, even though he could have been a victor in battle, his greater challenge lies in controlling his own desires.

Panels five and six demonstrate that the enemy has not yet learned this lesson. As we close in on the face of the opponent, we are conscious of him as a person. The panel is a strong parallel to the angry face we see in the second panel. Contrary to Ali's blank visage, upon which we can project any number of visions – and which symbolizes a loss of the individual self into the divine[77] – his adversary is still very much grounded in this world. He is sure of himself and indicates that he will follow Ali. For the adversary, to submit to another person is a sign of obedience, but he remains a man, attentive to the world. Ali's response in panel seven is to turn his back on the enemy, which indicates a cutting off of the relationship. He does not even return to battle, and appears to walk away. As he leaves, Ali says that his opponent should follow principles, not people. This message is a chastisement that people are still of this world but that principles are eternal. It is an implicit call to convert to Islam and to recognize God.

There is a third character in this story, Ali's sword Dhulfiqar. In the first panel, it is between the two duelers, with its distinctive two blades at the end. It is intimately linked with Ali, so much so that the angel Gabriel

---

74. Lakhani 2006, 44; cf. Shah-Kazemi 2006a, 80.

75. Shah-Kazemi 2006a, 72–77.

76. Lewisohn 2006, 135–136. Cf. the letter to Malik al-Ashtar, which says to find a commander of the army who is slow to anger and quick to forgive.

77. Shah-Kazemi 2006a, 77.

once says that there is "no hero except for Ali, and no sword except for Dhulfiqar."[78] For his enemy to ask for it is to ask for an extreme sacrifice from Ali. However, Ali must comply because a beggar cannot be refused, as we read in the story of Ali and the pomegranate. It is for this reason that Ali hands the sword over. In the third panel, Dhulfiqar is in the center, but on its side, poised not to kill the body of the enemy, but to kill his ignorance. Ali is attempting to demonstrate correct behavior rather than explain it to his enemy. Once the blade is handed over, and the adversary brings it close to himself, Ali is able to cause his enemy to lay down the sword. The power is not in the sword but in the intent with which it is wielded. For Ali, the power is God, and that power flows through Ali and into the blade. For the opponent, a blade is a blade, and without a weapon, Ali should be defenseless. However, in panel four, when Ali points out how impotent the enemy is compared to God, Dhulfiqar disappears from the comic. Ali's power is not in the sword.

The informed reader knows that there is a deeper history of Dhulfiqar. The origin of the sword is unclear. In some tellings, it is Adam's sword that is passed along the line of prophets until it goes from Muhammad to Ali.[79] Other versions have Muhammad receiving the sword directly from God, during Muhammad's Night Journey.[80] Muhammad then passes the sword on to Ali during a battle, when Ali's own sword breaks. In any version, the sword has a mythic quality to it, denoting Ali's special status. There is a story that says Ali had a small scroll attached to Dhulfiqar, in which was written, "may God curse whoever slaughters for other than God."[81] This parchment serves as a reminder to Ali that when he wields the blade he must remain God-conscious, and emphasizes Ali's rationale in sheathing the sword.

Ali and his sword become the epitome of a *jawanmard*, engaging in chivalrous acts, or in the case of Dhulfiqar, being a vehicle for the establishment of virtue. However, Ali's heroism is not based on his prowess with a sword. Even in combat, he must be in control of himself and be God-conscious. It is when his human nature would call him to strike that he must refrain from doing so, as there is a higher obligation. In one version of the story, his obligation is to stop his anger. In another version of the story, the obligation is to give charity. Ali's heroism, defined by his relationship with the divine, is about knowing when not to attack as much as it is by his great victories in battle.

78. Shah-Kazemi 2006b, 15.
79. Renard 1993, 96.
80. Knappert 1985, 241.
81. Knappert 1985, 241; Bahmanpour 2008, 8.

Conclusion

Ali says "no individual is lost and no nation is refused prosperity and success if the foundations of their thought and actions rest upon piety and godliness, and upon *truth and justice*."[82] There is an unmistakable, if superficial, parallel with the famous Superman catchphrase about his fight for "truth, justice, and the American way." However, Superman's heroism is dependent on secret identities, costumes, and his own strength and will. Ali's truth and justice are defined by his religion, Islam, and his relationship with God. He must be public about his identity and actions. His humanity, and the concordant human struggle to obey God, is the source of his heroism.

In Muslim traditions, Ali is the first hero. The angel Gabriel vouchsafes him as such, saying that he is a peerless hero. His heroism is based on his valor in battle but also his refusal to fight, his erudition, and his leadership. These qualities eventually take on a super-human dimension in mythic tales. These stories often incorporate details of historical events, granting them a semblance of veracity. The super-human stories, while meant to entertain, also have a moral value.

It is in the more human stories, of Ali as a hero, that the reader/listener receives moral edification. Certain characteristics of Ali can be achieved by a committed believer. Yet, many attributes are reserved for Ali and his family alone, because of their relationship to Muhammad and God. This special status is depicted through a halo-like effect, whether a gold ring, a crown of fire, or a blank face. In Islamicate tales, the hero is never dependent on super powers. Rather, the hero can do fantastical things, but is grounded in an approachable humanity to encourage the consumer to better her own life. As a result, Ali is best described as a super-hero, a hero who sometimes appears with uncanny abilities given by God.

Sufi Comics continues a long history of illustrating heroic stories from Islamicate traditions. The shift to a comics format allows for a more detailed telling of these stories. Traditionally, the image would be of a key moment in the tale, with text driving the manuscript.[83] The comics medium merges the narrative and illustrative elements in a more seamless fashion. The result is a dense version of stories that can engage with greater intertextual knowledge. At the same time, the core of Ali's morality persists throughout the stories. He is the first (super-)hero for Muslims. He has his signature sword, and fights for truth, justice, and the spiritual way.

That there is an alternative concept of what heroism is should not de-

82. Lakhani 2006, 3. Emphasis added.
83. Nasr 1987, 178–180.

tract from the emergence of characters like Simon Baz or Monet St. Croix in the American comic industry. However, it would be disingenuous to speak of Muslim superheroes without recognizing that there is a long and diverse history of what the idea of the hero means to Muslims. The point is not to establish competing visions of the hero, but to recognize the plurality of heroic models. As Muslim creators like G. Willow Wilson and Sana Amanat work on characters like Kamala Khan, we may also witness an expansion of what defines the Islamicate hero or an organic integration of different understandings of the hero.

Works Cited

Ali b. Abi Talib. 1984. *Nahjul Balagha: Peak of Eloquence: Sermons, Letters, and Sayings of Imam Ali ibn Abu [sic] Talib.* Elmhurst, NY.

Allison, S. T., and G. R. Goethals. 2011. *Heroes: What They Do & Why We Need Them.* New York.

Amir-Moezzi, M. A. 2011. *The Spirituality of Shi'i Islam: Beliefs and Practices.* London.

Bahmanpour, M. S. 2008. "The Book of Imam 'Ali (as) (Kitabu 'Ali): Al-Jami'ah." *Journal of Shia Islamic Studies* 1, no. 1: 3–28.

Benjamin, W. 1973. "The Work of Art in the Age of Mechanical Reproduction," In *Illuminations,* edited by H. Arendt. New York.

Berger, J. 1973. *Ways of Seeing.* New York.

Bhabha, H. K. 1994. *The Location of Culture.* New York.

Campbell, J. 2004. *The Hero With a Thousand Faces.* Princeton.

Coogan, P. M. 2013. "The Hero Defines the Genre, the Genre Defines the Hero." In *What is a Superhero?,* edited by R. S. Rosenberg, and P. M. Coogan, 3–10. New York.

Coogan, P. M. 2006. *Superhero: The Secret Origin of a Genre.* Austin.

Eco, U. 2004. "The Myth of Superman," In *Arguing Comics: Literary Masters on a Popular Medium,* edited by J. Heer, and K. Worcester, 146–164. Jackson, MS.

Flaskerud, I. 2010. *Visualizing Belief and Piety in Iranian Shiism.* New York.

Hagen, G. 2009. "Heroes and Saints in Anatolian Turkish Literature." *Oriente Moderno* (2009): 349–361.

Iloliev, A. 2015. "King of Men: 'Ali Ibn Abi Talib in Pamiri Folktales." *Journal of Shi'a Islamic Studies* 8, no. 3: 307–323.

Kaveney, R. 2008 *Superheroes!: Capes and Crusaders in Comics and Films.* London, New York.

Klock, G. 2013a. "The Revisionary Superhero Narrative," In *The Superhero Reader,* edited by C. Hatfield, J. Heer, and K. Worcester, 116–135. Jackson, MS.

———. 2013b. "What is a Superhero? No One Knows – That's What Makes 'Em Great," In *What is a Superhero?,* edited by R. S. Rosenberg, and P. M. Coogan, 71–75. New York.

Knappert, J. 1967. *Traditional Swahili Poetry: An Investigation into the Concepts of East African Islam as Reflected in the Utenzi Literature.* Leiden.

———. 1985. *Islamic Legends: Histories of the Heroes, Saints, and Prophets of Islam.* Leiden.

———. 1999. *A Survey of Swahili Islamic Epic Sagas.* Lewiston, NY.

Lakhani, M. A. 2006. "The Metaphysics of Human Governance: Imam ʿAli, Truth and Justice." In *The Sacred Foundations of Justice in Islam: The Teachings of ʿAlī Ibn Abī Ṭālib*, edited by M. A. Lakhani, 3–60. Bloomington.

Lewisohn, L. 2006. "ʿAli Ibn Abi Talib's Ethics of Mercy in the Mirror of the Persian Sufi Tradition." In *The Sacred Foundations of Justice in Islam: The Teachings of ʿAlī Ibn Abī Ṭālib*, edited by M. A. Lakhani, 109–146. Bloomington.

Li, S., and K. W. Luckert. 1994. *Mythology and Folklore of the Hui, a Muslim Chinese People*. Albany.

Madelung, W. 2014. "Introduction." In *The Study of Shi'i Islam: History, Theology and Law*, edited by F. Daftary, and G. Miskinzoda, 3–16. London.

McLuhan, M. 2004. "From *the Mechanical Bride: Folklore of Industrial Man*." In *Arguing Comics: Literary Masters on a Popular Medium*, edited by Jeet Heer, and Kent Worcester, 102–106. Jackson, MS.

Meisami, J. S. 1987. *Medieval Persian Court Poetry*. Princeton.

Morris, T., and J. Loeb. 2005. "Heroes and Superheroes." In *Superheroes and Philosophy: Truth, Justice, and the Socratic Way*, edited by T. V. Morris, and M. Morris, 11–20. Chicago.

Nasir-i Khusraw. 2012. *Between Reason and Revelation: Twin Wisdoms Reconciled: An Annotated English Translation of Nasir-i Khusraw's* Kitāb-i Jāmiʿ al-Ḥikmatayn. Translated by E. L. Ormsby. London.

Nasr, S. H. 1987. *Islamic Art and Spirituality*. Albany.

Paya, A. 2013. "Imam ʿAli's Theory of Justice Revisited." *Journal of Shi'a Islamic Studies* 6 (1): 5–30.

al-Qadi al-Nu'man. 2002. *The Pillars of Islam: Daʿāʾim al-Islām of al-Qāḍī al-Nuʿmān*. Translated by I. K. H. Poonawala. Oxford.

Rahim, H. 1989. "Perfection Manifested: ʿAli B. Abi Talib's Image in Classical Persian and Modern Indian Muslim Poetry." PhD diss., Harvard University.

Renard, J. 1993. *Islam and the Heroic Image: Themes in Literature and the Visual Arts*. Columbia, SC.

——. 2008. "Heroic Themes: An Invitation to Muslim Worlds." In *Muslim Modernities: Expressions of the Civil Imagination*, edited by A. B. Sajoo, 51–72. London.

Ridgeon, L. V. J. 2011. *Jawanmardi: A Sufi Code of Honour*. Edinburgh.

Roberts, A. F., M. N. Roberts, G. Armenian, and O. Guáeye. 2003. *A Saint in the City: Sufi Arts of Urban Senegal*. Los Angeles.

Rumi, J. 1989. "On Ali's Forebearance." *Wikisource*. http://en.wikisource. org/wiki/Masnavi_I_Ma%27navi_Book_I#STORY_XVI._.27Ali.27s_Forebearance.

Shah-Kazemi, R. 2006a. "A Sacred Conception of Justice: Imam 'Ali's Letter to Malik Al-Ashtar." In *The Sacred Foundations of Justice in Islam: The Teachings of 'Alī Ibn Abī Ṭālib*, edited by M. A. Lakhani, 61–108. Bloomington.

———. 2006b. *Justice and Remembrance: Introducing the Spirituality of Imam Ali*. London.

———. 2011. *Spiritual Quest: Reflections on Qur'ānic Prayer According to the Teachings of Imam 'Alī*. London.

———. 2015. "Imam Ali." In *The Shi'i World: Pathways in Tradition and Modernity*, edited by F. Daftary, A. B. Sajoo, and S. Jiwas, 33–55. New York.

Soenarto, E. "From Saints to Superheroes: The Wali Songo Myth in Contemporary Indonesia's Popular Genres." *Journal of the Malaysian Branch of the Royal Asiatic Society* 78 2 (289): 33–82.

Stuller, J. K. 2010. *Ink-Stained Amazons and Cinematic Warriors: Superwomen in Modern Mythology*. New York.

———. 2013. "What is a Female Superhero?." In *What is a Superhero?*, edited by R. S. Rosenberg, and P. M. Coogan, 19–23. New York.

Unknown. 2012. "About – Sufi Comics." Sufi Comics. http://www.suficomics.com/about/.

Vakil, M. A., and M. A. Vakil. 2011. *40 Sufi Comics*. Bangalore.

Weinstein, S. 2006. *Up, Up, and Oy Vey!: How Jewish History, Culture, and Values Shaped the Comic Book Superhero*. Baltimore.

From Book to Tool:
Editorial Remarks

A. David Lewis and Martin Lund

THE BOOK YOU HAVE JUST READ is a snapshot – or, better yet, a select series of panels. As such, while everyone involved has tried to do justice to the Muslim superhero as it exists today, we have, by necessity, had to leave much by the wayside. There is no mention in these pages of Silver Scorpion, Buraaq, or any of the many other independent or one-off Muslim superheroes that are out there. The book has not touched upon, for example, the Burka Avenger or Aquaman teammate Kahina the Seer. The book also leaves out things like Frank Miller's *Holy Terror!* and Bosch Fawstin's *The Infidel*, comics that are, at best, "critical" of Islam and, at worst, outright Islamophobic. These are not so much oversights – or, alternately, censoring omissions – as they are conscious choices for the foundation of *Muslim Superheroes*: What needs to be addressed first? What has to be synthesized before all the rest? What might serve as a distraction instead of a pillar? Toward that balance, also, while we have tried to not give the character too much room, we have returned time and time again to Ms. Marvel, Kamala Khan, despite her novelty and the uncertainty that still surrounds her staying power.[1]

Muslim Superheroes, then, presents only an incomplete view of a larger landscape, indelibly marked by the time in which it was produced. However, as noted in our introduction, we have had no ambition to give the final word on the subject. Nonetheless, we feel that our writers have made significant contributions to our understanding of who and what the Muslim superhero is. While the chapters speak more than eloquently enough for themselves, there are, nonetheless, some common themes that we, as editors, would like to address briefly before leaving the reader to digest the volume. Since several contributors have engaged issues of essentialism and hybridity through their chosen texts, we want to add a broader perspective to such thoughts. And, since multiple contributors have explicitly deconstructed the super-

1. Lund 2016b.

hero genre and its conventions, while many more have questioned these implicitly, we want to stress how these critiques can apply far beyond the covers of this volume. We also point to how *Muslim Superheroes* can have practical applications, by suggesting ways of bringing its subjects into the classroom. Finally, we aim to wrap this project up by considering where we can all go next, in terms of future research and new ground that Muslim superheroes past, present, and future, can chart.

Essentializing the Muslim Superhero

We wrote in our introduction that the term "Muslim superhero" refers here only to the fact that there exist characters that have been inscribed with one or several markers meant to signify a "Muslim" identity, based in one conception of Islam or another. No judgment was given as to the "authenticity" either of the characters depicted or treated as Muslim superheroes or of the conceptions of Islam that they are made to embody. We wanted simply to acknowledge that many Muslim and non-Muslim creators and critics have used these characters to produce, reproduce, represent, and embody many different discursive conceptions of Islam and Muslimness.

Nevertheless, it is important to keep in mind when working on any given social, cultural, religious, or ethnic group, that there is always a danger of essentializing the group. In a social constructivist perspective, all group identities are socially constructed, organized into useful fictions sharing a stock of stories and symbols. Whether it is made about families or about entire ethnic groups asserting a shared heritage – small groups formed around mutual interests, nations referring to a common past, or religious traditions that invoke an elect status by virtue of divine edict or personal salvation – the claim is always to a collective essence that is anchored in something above and beyond the idiosyncrasies of history and biology.[2] When elevated in this way, shared traits can serve as the basis for the construction of "imagined communities," the supposed members of which are perceived as being connected and alike, even though they are separated by time and geography to such an extent that they can or will never meet.[3] Such communities are often structured and represented on the basis of notions of "authenticity." Symbols central to the communities are regarded as having been static throughout history, despite the fact that many supposedly shared traits, ideologies, or practices (or at least their meanings at any given time) are always products of a particular context. The corollary to this type of essentialized

2. Cf. Berger and Luckmann 1991; Anderson 2006; Baumann 1999; Satlow 2006.
3. Anderson 2006, 6.

traits is the construction of stereotypes about Others, who are perceived to all be alike and indelibly different from oneself.

Acknowledging that essentialized communities are social constructions, however, does not mean that they should be dismissed. No matter how much evidence there is to support the conclusion that categories like "race" do not describe any significant differences, they are historically and socioculturally real and remain so in people's minds; they have meaning, simply, because people act as if they do.[4] Thus, while categories and collectives are socially constructed, they are also experienced as social realities. They are emphatically felt and constantly reproduced as structures, commonly built on a solid foundation of "insider" support and, just as often, serve as the basis for social inequalities and discrimination.

This is a key reason why a title like *Ms. Marvel* could be so widely hailed and so roundly denounced even before it had been introduced. It is a key reason why *The 99* has been both praised and reviled. For one section of the audience, they represent a corrective of the wrongful image attached to Islam; for another, they hide the "supposed 'true' nature of Islam – violent, oppressive, hateful."[5] Here, reception is centered on different conceptions of what an "authentic" Islam is. On this topic, scholar of religion Stuart Charmé has discussed varieties of authenticity in contemporary American Judaism, focusing on what he labels "essentialistic authenticities" and "existentialist authenticities."[6] Adherents to the essentialistic model make prescriptive claims about the normative superiority of one form of Jewish life over another, based on descriptive claims about historical continuity. What matters is that the identity is "authentically Jewish," as expressed in a depth of personal Jewish knowledge, observance, and commitment, and that it is rooted in tradition. Conversely, adherents to the existentialist model choose instead to regard the word "authentic" as modifying the noun, "identity," rather than the adjective. An authentic Jewish identity in this model is one that embraces the individual's sociocultural context wholly, and does so in a way that makes sense for them, rather than being guided by a surface acceptance in "bad faith" of traditions not perceived as meaningful.

Charmé's model, in a slightly modified version, can be applied both to contemporary Islam and to superhero production.[7] Most of the discussed Muslim superheroes created by non-Muslims fall under an essentialist perspective. They are often represented as representatives of "Islam" as

4. Cf. Omi and Winant 1994.
5. Santo 2014, 689.
6. Charmé 2000.
7. See Otterbeck 2010; Lund 2016a for examples.

a whole, and do so by embodying one or two traits taken to an extreme. Dust, of course, is the prime example of this, but other superheroes from the preceding pages function in a similar way, to a greater or lesser extent. Characters that instead embody an existential authenticity are often marked by a more developed and deeper characterization. When Mercedes Yanora calls Kamala Khan an "authentic superhero" and when Chris Reyns-Chikuma and Dérirée Lorenz say that she is "represented as courageously choosing the Muslim feminist option," they are, in part, pointing towards such a conception of identity.

But it is also the near-inescapable curse of the minority writer or character to be expected to stand as a representative of their whole group. To the extent that the Muslim superheroes by Muslim creators can be said to serve such a purpose, they can be regarded as expressions of what anthropologist Talal Asad has labeled "discursive traditions":

> A tradition consists essentially of discourses that seek to instruct practitioners regarding the correct form and purpose of a given practice that, precisely because it is established, has a history. These discourses relate conceptually to *a past* (when the practice was instituted, and from which the knowledge of its point and proper performance has been transmitted) and *a future* (how the point of that practice can best be secured in the long term, or why it should be modified or abandoned), through a *present* (how it is linked to other practices, institutions, and social conditions).[8]

In the case of *The 99*, the discursive tradition at the root of the series is a cosmopolitan and universalist Islam in the present, presented with reference to certain Islamic and Islamicate practices in the past. By offering characters who embody the faith as role models, al-Mutawa hopes to see these particular practices continuing into the future. In *Ms. Marvel*, the discursive tradition promoted is more clearly evident when Kamala sets herself on the superhero path with reference to a Quranic verse or when she questions the gender segregation in the *masjid*. In other cases, the discursive traditions promoted are less identifiably Islamicate and more pronouncedly Western. As seen in Kevin Wanner's chapter, for instance, Faiza Hussein is tied to a discourse of tolerance rooted in Western liberalism.

This brings us to an important crux in the matter of Muslim superheroes: hybridity. Ken Chitwood argues that *The 99* is a hybrid creation, located in the borderlands between religion and popular culture. This argument prompts us to ask, to what degree are all superhero characters and all super-

8. Asad 1986, 14.

hero creators "hybrid?" And is the Muslim superhero especially so? This is a difficult question to answer, but we can at least point to where this volume has begun to formulate a response.

In its simplest definition, comics itself is a hybrid medium, with its melding of words and images. The superhero was born out of a meeting of genre conventions and previous representations, and has remained such ever since; as such, this genre can also be considered a hybrid creation. Adding to this constitutive hybridity, the superhero is almost always the result of multiple creators; writers, artists, inkers, letterers, and editors all help create almost every new superhero story, and sometimes fans' input helps change a character's trajectory further. Finally, as Pumphrey so ably describes in his chapter about Dust, superheroes with a longer publication history also begin collecting conflicting characterizations, as creators try to reconcile their own ideas about characters with older versions.

The case of Dust is also a good illustration of how conflicting conceptions of Islam and Muslimness can appear in a Muslim superhero. Of course, she is still a character who has only been handled by non-Muslims to date, so her hybridity is still one rooted in the dominant culture. Conversely, characters like Kamala Khan and The 99 are, as noted, rooted in Islamicate discursive traditions, while also adhering to the superhero genre's conventions. The same applies to Qahera, whose dual contexts Aymon Kreil elucidates in his chapter. As such, these three, as well as, for example, Buraaq or The Silver Scorpion, might be classified as a form of "autoethnography" – "text[s] in which people undertake to describe themselves in ways that engage with representations others have made of them."[9] Comics such as these use the superhero genre to speak to Muslims and to non-Muslims alike, in both explicit and implicit ways. By doing this, their creators somewhat subversively use a genre that belongs to the dominant culture and that has been frequently used for conservative aims to symbolically police "the borders between key cultural concepts: good and evil, right and wrong, us and them."[10]

Through this type of hybrid superhero storytelling, creators (and their receptive audiences) can work in a "contact zone." The term "refer[s] to social spaces where cultures, meet, clash and grapple with each other, often in contexts of highly asymmetrical relations of power, such as colonialism, slavery, or their aftermaths as they are lived out in many parts of the world today."[11] These Muslim superheroes thus create opportunities for the subaltern to speak through a language belonging to the dominant culture and,

9. Pratt 1991, 35.
10. Brown 2011, 78.
11. Pratt 1991, 34.

in turn, more familiar to the cultural "mainstream," in order to intervene in prevailing ways of understanding Muslims and Islam. In a cultural moment when symbolic border policing is often framed in terms of keeping a Muslim "them" out, this is a risky enterprise, as the vehement opposition each new Muslim superhero encounters testifies. It is also a difficult one: as Strömberg's chapter shows, it is not easy to successfully meld an Islamic discursive tradition with that of the superhero. But, as Yanora's chapter suggests, by trying, creators of Muslim superheroes can help challenge reigning conceptions of Muslims and Islam and to destabilize the white, male norm that is deeply embedded in the superhero genre's figuration of heroism.

Muslim Superheroes and the Shape of Heroism

There have been numerous attempts to determine what, exactly, a superhero is, and what it is supposed to embody.[12] Most definitions have flaws, and the precise character type remains elusive. Of course, as comics scholar Geoff Klock points out, it is perhaps not necessary to define superheroes; the inability to capture the superhero in words is part of "what makes them great."[13] Indeed, it is possible that a final definition may never be determined, and for the reader of superhero comics, this need not matter greatly. It is it entirely sufficient, as a casual reader, to simply maintain that one knows a superhero when one sees it.

That position, however, is untenable for a critical reading. Simply because nobody has managed to capture ˙perfectly what superheroes – all superheroes, at all times – are, does not mean either that "[t]hey defy conventional definitions because they contain too many conventions,"[14] or that we should discourage all attempts at defining them. The extant definitions of the superhero are imperfect, but they are not meant to be all-encompassing. As attempts to capture the superhero, they are entirely sufficient for any study of their exploits, if one keeps in mind what scholar of religion Bruce Lincoln has noted: language is imperfect, and definitions cannot ultimately escape their own origin as "the historical product of discursive processes." This, Lincoln concludes, "hardly renders futile all efforts at definition, however, particularly when one understands these as provisional attempts to clarify one's thought, not to capture the innate essence of things."[15]

In some ways, the difficulty of negotiating a word like "superhero" is

---

12. Cf. Reynolds 1992; Coogan 2006; McLain 2009; Rosenberg and Coogan 2013; Lewis 2014a.

13. Klock 2013.

14. Gavaler 2015, 3.

15. Lincoln 2006, 2.

much like the difficulty of sizing up a seemingly universal word like "magic," as essayist and Islamic studies scholar Michael Muhammad Knight attempts in his book *Magic in Islam*. In it, Knight demonstrates how his primary term, "magic," from the Greek root *mageia* and perhaps an earlier Persian source of *magav*, can be deconstructed to the point of nothingness. For that matter, he notes, so can the words "Islam" or even "religion." The key, he suggests, is finding a "workable center,"[16] a point at which to tether the discussion lest it be entirely unanchored. The dilemmas that arise with pinning down such a "workable center," however, are its often unacknowledged arbitrariness, at best, and its deep biases, at worst. That was, for Knight, a crucial reason for writing *Magic in Islam* and pushing back against a flood of "Introduction to Islam" texts: "By presenting what s/he has judged to be essential knowledge, the author of the intro genre does not simply privilege the mainstream, but invents it."[17]

Two *Muslim Superheroes* chapters in particular are important guides for how to think about such characters, as well as about superheroes more generally. In his chapter, Fredrik Strömberg offers a synthesis and revision of earlier definition attempts, in which he identifies seven traits that are common to genre characters. Stressing that his is a "prototype definition" in that not every genre element convention needs to be present, Strömberg lists his conventions: superheroes (and supervillains) have superhuman abilities; superheroes have a strong moral code as their driving force; they have an origin story that explains their powers and moral codes; they have a clear visual branding, often through costume design; they have a mundane secret identity that contrasts with the superhuman one; they are engaged in recurring violent clashes with villains; they are sexualized, often through the male gaze; and their stories take place in a contemporary, although alternative, version of the reader's world. All characters in this volume measure up to this definition, but the way they do so varies between different Muslim superheroes and, more important, between many Muslim superheroes and their non-Muslim counterparts.

Mercedes Yanora's chapter gives us another important key for future work on superheroes, Muslim and non-Muslim alike. After a survey of critical studies of superheroes, Yanora summarizes the U.S. superhero industry's answer to who the "classic superhero" is: "the white heterosexual man." These two chapters offer a workable center, supported by myriad studies, from which future superhero scholarship would do well to take inspiration: how does the fulfilment of Strömberg's criteria relate to the white, straight

16. Knight 2016, 2.
17. Knight 2016, 4.

maleness of the "classic" superhero, and how are conventions used to up-hold the center or to destabilize it? In this volume, we have seen countless examples of Muslim superheroes being used for either end.

A questioning of the way superhero conventions are fulfilled and a destabilization of the white, male norm for the superhero genre leads to a further consideration, namely the dimensions and shape of heroism it-self. Indeed, it must be recognized that heroism and superheroism are not strictly synonymous. Therefore, just as the "superhero" must be probed for its complexities in an Islamicate context, so, too, must the distinct root of the "hero." Ultimately, we, as editors of *Muslim Superheroes*, are confronted by the question of whether there are significant differences to be discerned between the Western hero – however real or hyperreal that concept may be – and the Islamic hero.

Returning to Knight's reasoning, one might ask: When we, as the editors of *Muslim Superheroes*, evaluate the contours of the "superhero," what do we also see as the defining characteristics of the root "hero?" In turn, what kind of "heroism" are we thereby inventing? As much as possible, we have attempted to keep our editorial fingerprints light, as it were, but we can-not entirely disavow nor discount an inadvertent influencing. Rather than attempting to maintain a rigid objectivity and making the book a purely academic exercise, then, some discussion of the slipperiness of heroism feels as necessary as its descendent, the titular "superhero."

In a collection of essays about a topic like superheroes, a chapter like Hussein Rashid's, in which the very notion of the Muslim superhero is re-framed and replaced by the Islamic super-hero, may seem odd. Why include a piece that, in some ways, undercuts the premise of the book itself? The critical hyphen that Rashid introduces carries a great deal of significance, an acknowledgment not only of the superhero's modern and Americentric prominence but also of its pre-history. For this reason, Rashid's chapter is a reminder that the volume's premises are both steeped almost exclusively in the twentieth/twenty-first century as well as open to necessary scrutiny.

Therefore, if pressed to elucidate how we see "heroism" functioning in terms of "superheroism" – and, more specifically, how an Islamic con-cept of the hero can confront some Muslim iteration of the superhero genre – we would have to point to co-editor A. David Lewis's own previously pub-lished thoughts on the subject. As unseemly as self-citation may be, it is nonetheless the case that these earlier thoughts have influenced some of the navigation and charting offered to the contributors. Elsewhere, Lewis has remarked on the Western or (Judeo-)Christian image of heroes as those who confront peril and even death on a community's behalf: the activist, the police officer, the firefighter, the soldier, etc. Taking as his point of departure theorist Ernest Becker's *The Denial of Death*, Lewis considers this form of heroism to be marked by a pronounced cultural phobia of facing death, combined with the privileging of sacrifice as a guiding religious principle, which in the U.S. often takes on a distinctly Christian flavor.[18] Sacrifice is also a central tenet of U.S. civil religion. It can easily be attached to notions of blood and the land upon which it has been spilled, that is, expressed in a "tribal" understanding of national identity that privileges white Christians.[19] Such a Judeo-Christian or civil-religious notion of heroism, which is recurrent in superhero comics,[20] can have powerful, problematic "mythopolitical" consequences; as anthropologist Katherine Donahue wrote about the media creation of heroes in the weeks after 9/11, "[m]ythopolitics encompasses the creation by societies of heroes as reflections of desired qualities considered useful in future actions against those who threaten the state."[21] The willingness to sacrifice and to take action that heroes of this kind embody, "the ideal of citizenship as the heroic loss of life," can be mobilized to quiet deliberation, quell dissent, and disregard concerns about safety or life, as it did in the lead-up to the invasion of Afghanistan.[22]

Such a narrowly defined, nationalistically framed, and ideologically useful notion of heroism seems undesirable. It excludes more and more people, as multiculturalism and globalization are becoming ever more inescapable (if still, in some circles, strongly opposed) facts of life across the world. It can motivate, or even promote, conflict. The problem, then, comes in realigning this form of heroism with one located outside the United States and of Christianity. For that, Lewis suggests jettisoning the dominant Beckerian system of the hero and, instead, focusing on the virtues supposedly inherent cross-culturally in such a figure. Synthesizing from an array of works, Lewis distills two main virtues of a cross-cultural hero: bravery and honesty.[23] Whether the hero sustains harm or prevents others from harm is a potential after-effect of these virtues; likewise, whether a superhero does that which is impossible to the average individual is also entirely secondary to these attributes. A hero who deals without bravery or honesty is unworthy of the

18. Lewis 2014c.

19. Bellah 1967, 10–11; Williams 2013.

20. Cf. Ahmed and Lund 2016, where the authors discuss Marvel's 2011 crossover event "Fear Itself," in which such sacrifices are performed at least three times.

21. Donahue 2011.

22. Quote from Clark 2011, 84–85; cf. Donahue 2011; Lule 2002; Willis 2006, 141–184.

23. Lewis 2014b. Again we caution against essentializing. These virtues are intentionally broad and widely interpretable, leaving them proverbial space to breathe without belonging to any one group or minority.

name, in whatever context. As linguist and translator Jan Knappert has documented, these have been the "twin virtues" of the *umma*'s lore, present in the cultural milieu already in the pre-Islamic days of *jahiliyya* (roughly, "ignorance of divine guidance"), and embraced by Islamicate cultures throughout the spread of Islam, and up to the present.[24] Moreover, in a modern context, these virtues can be more easily stressed without leading into recklessness, Christ-like or civil religious sacrifice, ideological manipulation, or nationalism, opening up the realm of heroism to those who have for so long been excluded from it and from the body politic. Bravery and honesty, carefully defined, are not guarantors for a more equitable heroism, but, theoretically, they allow for the creation of heroes who are less easy to use for reactionary ends and who can instead strive for change, as outlined more below.

The one additional form of heroism, if we want to call it that, that emerges from this volume and which bears a moment of discussion is that of the super*heroine*. Stressing this gendered term is not to suggest that the heroine or superheroine *should* be a distinct and separate class from her male counterpart. In fact, we are ill at ease with the initial terms, with "superhero" suggesting a default male character, while the feminine descriptor seemingly names some kind of derivative category. Yet, as our contributors Reyns-Chikuma, Lorenz, Strömberg, and Yanora all testify, to be blind to the hyper-masculinity or hyper-sexualization inherent in the superhero genre is to put our personal principles ahead of the scholarship.

Even a brief glance at this volume's table of contents or a passing familiarity with its subject matter should yield the obvious but little-spoken observation that Muslim superheroes are, in strange disproportion to the rest of the genre, frequently superheroines. We can only speculate on why this might be, but, in all likelihood, Reyns-Chikuma and Lorenz are close to the mark in suggesting that part of Ms. Marvel's success may lie in her being both a teenager and a girl; certainly, G. Willow Wilson and company have made Kamala's into a story of empowerment, but that suggests that the character came from an unempowered state – a "safer" space for readers with latent Islamophobia, perhaps? Pumphrey details the problems surrounding Dust's introduction and handling by writers, but she has still remained a semi-regular presence in Marvel publications for more than a decade and a half. Granted, neither M nor Faiza Hassan, the Janissary nor Kahina the Seer, have reached either Ms. Marvel or even Dust's level of popular notoriety; yet, at the same time, they have enjoyed a greater, more consistent profile than that of their aggressive male counterparts such as Josiah X, Simon Baz, or Wise Son.

The trend, one feels, is that readers still need their Muslim superheroes

24. Knappert 1985.

minimized – we hesitantly use the term *feminized* – in order to be made more palatable to mass audiences. *Ms. Marvel* is a success unto itself, whereas many prior attempts at creating "the Muslim superhero" have not been. To what degree is it the character's age, her sex, even her assimilation into American culture that has positioned her for success?[25] She is brave, and she is honest, unquestionably a hero. And, she is immensely powerful, fighting in defense of the weak and overcoming impossible odds, most certainly a superhero. But is she only allowed to be a Muslim superhero while she is young, because she is a girl, and because she upholds "the American way?"

The purpose of questioning the superhero, the hero, and even the superheroine is to point to assumptions that are being left untested by superhero stories and in their analysis. The discussion of the "superhero" or "hero" in one cultural context is not necessarily the same as discussing it in another; this seems like a truism, but our unpacking of these terms suggests the layers of meaning and assumption that lurk beneath them, many of them tied to particular national or philosophical viewpoints. Just as this volume has explored the intersections of the superhero with the world religion Islam, future engagements between the genre and other contexts need to have a similar sensitivity as to what might undergird each.

Muslim Superheroes in the Classroom

Historically, comics, as a medium and as cultural artifacts, have in many nations been marked with a stigma. They have been considered as childish trash that is, at best, frivolous, and, at worst, harmful. In recent years, this perception has changed.[26] Comics are increasingly being welcomed into the cultural pages of newspapers and magazines, into libraries, and, most importantly, into classrooms. One can easily today put together a comics reading list on almost any topic and bring this list into a primary school, secondary school, or higher education environment. Ranging from edited volumes to websites to a dedicated scholarly journal (e.g. *SANE Journal: Sequential Art Narrative in Education*), there are now myriad resources for the interested teacher.[27] We encourage our readers to seek out these resources and to use them to include Muslim superheroes in their own lesson plans. To that end, we want to present a few suggestions for how this can be done and what can be achieved by doing so. Our focus below is on how the chapters in this book can help teachers get started.

In addition to being a comics scholar, *Muslim Superheroes* contributor

25. Cf. Kent 2015.
26. See Beaty 2005; Beaty 2012; Sabin 2001; Gabilliet 2010.
27. E. g. Tabachnick 2009; Syma and Weiner 2013; http://comicsintheclassroom.net/; http://www.graphicclassroom.org/p/best-comics-for-your-classroom-list-for.html

Fredrik Strömberg is also the president of the Swedish Comics Association, founder of the Comics Art School in Malmö, Sweden, and an advocate of comics as an art form and as a teaching resource. In his Swedish-language pamphlet *Serier i skolan: Lärarhandledning för grundskolan* (*Comics in School: A Teacher's Tutorial for Primary Schools*), he stresses the usefulness of comics as a pedagogical tool.[28] Although the pamphlet is written with the national Swedish public school curriculum in mind, many of Strömberg's insights are applicable internationally.

Strömberg summarizes recent research on comics to illustrate why comics are such a good teaching tool. They are often easier to get students to read, as they seem less of a chore than prose text. More importantly, they promote reader engagement. They also appear easier to remember than longer texts. Further, comics stimulate the reader's reading comprehension, visual interpretive skills, and associative ability. The fact that comics can be read faster than a work of prose also allows for their reading in a classroom setting in a way that includes weaker readers. This also allows for them to be reread, which makes possible a deeper analysis and discussion about themes, visual storytelling, and more.[29]

Muslim superheroes can be used in a wide variety of courses, from religion classes and Islamic studies, to history, social studies and social sciences, to media and literature classes, and far beyond. The simplest way of bringing comics, and Muslim superheroes, into the classroom is to assign a single comic book for the class to read and then lead a discussion about the content.[30] This kind of assignment opens up all manner of foci, from questions about factual and historical accuracy, to representation, to issues like Islamophobia in comic books. On the topic of historical accuracy, perhaps the best comic book to use is *The 99: Origins* special, which is available for free download.[31] As discussed in Ken Chitwood's chapter in this volume, this issue presents an image of Islamic history that is both useful for an overview of the topic and a selective retelling of that history, making it a perfect starting point for deeper discussion.[32] This issue along with the first issue of *Ms. Marvel* also lend themselves to discussions about representation. Questions for discussion can include how the writers and artists construct the everyday life of Muslims and how they show Muslims' interactions with non-Muslims.

28. Strömberg 2016.

29. Strömberg 2016, 15–16.

30. Strömberg 2016, 27. Martin Lund would like to thank Jonas Otterbeck, Andreas Gabrielsson, and Fredrik Carrasco for their helpful suggestions.

31. http://www.qmags.com/d.asp?pub=T99&upid=12648&fl=others/The99/T99_20070501_May_2007.pdf

32. Also useful in this connection is Clements and Gauvain 2014.

Fredrik Strömberg's and Aymon Kreil's chapters are also particularly helpful for the first topic,[33] while Chris Reyns-Chikuma's and Désirée Lorenz's, as well as Nicholaus Pumphrey's chapters can be very helpful in the latter case. Pumphrey's chapter and Dust can also be used as a starting point for discussions about veiling and its representations, as well as Orientalism in popular culture; for this, all one really needs is a single panel depicting the character in her *niqab* and a tight-fitting, form-revealing *abaya*.

Ms. Marvel, in particular, can also be used in teaching about and against Islamophobia, particularly in relation to Kamala's interactions with Zoe. This discussion can also work well in conjunction with Islam-critical or Islamophobic comics like *Holy Terror!* or *The Infidel*. When discussing immigration, integration, or Muslim diasporas in religion, social studies, or social sciences classes, Kevin Wanner's and Mercedes Yanora's chapters provide particularly well-suited insights, while Dwain Pruitt's chapter will help any teacher who wants to teach the much-overlooked topic of black Islam in America. And, of course, any comic book with a Muslim superhero in it can be a springboard into discussions about how Muslims are represented in the media; using any two comics with different portrayals allows for a comparative reading that should lead to fruitful discussion. If there is time, the class can even follow one or a few characters in a series to see how religiosity, ethnicity, and other identities are represented and change over time. The gaps, continuities, and changes that arise in such a reading leave much room for tailoring the discussion to fit teaching goals while still inviting discussion.[34]

There are certain pedagogies that might fit particularly well with this type of teaching. So-called "windows and mirrors" teaching, for example, would allow for a multicultural, critical teaching; self-identifying Muslim students would get a chance to engage with material that represents characters that, in a sense, mirror themselves, while other students would have a chance to look, as if through a window, into the world of their Others.[35] This is particularly good for groups with students of mixed heritages, where it is often easy for minority students to feel overlooked because of a lack of diverse representation in popular culture. For younger students in religion classes, it is also possible to have them create their own Muslim superhero characters, using what they have learned about Islam as a guide. These new superheroes can, in turn, be used in further discussions.

33. See also Edwin 2012.

34. It is also a good idea for teachers to familiarize themselves with how comics work. There are several good resources for this, but we would suggest as a starting point that they look to McCloud 1993; or Eisner 2008.

35. Bishop 1990. Our thanks to C. Darius Stonebanks and Melanie Bennett-Stonebanks for introducing us to this pedagogy.

For older students, in classes that focus on identity or diversity, and in which there is a mixed student body, it can be fruitful to employ a "contact zones" pedagogy. In a classroom setting, Muslim superheroes can be used to discuss the clashes discussed above, if one focuses particularly on the problematic aspects of the comics' representations. Particularly *Ms. Marvel* or *The 99* can be held up as "autoethnographic" texts. If this is coupled with a discussion about how the dominant culture has represented and keeps representing Muslims, this is likely to lead to new and lasting insights for the students. This works best if it is coupled with representations of other groups as well. One should keep in mind, however, that this type of exercise can be highly emotionally taxing and can lead to confrontation, so it should not be undertaken without proper preparation, and even then only with student groups that are likely to handle it well.

Every classroom is different, of course, and our purpose is not to tell anyone how to teach Muslim superheroes or the contents of this volume. But, given the tensions of our time, we want to stress that *Muslim Superheroes* is offered as a tool to those who look to welcome rather than condemn, to build rather than destroy. Therefore, while we leave the pedagogical method(s) open to the individual instructor and his/her circumstances, we do so with a caveat: the teacher who wants to bring Muslim superheroes into the classroom is charged with the responsibility of showing them the same respect we have earnestly endeavored to maintain in this volume.

The Tool of *Muslim Superheroes*

Muslim Superheroes is intended to fill a void – or, if not a true void, then a sparsely populated zone with little in the way of a map, as yet. Hopefully, this volume can be, if not the map itself, then the compass for further charting this space. It is intended to be as much a short chronicle of our subject in the current global climate as it is a tool for audiences' use. That is, once one has finished *reading* our book, it is time to start *using* it – testing our ideas and putting them to work.

Before entirely handing over that tool, however, we would like to offer a parting observation: a course heading, if you will. A friend of one of the co-editors made the comment that Muslim superheroes appear to be more openly religious than other characters. There are, of course, exceptions in the genre, such as Nightcrawler's Catholicism, Punisher's brief stint as an avenging angel, or Kitty Pryde's quiet Judaism. (We note that these are all Marvel characters, curiously enough.) Even more rare than superheroes whose mainstream religion guides them is the Muslim superhero whose faith does not.

Even if we accept this claim, superheroes with a commitment to Islam tend to be light on theology. Again, this is relatively true of a superhero from nearly any religion. Kitty Pryde's Judaism does not prevent her from eating extraterrestrial foods for fear of breaking kosher law, nor does Batman take great solace in his parents' souls receiving their eternal reward in heaven despite their murders. Admittedly, then, superhero comics seem to concern themselves with religion selectively. Yet, if the Muslim superhero is largely to be characterized in terms of his or her religion, then greater attention could be paid to the variety of Muslim thought.

A simplification of Islam might have been necessary for Muslims to make initial inroads into superhero stories and to themselves emerge as superheroes, but the future may lie with layering the faith's representations. Indeed, the recent proliferation of Muslim superheroes might already be accomplishing this. That is, by their growing numbers and variety, and despite many of them leaving much to be desired in terms of depth and representation, they are starting to add dimensions to Muslim and Islamicate representation in the genre. By not talking just about any single "Muslim superhero" in isolation, but instead collecting work about some of the many different representations of Islam and Muslim superheroes that exist today, this volume has demonstrated how Muslim superheroes are slowly coming into their own and has charted the landscape more thoroughly than has been done before. Wanner's comments on Ms. Marvel's options are telling, repeated here again for emphasis:

> Muslims will have either to choose between what liberalism and
> what their faith demands, or else accept the compromise solution
> of minimalism, which avoids confrontation between religious and
> competing claims and values by segregating them in separate spheres
> of life, zones which align roughly with the private versus the public.

Perhaps this has been true thus far of the Muslim superhero in the monthly comic book, maybe even of the immigrant Muslim or Muslim American in the post-9/11 context. Choose liberalism or faith, the public or the private, a compromise satisfying neither.

We would ask, however: Is there no *hybrid* way? Using the visual-verbal blend of comics as either a metaphorical, metaphysical, or conceptual guide, there should be, eventually, a way by which individuals can fulfill their faith and move fluidly through U.S. culture. We reject the Huntington hypothesis that Islam and the U.S. are antithetical to each other; Muslim superheroes are prime examples and tantalizing spaces where, instead of clashing, cultures are coming together and finding what they share in common. Doing so is not easy, but it can be done, and these characters and their like can help. Progress must be a collective effort. One way to further this aim could be for more Muslim writers and artists to embrace autoethnography, to challenge others' representation of Islam and Muslims head on, rather than seeking to "normalize," which is always an awkward prospect, not least because often in "their gambits to 'disavow their deviance,' normalizers must continually manage and contend with the inescapable tension of an interaction which is fragile, problematic, and easily subject to 'slips' and disruptions."[36]

Non-Muslim creators, in turn, could do better at taking Islam and Muslims seriously, learning more about them before putting pen to paper. The inability or unwillingness to "shift identities imaginatively" and to inhabit the position of the Other that has seemingly marked much Muslim superhero representation will only compound the many failures of identity that mar the history our contributors have outlined.[37] The world does not need another Dust. The superhero industry itself can further these developments by giving more space for this type of activity and incentivizing contributors, regardless of threat to their financial bottom line. Fans and critics, on the other hand, can continue to be vocal about what they like and dislike, and to push back against those detractors who might otherwise seem like representatives of the audience, thus showing the powers that be that their efforts are having a positive impact.

The Islam embodied by Muslim superheroes is not, in truth, monolithic – nor is the Islam of the real world. Our fictions can explore real-world tensions and envision the progress that, in time, our reality can follow. But that only happens if we listen to them and regard their narratives as meaningful. Otherwise, a work like *Muslim Superheroes* is *only* a chronicle of time and of lessons ready to be lost.

36. Anspach 1979, 769.
37. Michael 2008, 18–20.

Works Cited

Ahmed, M., and M. Lund. 2016. "'We're *All* Avengers Now': Community-Building, Civil Religion and Nominal Multiculturalism in Marvel Comics' *Fear Itself.*" *European Journal of American Culture* 35 (2): 77–95.

Anderson, B. 2006. *Imagined Communities: Reflections on the Origin and Spread of Nationalism.* Rev. ed. London.

Anspach, R. R. 1979. "From Stigma to Identity Politics: Political Activism Among the Physically Disabled and Former Mental Patients." *Social Science & Medicine. Part A: Medical Psychology & Medical Sociology* 13: 765–773.

Asad, T. 1986. *The Idea of an Anthropology of Islam.* Washington D.C.

Baumann, G. 1999. *The Multicultural Riddle: Rethinking National, Ethnic, and Religious Identities.* New York.

Beaty, B. 2005. *Fredric Wertham and the Critique of Mass Culture.* Jackson, MS.

———. 2012. *Comics Versus Art: Comics in the Art World.* Toronto.

Bellah, R. N. 1967. "Civil Religion in America." *Daedalus* 96: 1–21.

Berger, P., and T. Luckmann 1991. *The Social Construction of Reality: A Treatise in the Sociology of Knowledge.* London.

Bishop, R. S. 1990. "Mirrors, Windows, and Sliding Glass Doors." *Perspectives* 6 (3): ix–xi.

Brown, J. A. 2011. "Supermoms? Maternity and the Monstrous-Feminine in Superhero Comics." *Journal of Graphic Novels and Comics* 2 (1): 77–87.

Charmé, S. Z. 2000. "Varieties of Authenticity in Contemporary Jewish Identity." *Jewish Social Studies* 6 (2): 133–155.

Clark, M. M. 2011. "Herodotus Reconsidered: An Oral History of September 11, 2001, in New York City." *Radical History Review* 2011 (111): 79–89.

Clements, J., and R. Gauvain. 2014. "The Marvel of Islam: Reconciling Muslim Epistemologies through a New Islamic Origin Saga in Naif Al-Mutawa's the 99." *Journal of Religion and Popular Culture* 26 (1): 36–70.

Coogan, P. 2006. *Superhero: The Secret Origin of a Genre.* Austin.

Donahue, K. C. 2011. "What Are Heroes For? Commemoration and the Creation of Heroes after September 11." *Anthropology News,* September, 6.

Edwin, S. 2012. "Islam's Trojan Horse: Battling Perceptions of Muslim Women in *The 99.*" *Journal of Graphic Novels & Comics* 3 (2): 171–199.

Eisner, W. 2008. *Comics and Sequential Art: Principles and Practices from the Legendary Cartoonist.* New York.

Gabilliet, J-P. 2010. *Of Comics and Men: A Cultural History of American Comic Books,* translated by B. Beaty and N. Nguyen. Jackson, MS.

Gavaler, C. 2015. *On the Origin of Superheroes: From the Big Bang to Action Comics No. 1.* Iowa City.

Kent, M. 2015. "Unveiling Marvels: Ms. Marvel and the Reception of the New Muslim Superheroine." *Feminist Media Studies* 15 (3): 522–527.

Klock, G. 2013. "What Is a Superhero? No One Knows–And That's What Makes 'em Great." In *What Is a Superhero?*, edited by R. S. Rosenberg, and P. Coogan, 71–76. Oxford.

Knappert, J. 1985. *Islamic Legends: Histories of the Heroes, Saints, and Prophets of Islam*. Leiden.

Knight, M. M. 2016. *Magic In Islam*. New York.

Lewis, A. D. 2014a. *American Comics, Literary Theory, and Religion: The Superhero Afterlife*. New York.

———. 2014b. "Whither the Muslim Superhero?" *ISLAMiCommentary*, June 3. http://islamicommentary.org/2014/06/whither-the-muslim-superhero/.

———. 2014c. "Putting the 'Hero' Back in 'Superhero': How the Muslim Superhero Can Save the Genre." *ISLAMiCommentary*, September 5. http://islamicommentary.org/2014/09/putting-the-hero-back-in-superhero-how-the-muslim-superhero-can-save-the-genre/.

Lincoln, B. 2006. *Holy Terrors: Thinking about Religion after September 11*. Chicago.

Lule, J. 2002. "Myth and Terror on the Editorial Page: The *New York Times* Responds to September 11, 2001." *Journalism & Mass Communication Quarterly* 79 (2): 275–293.

Lund, M. 2016a. *Re-Constructing the Man of Steel: Superman 1938-1941, Jewish American History, and the Invention of the Jewish-Comics Connection*. New York.

———. 2016b. "On the Ms. Marvel Moment." *Mizan*, June 20. http://www.mizanproject.org/pop-post/muslim-superheroes/.

McCloud, S. 1993. *Understanding Comics: The Invisible Art*. New York.

McLain, K. 2009. *India's Immortal Comic Books: Gods, Kings, and Other Heroes*. Bloomington.

Michael, J. 2008. *Identity and the Failure of America: From Thomas Jefferson to the War on Terror*. Minneapolis.

Omi, M., and H. Winant. 1994. *Racial Formation in the United States: From the 1960s to the 1990s*. 2nd ed. New York.

Otterbeck, J. 2010. *Samtidsislam: Unga Muslimer I Malmö Och Köpenhamn*. Stockholm.

Pratt, M. L. 1991. "Arts of the Contact Zone." *Profession*, 33–40.

Reynolds, R. 1992. *Super Heroes: A Modern Mythology*. Jackson, MS.

Rosenberg, R. S., and P. Coogan, eds. 2013. *What Is a Superhero?* Oxford.

Sabin, R. 2001. *Comics, Comix & Graphic Novels: A History of Graphic Novels*. London.

Santo, A. 2014. "'Is It a Camel? Is It a Turban? No, It's The 99': Branding Islamic Superheroes as Authentic Global Cultural Commodities." *Television & New Media* 15 (7): 679–695.

Satlow, M. L. 2006. *Creating Judaism: History, Tradition, Practice.* New York.

Strömberg, F. 2016. *Serier i skolan: Lärarhandledning för grundskolan.* Malmö:.

Syma, C. K., and R. G. Weiner. 2013. *Graphic Novels and Comics in the Classroom: Essays on the Educational Power of Sequential Art.* Jefferson, NC.

Tabachnick, S. E. 2009. *Teaching the Graphic Novel.* New York.

Williams, R. H. 2013. "Civil Religion and the Cultural Politics of National Identity in Obama's America." *Journal for the Scientific Study of Religion* 52 (2): 239–257.

Willis, C. R. 2006. "Tempered by Flame: Heroism, Nationalism, and the New York Firefighter on 9/11 and Beyond." PhD dissertation, University of Southern California, Los Angeles.

Index

12/18